The Illustrated Book of
WILD FLOWERS

The Illustrated Book of
WILD FLOWERS

edited and with additional
material by

Pamela Bristow

from a text by

Zdenka Podhajská

illustrated by

Květoslav Hísek

OCTOPUS BOOKS

Translated by Simon Pellar
English edition first published 1985 by
Octopus Books Limited
59 Grosvenor Street
London W1

© Artia, Prague
(except 'Folk Lore' p. 27 and 'Conservation' p. 31,
© Octopus Books Limited)

ISBN 0 7064 2333 X

Printed in Czechoslovakia by TSNP Martin

3/13/10/51-01

CONTENTS

Man and Nature

The landscape that we see today in Britain and continental Europe is very different to the original wild land that was there before men arrived. The natural vegetation of the area is mixed deciduous woodland in the more southerly regions merging into coniferous forests further north. It is the influence of man that has transformed these forests into the familiar countryside of today.

Prehistoric men lived in caves, in close contact with the local environment, dependent on a favourable climate and natural resources like stone chips and animal bones. As their lifestyle changed from the hunters and gatherers of fruits to the shepherds and settlers who raised domestic animals and grew crops, they began to transform the landscape.

Prehistoric men used natural resources like any other animals – they took only what they needed for food, housing and clothing. At first no major changes occurred in the landscape. The first steps were taken by agricultural men, for they eliminated some of the extensive forests and converted the land into pastures, fields and gardens to grow cereals, vegetables and other crops and to make grazing land for their domestic animals. By burning and woodcutting they obtained humus-rich soil in lowlands and river valleys in which fertility was preserved by regular floods and organic manure. This land was cultivated with simple tools.

The elimination of forests continued slowly right up to the Middle Ages, when wood consumption suddenly increased. More land was needed for crop growing to support the growing population and many trees were cut down to be used in building the large fleets of ships possessed by many European nations.

Since then, the laborious cultivation of fields has been made easier by increasingly advanced mechanization. The advent of the scientific and technological revolution accelerated and perfected the processes of mechanization, electrification, automation and the introduction of chemicals into agriculture. Cultivated areas have been continually enlarged to permit the use of larger and larger machines and many of the remaining woods and hedgerows have been destroyed in the process. Not only has the aesthetic look of the landscape become impoverished but the protection constituted by the trees has diminished. Trees protect the soil from erosion by water and wind. Their roots trap soil on hillside slopes so that it is not carried away by torrential rains into valleys and rivers, which are then filled with sediments. The slopes in deforested areas are often laid bare to the underlying rocks and run-off water cuts deep erosive gulleys and ravines in the weathered rock.

Excessive use of dry slopes as grazing land for some domestic animals has often led to extensive erosion. On these slopes the vegetation takes a long time to regenerate and enormous arid areas have been created in the inland regions of Spain, Yugoslavia and Greece. Before the arrival of men the soil was covered with shrubby macchia, an impenetrable cover of evergreen, thorny bushes, 2–3 metres tall, protecting the lower growing ground cover of flowering plants. Grazing herds of goats and sheep with their small pointed hooves gradually denuded the fertile topsoil and caused its erosion. Absence of greenery then created a drier climate in the region. This is only one of many examples of human exploitation of the environment.

Men have often used natural resources in a profligate manner, without any forethought about their regeneration. This ruthless behaviour has accounted for the near extinction of many animals including bison in North America and Europe, tigers in Asia and many other furred species all over the world. Soil in many places has been exhausted, large stretches of forest have been eradicated, plant species have diminished in numbers or have become extinct. The industrial revolution in western Europe in the 18th century brought about another intensification in agricultural techniques and the application of artificial fertilizers and the use of pesticides has triggered off land and water pollution. Increasing industrialization has brought more and more disturbance into the balance of nature. Oil is found throughout the oceans; lakes and rivers are polluted by sewage and factory effluents; more and more land is covered by housing developments. The need to recognise that the ecological resources of the planet are not infinite, is more essential every day.

To a certain extent the balance of nature is self-maintaining and human intervention can be compensated for by the regeneration of natural vegetation and the ability of the land to break down man-made artifacts by oxidation and bacterial action. But in the 20th century we face an ecological crisis which can only be avoided by the realization that we cannot go on depleting our environment for ever. The natural world can only absorb so much abuse and since we are dependent on it like any other living organism, we will eventually be affected like the rest. Our planet Earth is a closed system which depends on clean healthy forests, pollution-free seas and fertile soil to maintain its life.

The present is characterized by growing artificial invasion of the natural world which is being transformed for the benefit of mankind alone. But many scientists feel a growing concern that pollution, erosion, the extinction of many species and the growth of the human population must be controlled. A multidisciplinary science has been developed to explore the inter-relationships of our world — ecology.

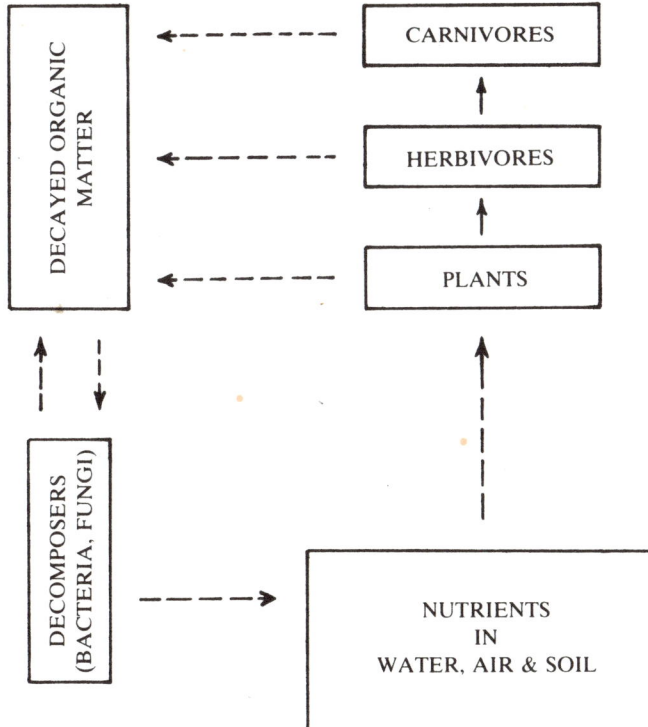

The circulation of nutrients in nature. Essential elements, like carbon, oxygen and nitrogen, are in a constant state of circulation in the natural world. Plants are capable of utilising these elements in their inorganic states by absorbing them from soil, air and water and converting them into organic molecules, using the energy from sunlight. The plants are often eaten by herbivores, which may then be eaten by carnivores. All are subject to eventual death and decay, when they are broken down by bacteria and fungi and the cycle begins again. In a rich, complex habitat the nutrients may be used by many different organisms before returning to their inorganic states.

Ecology

Ecology, a term recently known only from textbooks and scientific literature, now appears in everyday newspaper articles, in magazines, books and political reports. The fact, that this term is encountered so often, reflects the growing recognition of its importance.

Ecology deals with the relationships between animals and plants, between individual organisms and between the living communities and the environment. It studies the problems of the biological balance and tries to anticipate environmental conflicts. The term ecology was first introduced in scientific literature by the German biologist and philosopher Ernest Haeckel in 1866. He defined it as a biological science studying the relationship of organisms and their environments, which covered all existential conditions in the broad sense.

When examining organisms in an area, we observe groups of animals of the same species (populations) and stable plant communities occurring together. The occurrence of individual species is determined by ecological factors such as climate, soil, water, light, landscape morphology, altitude etc. Ecologists study the principles controlling the inter-relationships between the environmental factors and the living organisms. Depending on the subject of study, this branch of biology is divided into special, general and regional ecology. Special ecology is concerned with the biology of individual species (autecology) or communities and ecosystems (synecology) and includes growth, feeding habits, reproduction etc. General ecology is concerned with the relationships between species (competition, co-operation etc.) and the stability, adaptability and productivity of ecosystems and the relationships between one ecosystem and another. Regional (synthetic) ecology is concerned with the ecology of entire regions and with ecological syntheses, and participates in the protection and creation of landscapes and in environmental management according to defined objectives.

The plants illustrated and described in this book are arranged in groups, each group consisting of a number of species that occur most commonly in one, rather than another, of the different types of locality that make up our countryside — the habitats or biotopes. A habitat or biotope is the sum total of all factors, living or non-living, which exert an influence on organisms or their communities living in a particular place. For the purpose of this book, nine specific habitats have been chosen: waste places; roadsides and hedgerows; moist grassland; dry grassland; arable land; water and waterside; open woodland; shady woodland; moors and heaths. Other habitats (rocks and cliffs, dunes and shingle beaches) are mentioned in the texts, where relevant, accompanying the species. This classification is rather artificial in many instances as most plant species occur in the wild in several different habitats. We have tried, however, to place each species in the habitat in which it is most likely to be found but the others in which it might occur, albeit less commonly, are also indicated in the fact panel. The selection of species concentrates on inland herbaceous plants, particularly those with more or less conspicuous flowers. Grasses and grass-like plants are omitted although they constitute an important feature of all habitats.

Original, natural habitats are characterized by a rich variety of species, high stability and healthy plants. On the other hand, artificial man-made habitats or ones strongly affected by human activity, such as forest and field monocultures, cultivated 'improved' meadows etc., are characterized by few species, instability and vulnerability to infections and insect pests. Artificial biotopes require a great deal of care to preserve the plants in an optimum state.

Forest, unaffected by man's economic activity, is the original ecosystem of the temperate zones of Europe. It is a habitat of many woody species with a rich herbaceous undergrowth. According to the light requirements of the herbaceous plants, the forest is divided into open woodland and shady woodland. Grassland, another species-rich habitat, varies from wet humid meadows to dry grassy slopes, pastures and hayfields. Aquatic habitats include lakes, rivers and ponds, their margins and marshes and fens. The last natural habitat in this book includes moorlands, heaths and peat bogs. Artificial habitats include arable land and fields, as well as wasteland, roadsides and hedgerows, walls and fences.

Waste Places

Men have transformed many natural ecosystems into cultivated ones for food production and an ever greater profit. Many places have become concrete deserts with the construction of new housing estates and factories. Rivers have been dammed and coastal bays infilled or made into harbours. Not all the occupied space is used up, and many forgotten places remain, seen either as useless or used for storage of materials or waste. Plants soon invade these areas, not just single plants but entire plant communities, species that can survive in such areas. They are light-loving, vigorous and spread rapidly both by vegetative means (runners and creeping underground stems) and by producing great numbers of seeds. These communities have been found from time immemorial in the vicinity of human settlements. The plants grow in circumstances entirely created by man, although man does not directly control their existence. They grow in soils which are loose, well aerated and usually rich in compounds of nitrogen, potassium, calcium and phosphorus. Their environment is also 'enriched' by a variety of constantly accumulating inorganic waste. Such places include rubbish dumps, compost heaps, farmyards, stables, sometimes even neglected village greens and ponds. Similar situations are found in building sites, railway stations, dockyards and on disused railway tracks, road and railway embankments.

The common species of waste ground are distributed throughout the world. Their seeds are frequently dispersed by man; in trains, boats and planes, in cross-continental lorries and in the cars of holiday makers. Dockyards are often the first places to be colonised in new territories or continents. From there they spread by seed to other waste grounds, gradually invading the country. Waste ground species often include medicinal plants and culinary herbs like Stinging Nettle (*Urtica dioica*), burdocks (*Arctium* spp.), mugworts (*Artemisia* spp.), motherworts (*Leonurus*), mulleins (*Verbascum* spp.), dandelions (*Taraxacum* spp.), Smooth Rupture-wort (*Herniaria glabra*), melilots (*Melilotus* spp.), Greater Celandine (*Chelidonium majus*), and the cultivated escapes like Horse-radish (*Armoracia rusticana*). They have been carried from one place to another by the practitioners of herb medicine and apothecaries.

Plants of roadside verges have to withstand

extreme temperatures. In sunny weather, the stony asphalt road surface heats up to 50—80 °C. At night, the radiated heat from the road surface protects the area from frost and damp dews. The scorching daytime heat and mild nights combined with shallow, dry soil are suitable for warmth-loving, xerophilous species like Viper's Bugloss (*Echium vulgare*), Dark Mullein (*Verbascum nigrum*), Pink Coronilla (*Coronilla varia*) etc. In such habitats, the plants can be found at higher altitudes than in their usual areas of distribution.

Roadside verges also provide a suitable environment for plants demanding nutrients in the soil. Mud containing organic remains often drops from the wheels and undersides of passing vehicles, dust and rubbish accumulate in ditches. Materials used for road building and repairs supply the wayside soil with calcium, phosphorus, potassium and nitrogen. These elements are most concentrated near the road, diminishing rapidly even a few feet away. Where a ditch is present, the moisture content of the soil is high and encourages the growth of species such as Meadow Cranesbill (*Geranium pratense*) and Wild Teasel (*Dipsacus fullonum*). Chicory (*Cichorium intybus*) is another common inhabitant of roadsides; the striking blue colour of its flowers form the basis of a folk legend according to which the plant is a bewitched girl waiting beside the road for her lover.

Chemicals in the ground exert a significant influence on the distribution of plants and may explain their occurrence in unexpected places. For instance materials used in road building and repair (limestone gravel and cement) provide lime-rich patches even in areas with poor acid soils, encouraging the growth of lime-loving plants like *Centaurea rhenana*, which colonise the patches by seed.

However, the treating of ditches, roadside verges and adjacent fields with herbicides is often devastating to the wild plants. The regular winter protection of roads with salt results in oversalting of the soil and such an increase in the soil content of sodium and potassium can only be tolerated by a few weeds, such as Spear Orache (*Atriplex hastata*) or Glaucous Goosefoot (*Chenopodium glaucum*). Changes in the chemical content of the soil can cause a serious breakdown of soil fertility in roadside woodlands and trees lose vitality, some may even die. Many wayside plants growing on paths or between paving stones can tolerate trampling by people or being run over by cars. Such species include Knotgrass (*Polygonum aviculare*), Annual Meadow Grass (*Poa annua*), Great Plantain (*Plantago major*), Silverweed (*Potentilla anserina*) and Perennial Rye-grass (*Lolium perenne*). This last species survives even in playgrounds and airports.

Road traffic assists in the dispersal of roadside plant species. The fruits and seeds are carried on shoes or wheels of cars and tractors. Meadow species may be spread from pastures to verges by cattle at milking time on their hooves, caught in their hides or in their digestive tracts. On the broader roadside verges between roads and fields and meadows grow a number of weed species; Groundsel (*Senecio vulgaris*), Field Poppy (*Papaver rhoeas*), Field Thistle (*Cirsium arvense*) and others. The roadside verges become their homes when the fields and meadows are so highly controlled by the farmers that they cannot survive in their old habitats. The verges often become permanent refuges from which the plants may recolonise the fields.

Medicinal plants growing on roadsides are spoiled by wastes from road traffic, not only by dust and dirt, but also by residues of heavy metals from exhaust fumes, which the plants receive both from the soil and through their leaf surfaces to be stored in their bodies. They may become not just unwholesome but positively dangerous and should not be picked.

Grassland

Meadows are usually natural, although secondary, areas of perennial grasses. They have occupied stretches of land obtained from forest clearance by primitive shepherds and farmers. In such deforested areas farmers grew cereals and in others they kept cattle and grew hay. Meadows were originally formed only in the valleys of large rivers, where the spring torrents of water and ice did not allow for a continuous growth of woodland. Mountain grasslands form above the timber-line and include both long-stemmed grasses and short-stemmed grasses, growing in the cold upland areas where snow remains for the greater part of the year or on avalanche routes. Meadows near the sea are also of primary origin. There the growth and development of woodland is prevented by the high salt content of the soil and by the more or less continuous wind in exposed areas. American, Australian and Asian savannahs with long-stemmed grasses, and Asian and European steppes with short-stemmed grasses form enormous areas of natural grassland. At present they are mostly transformed into high-yielding corn fields.

The life of grassland plants is controlled by light intensity and water. The species in meadow communities are all light-loving plants and shading reduces their growth; only marginal species gradually blend with the communities of forest margins and open woodland which mark the boundaries of the meadows. A peculiar feature of meadow plants is their ability to withstand regular cutting, a process which may even increase their vigour. A cultivated meadow requires constant care and management, fertilizing and mowing twice a year. Semi-cultivated meadows are not fertilized, only the grass is harvested and grazing cattle provide manure. Uncut or ungrazed meadows gradually become overgrown with bushes, becoming scrubland and eventually reverting to the forest state.

The amount of water in the soil determines the type of grassland and the plant communities present. In lowland areas where the water table is high or alongside streams, moist meadows are common. Wet mountain meadows occur in river valleys. At higher altitudes the meadows are often covered by Globe Flowers (*Trollius europaeus*) and Pink Bistort (*Polygonum bistorta*); other conspicuous plants are thistles like *Cirsium heterophyllum* and *C. rivulare*. In high mountain ravines, wet mountain meadows form the home of various tall herbs and grasses which could not survive on the exposed mountain side. In their deep, humus-rich soil grow such species as the groundsel *Senecio nemorensis*, butterburs (*Petasites*), White False Hellebore (*Veratrum album*), leopard's banes (*Doronicum*), etc. Typical of medium-high areas are wet moorland and so-called orchid meadows. Low-lying meadows are often more monotonous because of grass predomination and modern cultivation methods but old-fashioned meadows may still contain such species as Ragged Robin (*Lychnis floscuculi*), Ox-eye Daisy (*Leucanthemum vulgare*), Tormentil (*Potentilla erecta*) and several different species of clover (*Trifolium*).

As moisture in a meadow decreases, more drought-loving species appear. The plants of dry stony grasslands are often low-growing, the cover is sparser, often discontinuous, interrupted by protruding rocks and arid patches of stony soil. Xerophilous cushion-forming herbs and low spreading tufts of grasses and sedges are abundant in such places. The plants of dry habitats are adapted to the water shortage; their glandular, felt-covered or curled foliage reduces water loss. Typical plants of dry grassland include pulsatillas (*Anemone*), wild thymes (*Thymus*), sages (*Salvia*), mugworts (*Artemisia*) etc. Water is a factor influencing the composition of species in hayfields and consequently the yield and quality of fodder. In these fields soil water is regulated; wet meadows are drained and dry meadows are irrigated. Industrial fertilizers are also applied and the whole field may be ploughed and re-seeded with high-yield grasses. Often the wild species disappear entirely. A wet meadow left without control may become a marsh or moor with acid stands of sedges and rushes. A dry meadow on a dry slope becomes a steppe slope and pasture.

Arable Land

Fields are an entirely artificial habitat, just like a garden. They were created by man as an environment for cultivating crops. The carefully treated crops, however, have always grown in the company of wild plants called weeds.

The ancient farmer grew cereals and pulses as food for himself and fodder for his animals. Textile, medicinal and oil-producing plants are also grown in fields today. Vegetables, which need regular watering and frequent weeding, are also cultivated on a large scale in fields as well as in gardens. Favourable growing conditions and the elimination of competitive plants have turned the original hardy wild species into cultural crops dependent on the farmers' care. Plant breeding has changed them so that selected edible parts of the plants have been enlarged sometimes at the expense of the rest of the plant. Cultivated crops are now found far from their native lands in the fields of other continents.

Inevitably the worldwide distribution of crops was accompanied by the spread of their pests and diseases and by the seeds of the weeds that grew with them. With their adaptability, vast quantities of seed and effective methods of vegetative reproduction like creeping underground stems, weed species quickly colonise fresh soils. Ploughing and harrowing of arable land chops their underground stems and roots into small portions, each of which may be able to produce a new plant. The most successful annual weeds have life cycles which coincide with flowering and ripening of the crop plants. Although weeds in fields are often undesirable, many are useful as medicinal plants, like Chamomile (*Chamaemelum nobile*), Bindweed (*Convolvulus arvensis*), poppies (*Papaver*), etc. A former weed of wheat fields — rye — later became a cereal grown in poorer European soils. Weeds like mustards (*Sinapis*) and vetches (*Vicia*) provide nectar and pollen for honey bees.

Weeds are eliminated from fields and gardens to prevent them from depriving the crops of space, moisture, nutrients and light and to ensure a higher, cleaner yield. Perennial weed species are particularly vigorous but the majority, perhaps four fifths, of all weedy plants are annuals producing an abundance of seed. For instance a single specimen of Shepherd's Purse forms some 14,000 seeds, Groundsel 40,000 and Field Poppy up to 50,000 seeds a year.

In one square metre of weed-contaminated soil, 34,000—45,000 seeds were found, almost all capable of germination. With effective dispersal mechanisms, these weeds can quickly invade fields and gardens. Consistent weed control, carried out mechanically and chemically, by massive doses of herbicides, has successfully killed weeds but it has also destroyed some botanical species which are now rarely found in the wild. Some of them may have been valuable medicinal plants or potential sources of food — we shall never know.

Water and Waterside

Water is not only necessary for every living organism — a plant body contains up to 90 % water — but it is also the favoured environment for many plant species. Aquatic plants are adapted to live in water through their internal structure (anatomically) and by their shape (morphologically). For example the leaves of water lilies have long elastic leaf-stalks made buoyant by the air which fills the intercellular spaces of the thin-walled tissues inside. The rounded leaf-blades are leathery and waxy, so that water runs off them, leaving the leaf floating on the water surface and the air-holes are on the upper air-facing surface (in land plants the air-holes of a leaf are on the lower surface). In submerged plants the leaves are divided into a number of linear segments which increase the total leaf surface and dissolved gases and plant nutrients diffuse directly into the leaf cells from the water — there are no special transport cells like those found in land plants. Through photosynthesis, aquatic plants enrich the water with oxygen and thus clean it.

Water plants form a great amount of organic matter which, after decaying, accumulates as detritus on the bottom of a pond or lake together with the remains of dead animals. Decomposition of these organic substances forms mud which accumulates in sediments on the bottoms of water reservoirs or, in shallow water overgrown with vegetation, near the banks. The substances released by decomposition serve as nutrients for the next season's growth. To maintain the uninterrupted cycle of nutrient substances in the water, all the components of the aquatic ecosystem must be balanced.

The aquatic environment can be divided into biotopes of running water and biotopes of still water. The running water of rivers and streams contains more oxygen but it is sometimes more polluted by sewage and factory wastes. Plants may find difficulty in rooting themselves to the bottom. Natural and artificial bodies of water with still water include ponds, lakes, reservoirs and marshes. Some aquatic plants, like water lilies and water crowfoots, use the whole water column from the muddy bottom, in which they are anchored by their roots, to the surface, where their leaves and flowers float on the water. Other species do not reach the surface and their leaves and flowers remain submerged, eg. pondweeds. Some water plants are not anchored to the bottom but their leaves float on the surface (duckweeds and frogbit) or in the topmost layers of the water (bladderworts, Ivy-leaved Duckweed). Plants are not found in deep water where the light cannot penetrate though oxygen is still present for they cannot photosynthesise their food where there is no light.

As the water becomes shallower, as in fens and marshes, communities of marsh plants develop including species like arrowheads (*Sagittaria*), bulrushes (*Typha*), reeds (*Phragmites*), Flowering Rushes (*Butomus umbellatus*) and Yellow Flags (*Iris pseudacorus*). Their dense stands and conspicuous flowers adorn the banks of ponds and ditches. The network of their roots strengthens the thin mud at the bottom and causes the pond or ditch to silt up. Where the bank is shallow and shelving, a succession of plants can be seen, with deep water plants growing in the centre of the pond or lake and shallow water plants nearer to the bank. As the marginal vegetation thickens it traps more silt and the margins become shallower and, because of evaporation in the summer, drier. In this way, every year the plants creep a little further out into the water until eventually, over hundreds of years, the pond becomes filled with vegetation and land plants grow where once was open water. On the banks themselves shallow water plants gradually pass into the terrestrial flora of meadow or woodland plant communities.

Artificial and shallow ponds are occasionally drained or they may dry out in a particularly dry season. The bottoms of dried-out ponds provide a suitable environment for certain kinds of plants which also grow on the edges of shallow ponds, species which can survive alternate drying out and drowning, plants like *Callitriche platycarpa*, *Eleocharis acicularis* and *Littorella uniflora*. Truly aquatic species may survive such periods of drought or draining by producing seeds which remain dormant in the cracked mud until the water returns.

Pond inhabitants tend to be intolerant of too much human interference. Fertilizers from nearby arable land enhance the growth of plankton − unicellular algae and protozoans that float in their hundreds of thousands in the water. Some sensitive species of water lilies and pondweeds perish, clogged with algae, while others tend to over-multiply and, when they inevitably die from lack of light and oxygen, their remains may be so numerous that normal decay cannot take place and the pond becomes stagnant and develops a characteristic evil smell.

A spring is a place where water flows out into a natural well or seeps through or into the soil. A concealed spring in a meadow or mountain forest can be recognised by the fresh greenery of the surrounding vegetation. In such places, characteristic communities of plants are formed which include Bittercress (*Cardamine amara*), Kingcup (*Caltha palustris*) and Blinks (*Montia fontana*) together with many sedges and rushes. Forest springs are surrounded by golden saxifrages (*Chrysosplenium*), Field Horsetail (*Equisetum sylvaticum*), *Mnium* and *Sphagnum* mosses, the knotgrasses *Polygonum hydropiper* and *P. lapathifolium*, *Juncus* spp., Corn Mint (*Mentha arvensis*) and many others.

Woodland

Woodland constitutes a well-balanced, highly organized ecosystem consisting of trees and bushes, herbs, mosses, fungi and soil bacteria, as well as mammals, birds and invertebrates, some of which loosen the soil by digging. Woodland and forests have always resisted transformation into arable land or pastures. As soon as human activities cease, then such fields and meadows first become weedy in nature, then the weedy species are gradually replaced by woodland plants and bushes, then individual trees invade the area until it becomes woodland again. The trees of the forest interact with invisible soil microorganisms to produce humus-rich, moist

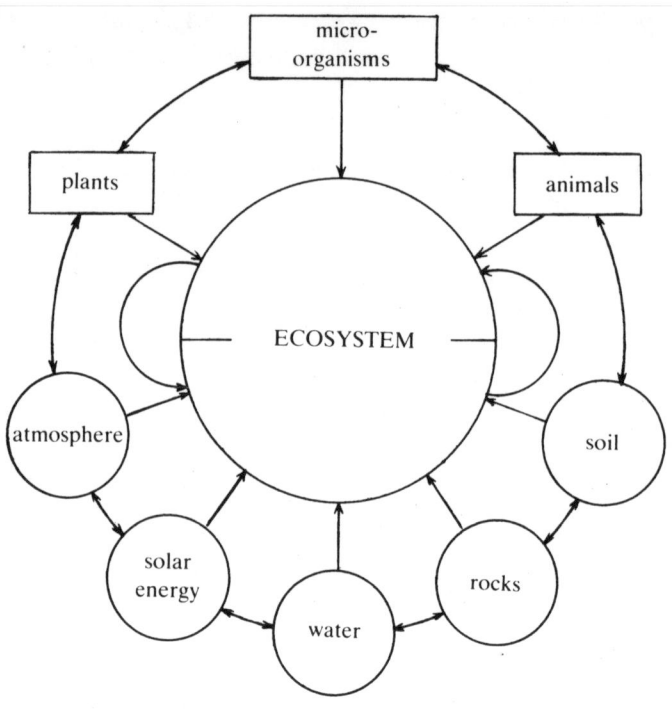

Ecosystem and its components. An ecosystem is an intricate system of inter-relationships between living organisms and their inanimate backgrounds. Rocks are broken down by the action of wind and water, and by bacteria and plant-roots until soil is formed. Plants grow prolifically in the soil and an animal community depends on the plants. Death returns their remains to the soil which becomes high in humus content and thus able to support a higher population of plants and animals. All elements in this ecosystem are essential to its continuing evolution. No ecosystem remains unchanged indefinitely but small or cyclical changes are part of a longer-term growth and stability. Major changes like total depletion of soil nutrients or removal of vegetation may be too great for maintenance of stability and the ecosystem may break down.

soils, an ideal substrate for woodland plants and fungi. Fungi are non-green plant-like organisms such as toadstools and mushrooms, which play an important role in the decomposition of organic matter during their feeding processes. Fungal threads and tree roots grow together in a form of co-existence called mycorrhiza (e.g. *Boletus scaber* occurs only around birch trees) and it is probable that neither can grow well without the close proximity of the other.

According to the dominant species, forests are divided into coniferous, deciduous or mixed woods and further subdivided into beech woods, hornbeam woods, oak woods etc., each with its own characteristic under-brush and ground flora. The composition and type of forest in any one area is determined by several factors including climate, altitude and soil type.

Lowlands (up to 200 metres above sea level) are the home of oak woods and occasional hornbeam woods, while the two trees may form a mixed oak-hornbeam wood in hilly regions (up to 500 metres) with heavy clay soils. Oak woods on limestone and dolomite bed rocks spread from the lowlands up to the warmer places in the hills. Beech woods are often found in the hills from 500 to 1,000 metres up, where they gradually pass into the spruce stands of mountain elevations (1,000 to 1,500 metres). The original climate-conditioned spruce forests extend to the timberline, the term that is used for the point at which trees become scarcer and more stunted in growth until they disappear altogether. Dwarf pine woods are found at subalpine elevations (1,500 to 1,800 metres).

Beech woods are often characteristic of the submontane regions but they are also found on uneven terrains in the lowlands. The dense crowns of beech trees intertwine to form an impenetrable canopy preventing the sun's rays from reaching the ground. Permanent shade and a low temperature means permanent moisture. Deep leaf litter affects the character of the herbaceous undergrowth. Only in early spring before the leaves emerge can the sunlight reach the ground layer of a beech forest. It is the flowering season for some of the undergrowth plants such as Coral-wort (*Dentaria*), Mezereon (*Daphne mezereum*), Asarabacca (*Asarum europaeum*), Wood Anemone (*Anemone nemorosa*) etc. Plants that bloom later in the spring and summer after the beech leaves have emerged, tend to grow in clearings or on the

woodland edges or to be lovers of deep shade. These include Baneberry (*Actaea spicata*), Wood Spurge (*Euphorbia amygdaloides*), Sweet Woodruff (*Galium odoratum*), Wood Sanicle (*Sanicula europaea*) together with the many ferns and mosses that like the conditions of almost permanent summer shade and high humidity in this kind of wood.

There are many plants that flower in early spring, growing in hornbeam and hornbeam-oak woods. They include Wood Anemones (*Anemone nemorosa*), Lesser Celandine (*Ranunculus ficaria*) and Dog's Mercury (*Mercurialis perennis*). Later-flowering species include Wood Forget-me-not (*Myosotis sylvatica*), Foxglove (*Digitalis purpurea*), willowherbs (*Epilobium* spp.), Enchanter's Nightshade (*Circaea*) and Yellow Archangel (*Lamiastrum galeobdolon*), most of them growing in clearings and on the edges of the woodland.

Oak woods are characteristic of lowland vegetation. The scattered trees allow the sun to warm up the soil and many drought-loving and light-demanding woodland plants are common. In cooler regions the herb layer may consist mainly of heathers and bilberries (*Erica* and *Vaccinium* spp.) but in warmer areas it becomes more varied. Bluebells (*Hyacinthoides non-scripta*) are often dominant in oceanic areas of Europe but their place is taken by *Corydalis solida* in more northern and central areas, and in many woods there are large stretches of Bracken (*Pteridium aquilinum*). Wood anemones, violets and primroses flower in spring and in summer the delicate white flowers of Wood Sorrel (*Oxalis acetosella*) and Heath Bedstraw (*Galium saxatile*) make their appearance.

Some forests are not influenced by the climate; they are azonal, that is they can occur at various altitudes. Fen woods are characteristic of moist situations, on soils that are regularly affected by spring floods and which often stay waterlogged throughout the winter. They are usually to be found in flat lowlands, but they may ascend alongside streams up to a height of 1,000 metres above sea level. The trees are highly characteristic. Exposed sites along lowland river reaches are colonised by willow trees (*Salix alba, S. fragilis* etc.), poplars (*Populus nigra, P. alba*) and sometimes ash trees (*Fraxinus* spp.). In the upper reaches of the rivers and alongside smaller streams in moist fen woodland grow the alders (*Alnus glutinosa* and *A. incana*). Moisture loving and shade-loving plants are found in the fen herb layer. Snowdrops (*Galanthus* spp.) and Snowflakes (*Leucojum* spp.), originally the inhabitants of scree forests, flower here in the spring, accompanied by the blue Two-leaved Squill (*Scilla bifolia*). Common species include Wood Anemones, the aromatic Ramsons (*Allium ursinum*), Comfrey (*Symphytum officinale*), Figwort (*Scrophularia nodosa*), Hemp Agrimony (*Eupatorium cannabinum*), Yellow Pimpernel (*Lysimachia nemorum*), Water Forget-me-nots (*Myosotis* spp.) and Kingcup (*Caltha palustris*).

Scree forests, likewise, are not bounded by any climatic zone but rather by their typical soil type consisting of stones, boulders and gravel and they extend from hillside habitats to true montane regions. Their trees are mostly maples and sycamores (*Acer* spp.), Large-leaved Lime and Small-leaved Lime (*Tilia grandiflora* and *T. parviflora*), Common Ash (*Fraxinus excelsior*) and Wych Elm (*Ulmus glabra*). Typical plants of the herb layer are Honesty (*Lunaria rediviva*), Dog's Mercury (*Mercurialis perennis*), Herb Robert (*Geranium robertianum*) and Yellow Balsam (*Impatiens noli-tangere*).

Coniferous forests differ from deciduous woodland in a marked way. Their trees are spruces, pines and firs, rarely yews. Spruce trees are often grown in monoculture in lowland and montane regions for their fast growth, which results in a considerable production of timber. Spruce wood is sold in large quantities at low cost, it has become a part of our civilization, a 'utility plant'. Artificial stands of spruce trees are found in places once occupied by fir, beech, pine and oak forests. The natural distribution of spruce lies in the montane vegetational belt, where it forms dense belts at altitudes of 1,000 to 1,200 metres in hills, on their shady slopes and in steep ravines. Monoculture growth of spruce has its problems for it is prone to attacks by pests, uprooting and damage caused by heavy snow and wind. It is better ecologically, but not economically, to grow it in mixed woodland together with beech, pine and larch.

The ground cover in coniferous spruce forests is very poor; many plants find the soil too acid for the spruce needles make it so and the shade is very dense while the trees are young. In a mature spruce forest there is more space and light, and plants such as wood sorrels (*Oxalis*), Hairy Woodrush (*Luzula pilosa*), European Trientalis (*Trientalis europaea*), Yellow Bird's-nest (*Monotropa hypopitys*), Milkweed Gentian (*Gentiana asclepiadea*), May Lily (*Maianthemum bifolium*), and ferns like *Dryopteris dilatata* may grow there.

Pine forests at lower altitudes also have a relatively poor herb layer due to the poor, often sandy, nutrient-deficient soil which is most favoured by pines. Pine is a light-loving species capable of extraordinary adaptation to various habitats. Its natural area of distribution is at heights of 500 to 700 metres. Its strong taproots penetrate deep into the soil or rocky crevices, anchoring it securely into the ground. In the undergrowth, pines are accompanied by Woodrush (*Luzula albida*), heathers and bilberries (*Erica* and *Vaccinium* spp.), Tormentil (*Potentilla erecta*) and occasionally Alpine Milkwort (*Chamaebuxus alpestris*).

In the highest vegetational belt around the timberline grow dwarf pines. Their twisted trailing branches are intertwined so densely that there is no room left for any undergrowth. The only other plants present are mosses, lichens, the grass *Festuca supina*, Blueberry (*Homogyne alpina*) and Common Goldenrod (*Solidago virgaurea* ssp. *alpestris*).

Borderlines between forests and meadows, forest margins or woodland edges have a characteristic flora of their own. The border is often much more densely overgrown with herbaceous plants than the forest floor itself, for the plants gain protection from the trees while enjoying the higher light intensity and the increased water supply without the competition of the tree roots. The natural forest does not end abruptly; its margins are often composed of many species of shrubs including Sloe (*Prunus spinosa*), Hawthorn (*Crataegus* spp.), Dog Rose (*Rosa canina*), Blackberry and Raspberry (*Rubus fruticosa, R. idaeus*), Barberry (*Berberis vulgaris*), Elder (*Sambucus nigra*), spindle trees (*Euonymus* spp.) and Bird-cherry (*Frangula alnus*).

Many of the herb layer species are characteristic meadow plants. They include knapweeds (*Centaurea* spp.), St. John's Worts (*Hypericum* spp.) and several species of orchids and daisies. Forest species found in the margins include Wood Anemones, Columbines (*Aquilegia vulgaris*), the campanulas *Campanula trachelium* and *C. persicifolia,* and several scrambling vetches (*Vicia dumetorum, V. sepium* and *V. cracca*).

Peat Bogs, Moors and Heaths

The peat bog is a monotonous habitat, poor in species, but with a complicated developmental background. It is a constantly developing biotope. Its origin and existence depends on the water system for peat bogs are formed in moist situations with shallow stagnant water, often on slightly undulating uplands with a high water table where rainfall is frequent and abundant. Peat bogs lack soil nutrients because dead organic remains of plants and animals sink beneath the water surface; they are cut off from air and therefore from oxygen and do not rot but decay only partly to form peat.

Sphagnum moss is the dominant plant of the peat bogs but other plants may be present, including sedges, rushes, heathers, bilberries, cranberries and Bladder Rush (*Scheuchzeria*). Their remains are mixed with the peat, as the plants die off at their bases while continuing to grow at the top. Deep peat pools tend to become overgrown from the edges and the banks are sometimes torn off and float as independent islets with peat vegetation. One of the most interesting, although minute, groups of plants of this biotope are the sundews (*Drosera* spp.). They grow on the verge of a pool, on the springy green carpet of *Sphagnum* moss, catching the mosquito larvae as they hatch into adults.

We may be able to learn from peat bogs what the surrounding countryside looked like long ago. Every year a thin layer of peat settles down, containing pollen grains of plants growing in the neighbourhood. Nearby wooded regions will be revealed by the presence of the pollen of the trees. The pollen grains are scattered over the peat bog by wind or dropped by passing birds. They are enclosed in a cellulose membrane which resists peat acids and peat has perfect preservative qualities; the pollen is kept intact for a long time. Identification of the type and number of pollen grains in peat is called 'pollen analysis', and this technique is of great value in determining the age of a peat bog.

A peat bog formed above the constant surface of underground water has a convex loaf-like shape. It is called a raised peat bog and is the home of some rare plant species like Marsh Tea (*Ledum palustre*), Marsh Andromeda (*Andromeda poliifolia*), the carnivorous sundews (*Drosera* spp.) and Bladder Rush (*Scheuchzeria palustris*).

Moorland is formed by the growth of reeds, sedges, horsetails and alders which cause the silting up of shallow ponds and marshes. *Sphagnum* is absent from moorland. The plants require constant, all-year moisture — particularly from undergound water — even throughout the summer months. Peat is also formed, but it has a different composition to that of peat bogs; it consists of the remains of reed-stalks, leaves and sedge blades with mud layers in between. Moorland soil is usually acid but may be alkaline where water runs in from close by limestone or magnesian rocks. These alkaline bogs contain unique communities of moisture-loving plants like Butterwort (*Pinguicula*), Cotton Grass (*Eriophorum latifolium*), Bog-rush (*Schoenus nigricans*) and Bog Myrtle (*Myrica gale*).

True moors and heaths have acid soils lacking minerals and nutrients, particularly calcium. The principal plant of this habitat, Heather (*Calluna vulgaris*) is a low shrub, 20—50 cm tall, in central Europe, but it can reach a height of up to one metre in the Atlantic parts of Europe and Britain. Continuous carpets of Heather are frequently complemented by Cross-leaved Heath (*Erica tetralix*), Bilberry (*Vaccinium myrtillus*), Gorse (*Ulex europaeus*) and other acid-loving herbs and grasses.

Heaths, like meadows, pastures and some bodies of water, are semi-natural habitats — localities in which the natural development of the ecosystem has been halted by human intervention, in an intermediate stage of an otherwise natural succession. The species are native to the area. A peat bog or heath, left to itself, is invaded by pine and birch and becomes open woodland in mountain areas, whereas in lowland areas it is invaded by alder and willow to become dense alder carr. The heaths were originally derived from similar woodland areas by deforestation followed by soil erosion, in which the calcium was carried away to leave a thin acid soil.

Plant Anatomy

An exhaustive survey of all types of plant organs and their mutual relationships is not the purpose of this book — it belongs to botany textbooks. We shall merely look at a variety of the anatomical features of plants and explain some of the terms used in the texts accompanying the featured species.

The root is the first part of the plant to emerge from a germinating seed. The first root soon thickens into the main root and produces a number of lateral roots, or it withers (as in grasses) and its function is taken over by many lateral roots. In addition to its basic functions — anchoring the plant in the soil and absorbtion of water and nutrients — the roots may also serve as food storage organs or as a means of vegetative propagation etc. Any change in function involves a change in form. Basic types of roots differ in shape, thickness and number: they may be tapering or cylindrical, taproots, lateral roots or adventitious roots, etc. Roots often reach to a great depth to obtain moisture and stability in a dry stony soil. The tip of the root is protected from damage caused by rough soil particles by a root cap. Immediately behind the cap is the region of root hairs — fragile outgrowths which absorb the soil moisture. As the root grows, new root hairs are constantly formed and the old ones are worn away by the soil — this process can be readily observed in spring on the roots of sprouting potatoes.

Shallow-rooted plants have roots spread close to the surface of the ground (maize, onions for example). The roots may be creeping and capable of growing into new plants if cut off from the parent. Bindweeds (*Convolvulus*) have creeping roots which deeply penetrate the ground. Other deep reaching roots are taproots like those found in dandelions (*Taraxacum*) and members of the carrot family (Umbelliferae). Adventitious roots grow directly from the nodes of creeping stems, like those of Creeping Buttercup (*Ranunculus repens*), or from the bases of bulbs.

Parasitic plants like the broomrapes

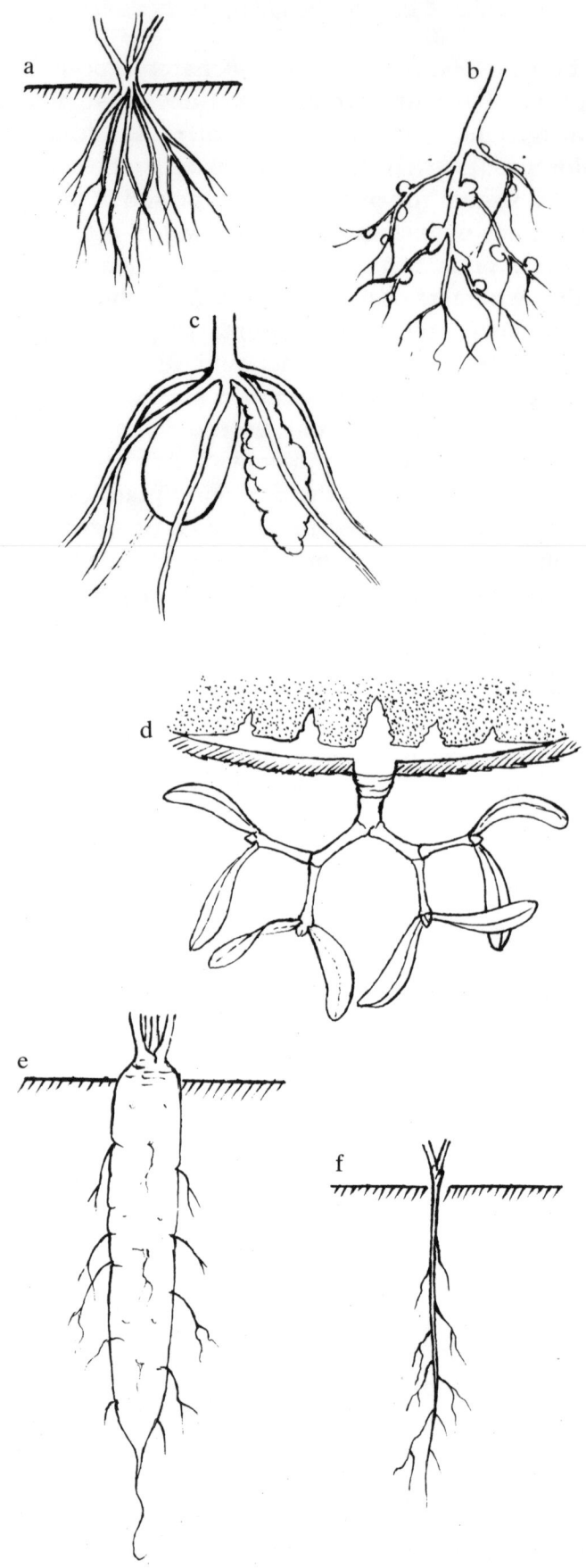

Roots: a) adventitious roots like those found in grasses b) roots of leguminous plant with nodules containing symbiotic bacteria c) roots and root tuber in which food is stored d) parasitic roots of mistletoe penetrating bark of tree e) taproot with stored food like that found in cultivated carrot f) taproot like that of dandelion

(*Orobanche*) have special roots called haustoria, adapted for sucking nutrients from the stems of their host plants. The roots of the members of the pea family (Leguminosae) bear tubercles with nitrogenous bacteria (*Rhizobium radicicola*) which supply the plants with nitrogen from the air. Storage roots become oval, globular or palmately divided into root tubers.

Root systems vary in proportional relationships with the rest of the plant. For instance, wheat has a root system much larger than the leaves and stalks with their ears, while conversely maize, although it may reach a height of up to 3 metres, has a very small shallow root system. The length and degree of branching of the roots is very much affected by the qualities of the soil. It is well known that root crops such as carrots grow much straighter in sandy soil where there is little soil resistance, than in dense clay soils. In most plants the roots grow from the region at the base of the stem.

The main function of the stem is to bear the leaves and to transport water and nutrients throughout the plant. Persistence of the stem depends on the plant's longevity. In ephemeral and annual or overwintering plants, the vegetative period is restricted to the several weeks or months required for the formation of seeds. Biennial plants need two seasons to complete their life cycle. Monocarpic plants take several years to grow, produce flowers and fruits, and die (*Agave americana* takes 40−50 years to flower, then it dies). The stems of perennial plants may last many years and bear flowers and fruits annually or the plants may persist underground in winter and produce new stems every year.

Stems may be erect, ascending, trailing, creeping, twining or climbing. Some stems are leafy, others (scapes) carry flowers only. Grasses have hollow stems with nodes. Creeping stems may grow above ground as long thin runners as in Creeping Cinquefoil (*Potentilla reptans*), or underground as in Ground Elder (*Aegopodium podagraria*). These are distinguished from roots by their ability to form adventitious roots and by the buds which may be found on them. Instead of leaves, creeping underground stems (called rhizomes) bear scales. Rhizomes often serve as underground food stores, when they are characteristically swollen and are called stem tubers (examples include potatoes and irises).

Stems are enormously varied. They may be winged, ribbed or triangular in cross-section,

they may be flattened and green and function as photosynthetic organs (*Lemna*), they may be thorny (roses), tall and woody as in many trees or, at the other extreme, they may be reduced to almost nothing as in many alpine species of saxifrages and primulas.

In cacti and other succulents, the stem is both a storage organ for water and a photosynthetic organ. The photosynthetic organs of most plants are the leaves. In the light, the leaves use the energy from the sunlight to drive a photochemical reaction between water and carbon dioxide in which the green pigment, chlorophyll, acts as a catalyst and oxygen is released. Photosynthesis produces sugars which are usually converted into

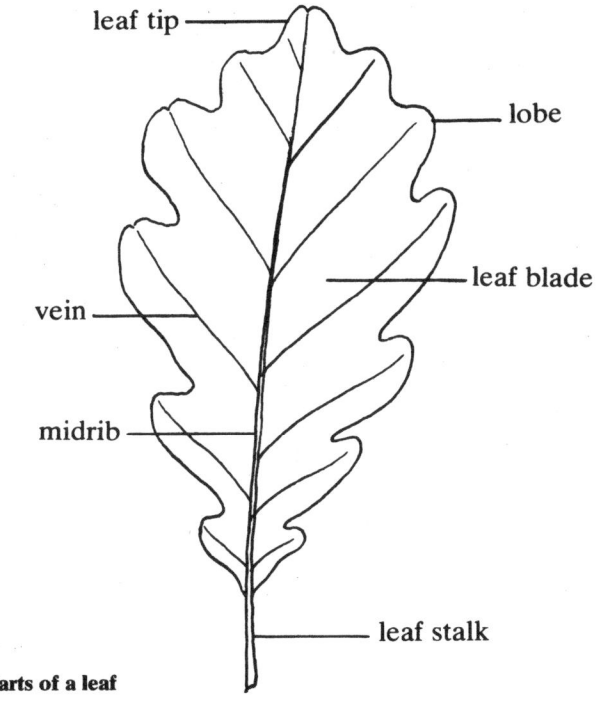

leaf tip · lobe · vein · leaf blade · midrib · leaf stalk

Parts of a leaf

starch and stored in food storage organs until needed. Starch is then broken down into soluble sugars which the plant can use to provide energy or as material for growth. During the breakdown of the sugars, carbon dioxide and water are released and the plant takes in oxygen from the air. The process is the same as animal respiration. In the daytime the plants' respiration is overshadowed by their photosynthetic assimilation, during which oxygen is produced and released. In this way plants are indispensable for all living organisms − they are responsible for maintaining the oxygen balance of the atmosphere. By transpiring excess water through the pores in the leaf surfaces, the plants also moisten the air. Leaves use solar energy to perfection. Their flat blades and arrangement on the plant present the maximum surface area to the sun.

Some monocotyledonous plants (sedges, grasses etc.) have linear blades without stalks, but each leaf has a sheath enclosing the stem and there is a membranous ligule between the sheath and the blade. Dicotyledonous plants (those in which the leaves have netted veins) have well-developed leaf-stalks. These may be very long, as in water lilies. In some species, like acacias, which are found in extremely dry situations the blade of the leaf has disappeared and the leaf-stalks are enlarged and leaf-like. Some families of plants have stipules − leaf-like structures at the junctions of the stems and leaves. In some central American acacias the stipules are modified into large hollow thorns serving as homes for ferocious ants. This symbiosis yields food for the ants (oily white particles on leaf tips), while the acacias are protected from herbivorous animals.

Bracts, underdeveloped leaves in the inflorescences protecting the flower buds, are also of leaf origin. Small opposite bracts on the flower stalks are called bracteoles.

Leaves may be adapted to serve various functions, for instance leaf tendrils of vetches enable the plants to cling to other plants and climb towards the light. The sticky leaves of the sundews (*Drosera*) and the bladder-traps of the carnivorous bladderworts (*Utricularia*) are both modified leaves designed to trap insects. The bulb, a storage and reproductive organ, is formed from thickened, scale-like leaves gathered around an extremely shortened base of a stem.

Leaves may be simple and undivided as in nightshades (*Solanum*), or simple and toothed as in the deadnettles (*Lamium*), or palmately lobed as in mallows (*Malva*) or pinnately lobed as in Groundsel (*Senecio vulgaris*). Compound leaves have blades composed of several to many leaflets; they may be palmate or pinnate in shape and the leaflets may be subdivided also. Compound palmate leaves are found in many of the cinquefoils (*Pottentilla*), pinnate compound leaves are found in vetches (*Vicia*) and compound divided leaves are found in many members of the carrot family (Umbelliferae).

Any description and classification of plants always includes the arrangement of the leaves on the stem and their attachment to it. The leaves may be alternate, opposite or whorled; they may be stalked, stalkless, clasping, sheathed etc. Sometimes the shape of the tip and the base of the blade is important as in Corn Mint (*Mentha arvensis*), where such a feature distinguishes the various subspecies. It is rare for both stem and leaves to be completely hairless; usually they are sparsely or densely covered with hairs of various lengths and thickness, from a few large scattered hairs to a dense covering of white felt. Similarly many plants bear glands − groups of cells which may look like small dots as in St. John's worts, or modified into thorns as in roses.

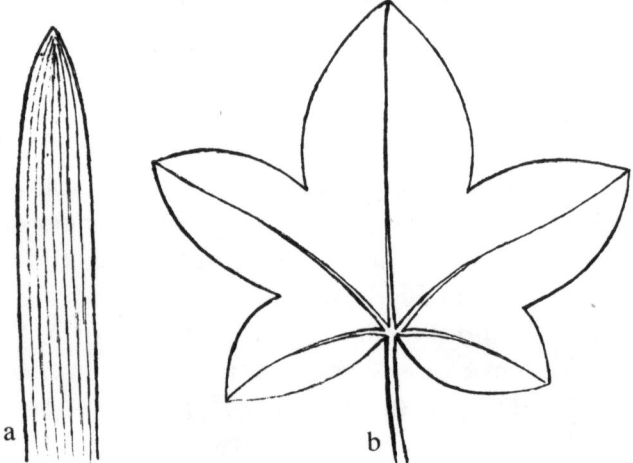

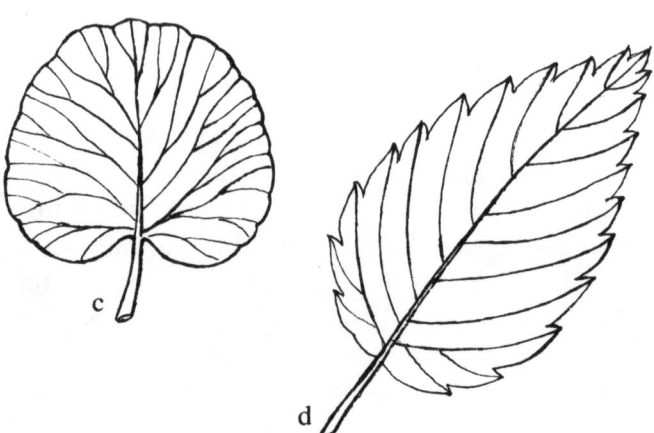

Leaf venation. There are two large groups of flowering plants, the Monocotyledones and the Dicotyledones. The first group, the Monocotyledones, often have long, straight, parallel-sided leaves with parallel veins like those of grasses, rushes and many members of the onion family; others of the group have more oval-shaped leaves but with the same parallel veins, as seen in orchids and lilies. Dicotyledonous leaves, however, vary considerably in shape from simple lance-shaped or oval leaves to palmate and compound leaves with many leaflets. In this group the veins are always in the form of a network.

a) parallel veins of a monocotyledonous leaf
b), c), and d) network-type venation patterns of dicotyledonous leaves

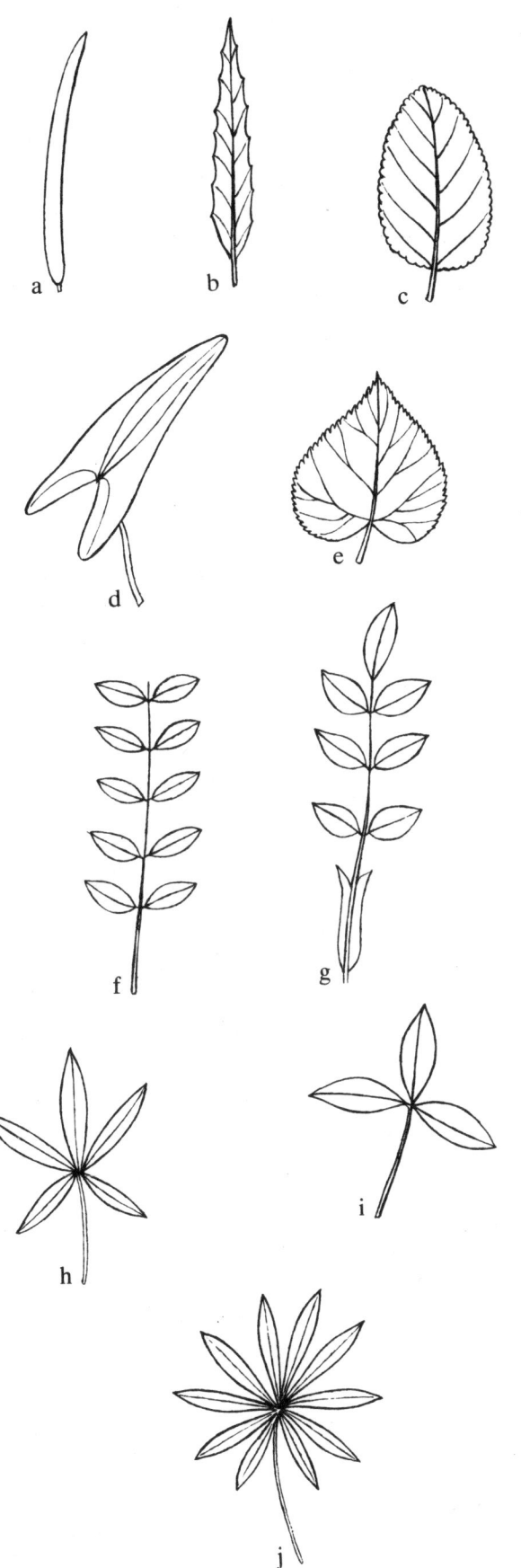

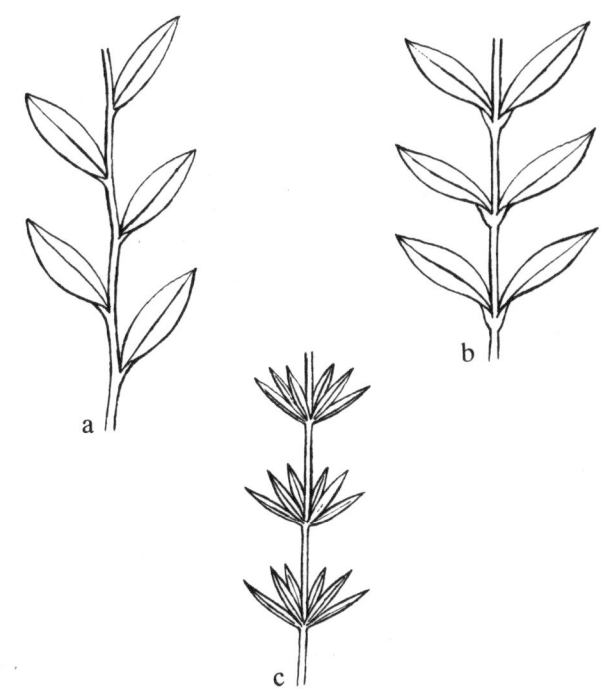

The arrangement of leaves on a stem: a) alternate b) opposite c) whorled

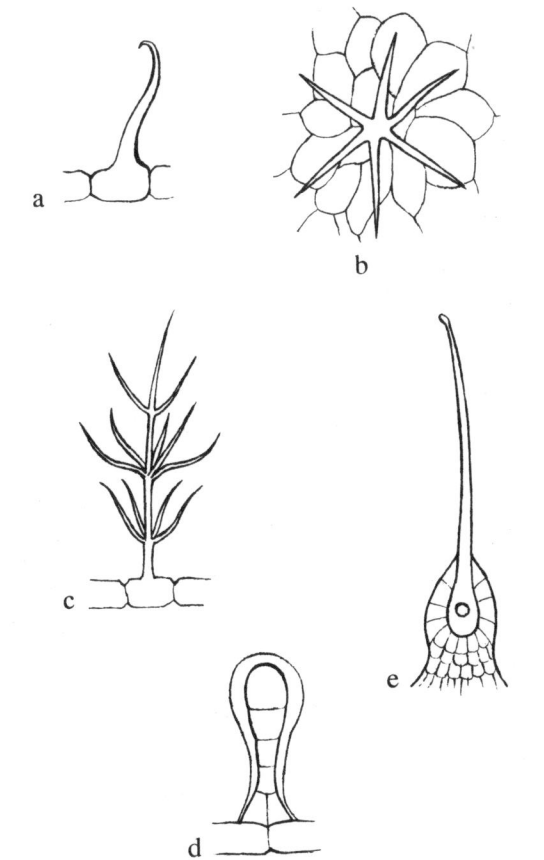

Simple leaves: a) linear b) lance-shaped c) oval d) arrow-shaped e) heart-shaped **Compound leaves:** f) pinnate leaf with an even number of leaflets g) pinnate leaf with an odd number of leaflets h) compound leaf with five leaflets i) compound with three leaflets j) compound leaf with many leaflets

Hair-types found on leaves and stems: a) hooked b) star-shaped c) candelabrum-like d) glandular e) stinging

Flowers are very shortened stems with restricted growth and with modified leaves. Each flower is formed from four whorls of modified leaves. The outermost whorl is composed of sepals, next there is a whorl of petals, inside that a whorl of stamens and the innermost whorl is one of carpels. The numbers and arrangement of the parts of the flower vary considerably and are of prime importance in the classification and identification of species.

The sepals are usually green and leaf-like, enclosing and protecting the bud and the base of the flower. They vary in number from two to six or more; they may be free (not joined) or united into a tube; they may resemble petals in form and function or they may be tiny or absent.

Petals are usually brightly coloured and serve to attract insects to the flowers so that pollination can occur. They often have guidelines on them, which direct the insect into the flower in such a way as to coat the insect with pollen that it will then carry to another flower. Many flowers produce nectar in nectaries on the bases of the petals or on the receptacle; this also attracts the insects. Petals vary in number from none at all up to 30 or more; they may all be free or partially united into a tube and some families have flowers with unequal petals, like the lipped flowers of the mint family (Labiatae) and orchids (Orchidaceae) and the pea flowers of the Leguminosae.

The leafy origin of the sepals and petals is usually clear but the stamens are less obviously leaf-like. Each one consists of a filament or stalk which varies according to species, and four sacs at the top of the filament which are called anthers. In the anthers grow the male sex cells, the pollen grains. There are often the same number of stamens as petals or twice as many stamens as petals, and their arrangement in the flower is an important distinguishing feature; they may grow on the petals or on the receptacle, they may be opposite the petals or alternate with them, there may be stamens with different length filaments in the same flower. The arrangement is often related to the method of pollination.

The central whorl of the flower is the pistil consisting of the carpels which vary in number from one to many, depending on the species. Frequently it appears as if there is only one carpel in the centre of the flower when, in fact, there may be several, so closely united as to appear to be one. Cutting open the pistil reveals

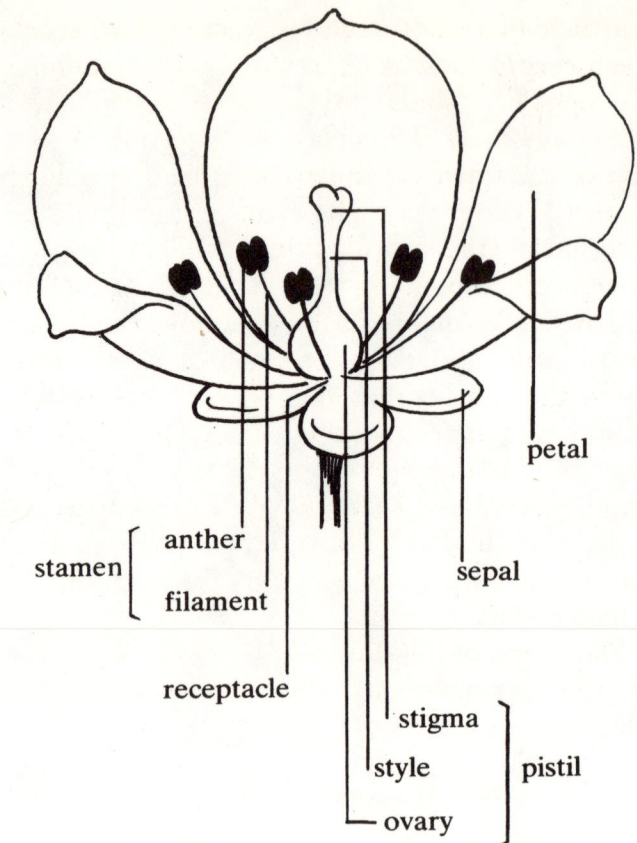

Parts of a flower

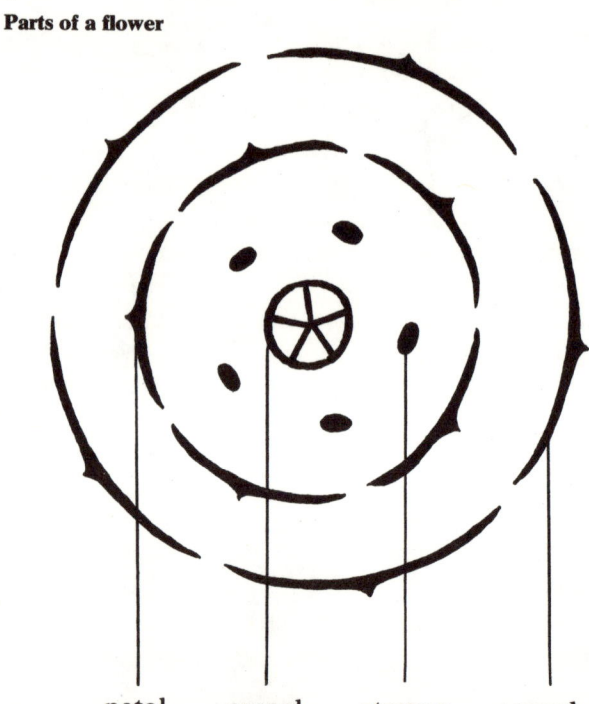

Floral diagram of a hypothetical flower. A great deal of information is contained in a floral diagram, which is a schematic representation of a flower. For instance, this diagram represents a flower in which the parts are all in fives; the sepals and petals are free (if they were united, then they would be drawn touching) and the sepals and stamens are inserted on the flower alternating with the petals, not opposite them. The stamens are drawn separately, meaning that they are growing directly on the receptacle; if they were growing on the petals (a common condition in many flowers) then a line would be drawn connecting each stamen to a petal. The ovary is formed of five fused carpels.

that it is in several sections, each one a carpel. Each carpel consists of a basal ovary containing the eggs, a tubular style and a stigma. The arrangement of the carpels with respect to the rest of the flower is an important distinguishing feature. They may grow on and above the receptacle (the more or less flat base of the flower corresponding to the shortened stem which forms the basis of the flower). If the ovary grows above the receptacle and therefore above the bases of the other flower parts (sepals, petals, stamens) it is called a superior ovary. It may grow below the receptacle and is therefore found below the bases of the other flower parts, it is then called an inferior ovary. In other flowers the flower parts grow only just below or on the same level as the ovary.

The shape of the flower and its parts is shown on the accompanying illustration and on the circular diagram known as the floral diagram.

Flowers rarely grow singly; more commonly they are gathered into a multiflowered inflorescence. There are two basic types of inflorescence, the raceme and the cyme. In the raceme the lateral flower-stalks are shorter than the main stem with its terminal flower and the flowers open from the bottom upwards. If the lateral flower-stalks are elongated so that all the flowers are in line, then the inflorescence is called a corymb (as in apple) and the individual flowers open from the margin towards the centre. If the main stem is shortened so that all flower-stalks grow from one point, then the inflorescence is called an umbel. This sort of inflorescence is typical of the family Umbelliferae. When a raceme is shortened it may form a flower-head as in clovers (*Trifolium*) or the family Compositae. This, the daisy family, has characteristic flat flower-heads in which the main stem of the head has been enlarged into a receptacle and the whole flower-head is called a capitulum, supported by a group of bracts called an involucre.

In the cyme, the main stem soon stops growing; it is terminated by a flower and the surrounding lateral stems grow beyond it so that the terminal flower is lower than the side stems. Flowers open from the top downwards or from the middle towards the sides (as in the houseleeks, *Sempervivum*). In a dichasial cyme, two opposite branches grow from beneath the short main stem and branch out in successive pairs, as in chickweeds (*Cerastium*). In the family Boraginaceae, lateral stems grow from one side

Types of flowers: a) open flower with free petals b) bell-shaped flower with united petals c) tubular flower d) two-lipped flower with a closed mouth and a spur e) hooded flower of the labiate family f) strapshaped flower of the daisy family g) hooded flower of the orchid family h) asymmetrical flower of the pea family showing (1) standard petal (11) wing petals (111) keel petals

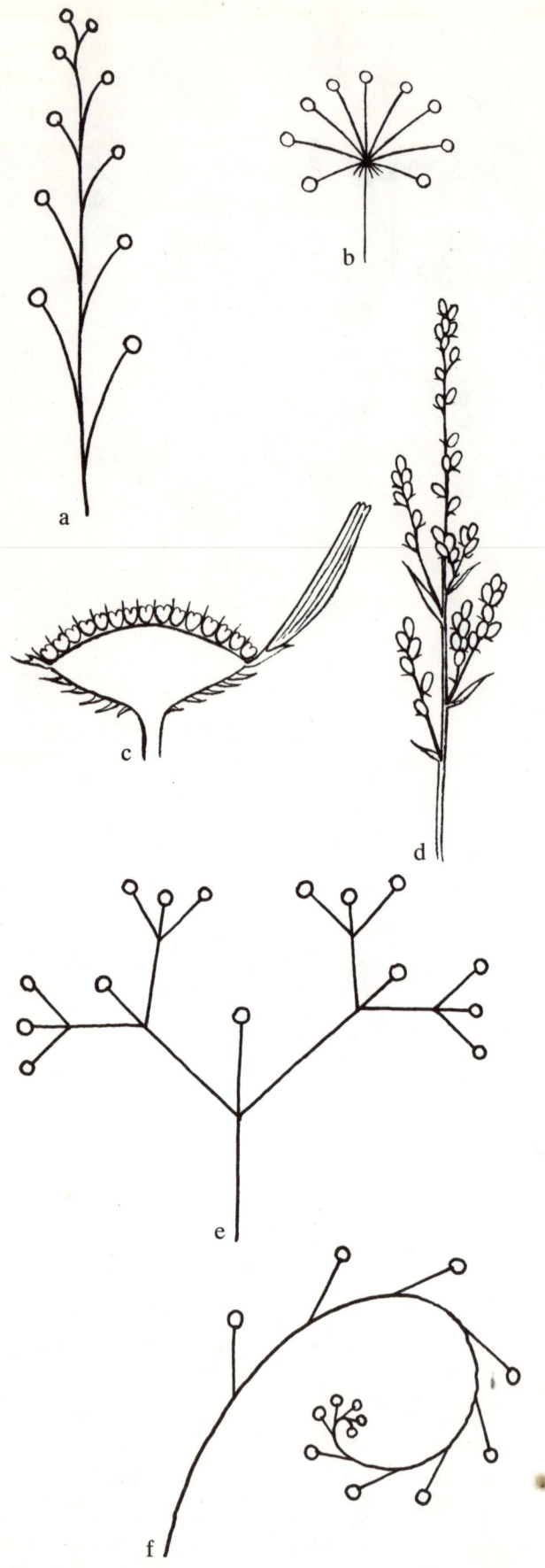

Types of inflorescences: a) raceme b) umbel c) head (capitulum) of the daisy family d) panicle of heads e) dichasial cyme as found in the chickweeds f) scorpioidal cyme as found in the borage family

of the cyme only, so that it forms a curl — this is a scorpioidal cyme.

Simple inflorescences may be gathered together into compound inflorescences, for instance a panicle is a compound inflorescence composed of many racemes, cymes, flowerheads etc. A compound umbel is composed of several smaller ones.

Most plants have bisexual flowers, that is with both stamens and carpels present. Unisexual flowers have either stamens (male flowers with anthers) or carpels (female pistillate flowers). A plant which bears separate male and female flowers on the same individual is called monoecious; many members of the daisy family have such flowers. In a dioecious species, male and female flowers are borne on separate plants (nettles, for instance).

Pollination occurs when pollen from ripe anthers is transferred from the anthers to the stigma. The small light pollen grains of wind-pollinated flowers (anemophilous flowers) are transported to distant flowers by the wind. The pollen of insect-pollinated flowers (entomophilous flowers) is carried by insects from the anthers to the stigma and is sticky or has tiny protruberances which catch on the insects' bodies. The transfer of pollen from one aquatic flower to another is usually carried out by water (hydrophilous flowers). In autogamy (self-pollination) the flower is fertilized by its own pollen. In special cases called cleistogamy, self-pollination takes place in an enclosed flower that never opens, as in violets for instance. Allogamy or cross-pollination, however, is more common and occurs when a flower is pollinated by pollen from another plant of the same species.

Plants often have various devices which prevent self-pollination. For instance, in many flowers the anthers ripen before the carpels. An insect attracted by nectar enters the flower of Wild Thyme (*Thymus praecox*), for instance, and is powdered by pollen from ripe anthers. As long as the anthers are ripe and powdery, the style is short. After the anthers are empty, the style starts growing and the stigmas ripen, ready to accept pollen from other, younger blossoms. The floral structure itself may also inhibit selfpollination. Heterostylic plants, primulas and Purple Loosestrife, for instance, have some individuals with long styles and short stamen filaments, while other individuals have short styles and long stamen filaments. The grains of the pollen differ in size as well, fitting into holes on the stigma, so that pollen from the short-styled flowers can only pollinate long-styled ones, thus assuring cross-pollination between two different plants.

Flowers often have vivid colours and may lure insects by an intense fragrance, sometimes even by an offensive smell, as in *Rafflesia* which attracts flies by smelling of rotting meat. Many flowers have nectaries and provide the insects with nectar, like many species of clover. Not only insects are involved in pollination; uncommon pollinators include bats and hummingbirds in tropical countries. Pollination of some species depends on a specific pollinator: *Yucca filamentosa*, for instance, is dependent on the tiny moth *Pronuba yuccasella*. Sage, like many other members of the family Labiatae and many orchids, has an automatic lever mechanism for cross-pollination and a landing surface for insects on the lower lip of the flower. Pollen grains of orchids are packed into a cluster (pollinium) to be transported as a parcel on insects' bodies.

Artificial pollination, that is human transfer of pollen from one plant to the stigma of another selected plant, serves as a cross-breeding method in hybridization, when the hybrid plant produced may yield choicer flowers or a higher crop than either of the parent plants. Pollen grains landing on the stigma grow down through the style, carrying the male sex cells to the ovary where the eggs are fertilized. The ovary and eggs then grow, the former becomes the fruit and the latter the seeds within it.

Seeds vary in size from the minute seeds of orchids, underdeveloped and lacking a store of nutrients, to the gigantic seeds of the rare palm *Lodoicea maldivica* from the Seychelles in the Indian Ocean, whose oval fruits reach a length of 40—50 cm and weigh up to 20 kg when fresh. Their single seed matures after five years.

Ripened dry fruits either dehisce (open) to release mature seeds or they do not open and the seed(s) remain enclosed. Dehiscent fruits include the follicles of the Ranunculaceae, the pods (legumes) of the Leguminosae, the siliquas of the Cruciferae and the capsules of many families of flowering plants. Fruits that do not open are usually one-seeded, like the achenes of the Compositae. They may occur in clusters like those of buttercups (*Ranunculus*) and cranesbills (*Geranium*) or in pairs like those found in the family Umbelliferae.

In succulent fruits the wall of the ovary becomes juicy and sweet, surrounding several seeds in berries (redcurrants), or a single seed in a stone as in the drupes of cherries and peaches. All the above-mentioned fruits are true fruits, that is the covering of the fruit is derived from the wall of the ovary whether it is dry or succulent. False fruits are those originating from another part of the flower, for instance the rose hip consists of a fleshy receptacle enclosing several carpels each with a seed, a strawberry is a pulpy sweet receptacle covered with achenes.

Plants often produce large numbers of seeds many of which would die for lack of space, water etc., if they were not carried away from the parent plant. Plants have various mechanisms to ensure the dispersal of their seeds. In those with dehiscent fruits the seeds may be flung out, for instance by the sudden explosive opening of the pod in vetches or by the pepper-shaker effect of the poppy capsules swaying in the wind on their long flexible stalks. These seeds do not travel far from the parent plant and may form colonies nearby, so that the species gradually spreads further afield each year. Plants with light seeds like those of orchids or *Campanula* which are dispersed by wind may be found far from the parent plant. Other wind-borne seeds or fruits may be adapted for flight by the presence of hairs (Dandelion, Rosebay Willowherb) or wings (Wild Angelica). The entire plant may participate in seed dispersal, for instance the upper parts of Field Eryngo (*Eryngium campestre*) die away in autumn and the plant is then rolled about by the wind. *Crambe* is another genus distributed in this way. These plants are called tumbleweeds.

Water plants also often have light seeds, frequently with flotation devices to carry them to the surface if the fruits are at the bottom, and to keep them afloat while they are carried away. Such seeds are produced by the White Water-lily (*Nymphaea alba*). Heavier seeds may be rolled along the bottom by the current, like those of Policeman's Helmet (*Impatiens glandulifera*).

Animals may disperse seeds and fruits great distances away from the parent plant. Some fruits form a common part of the diet of birds and mammals and their seeds germinate only after passing through the animal's digestive tract where they are processed by digestive juices. Such fruits are usually conspicuously coloured and have a juicy pulp. Other animals collect the seeds and transport them to their winter storage places (ants gather the seeds of violets, squirrels and mice hoard acorns and nuts) but only rarely are all the seeds eaten and those left over germinate to form new plants.

Seeds and fruits equipped with hooks, spines and thorns are carried by animals on their fur or feathers and by people on their clothing. For instance, bur marigolds (*Bidens*) have fruits with tough bristles and backwardly turned spines, burdocks (*Arctium*) have large hooked fruits (burrs) which catch on clothing, forming the basis for a favourite children's game.

All well-developed healthy ripe seeds are potentially capable of germinating into new plants but many do not survive. They may be eaten, attacked by bacteria or fungi, or land in unsuitable places where they die soon after germinating. Seeds are differentiated according to the number of seed leaves or cotyledons that they possess. Dicotyledonous plants have two fat rounded food-storing seed leaves and when the seed germinates the first shoot grows up between the two, while the main root and lateral roots grow downwards. In monocotyledonous plants, like lilies and irises, there is only one cotyledon present which is thin and without food. When the seed germinates the seed leaf remains within the seed, while the first shoot grows up from the side of the seed leaf and the main root is soon replaced by numerous additional roots. The food store in monocotyledonous seeds is provided by a special structure called the endosperm, or it may be absent as in the underdeveloped seeds of the orchids.

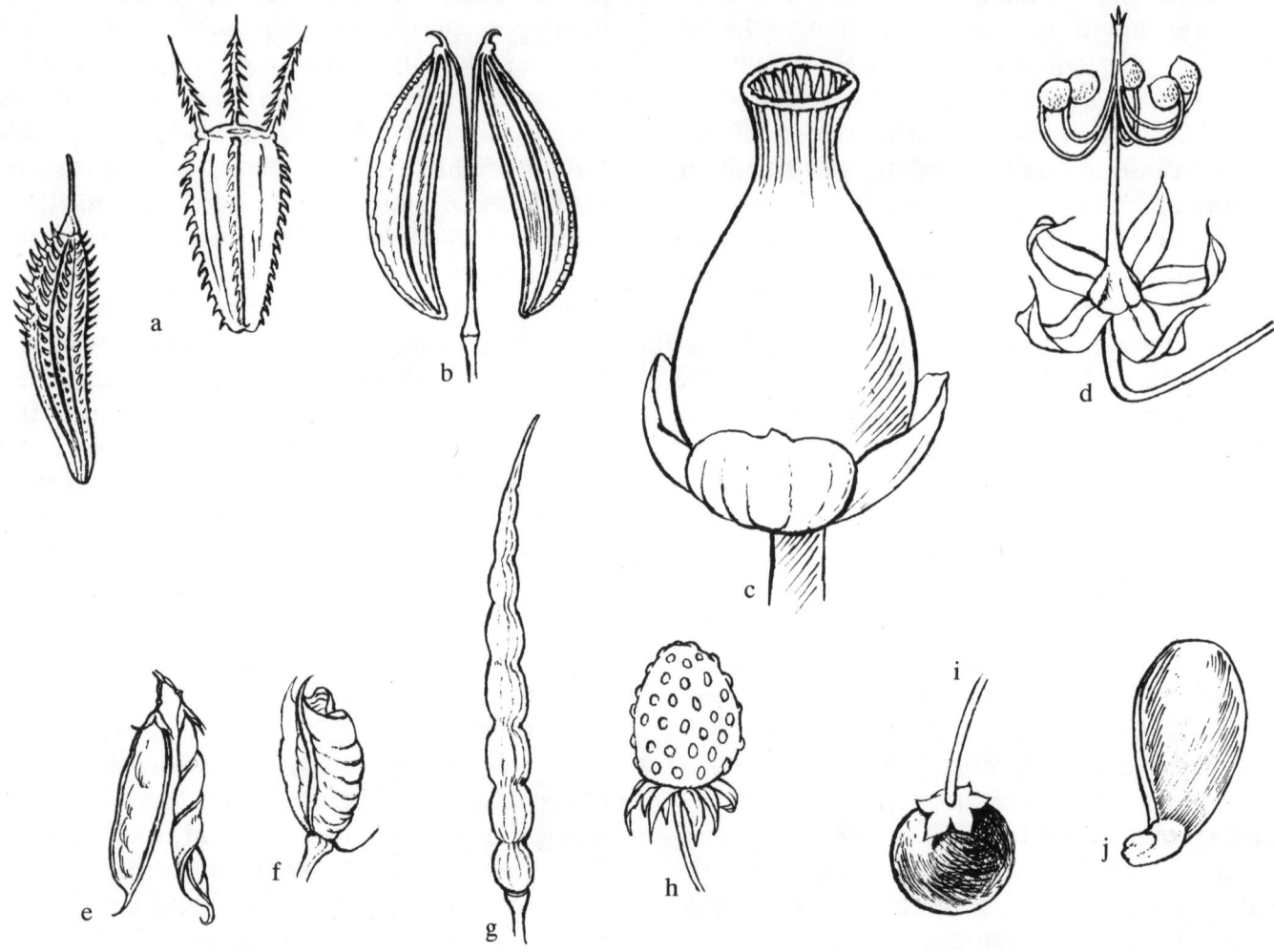

Types of fruits: a) achenes b) double achene of the umbellifer family c) capsule d) characteristic splitting (schizocarpic) fruit of the cranesbills e) pod of pea family f) follicle g) siliqua of crucifer family h) strawberry — a false fruit in which the sweet fleshy part is formed from the swollen receptacle and the 'pips' are achenes i) berry j) seed with caruncle

Botanical Nomenclature and the Classification of Plants

It seems quite natural today that all plants have two Latin names. This useful and simple method of naming plants and animals was introduced as late as the middle of the 18th century by the Swedish naturalist Carl von Linné, usually known today as Linnaeus (1707–1778). He gave each plant and animal known at that time a generic and a specific name, so that Biting Stonecrop, for example, has the generic name *Sedum* and the specific name *acre*. The generic name is a noun and the specific name is an adjective, often describing some aspect of the plant or animal. These brief and accurate names replaced the Latin superfluously descriptive names. For instance 'elder with black fruits in an umbel' (*Sambucus fructu in umbella nigro*) was shortened by Linnaeus to *Sambucus nigra* = Black Elder. Inconsistent and often contradictory terminology caused errors in identification, made communication among botanists and medical men difficult and sparked off unnecessary arguments which inhibited progress.

Many old names were based on useful substances yielded by the plant or on its similarity to something else, often a part of the body. In the 16th century, a French botanist mentioned three kinds of Lungwort, *Pulmonaria* I–III. Two of them were medicinal plants used to heal lung diseases; *Pulmonaria officinalis* and *P. angustifolia*. The third species was in fact the lichen *Lobaria pulmonaria* which was used for treating pulmonary diseases because of its external similarity to the lungs. This 'doctrine of similarity' was widespread in mediaeval medicine and many plants which resembled a part of the human body were used to treat illnesses of that part of the body. The lungworts already described were used for treating lung diseases since their spotted leaves resemble lung tissue.

Interest in plants, their usefulness and their classification, has been considerable since ancient times; first noticed were the plants yielding food and medicinal substances. The first attempts at a classification of plants according to conspicuous external traits appeared at the end of the 16th century; plants were divided into trees, shrubs and herbs and herbs were subdivided according to features like bulbs, tuberous roots, prominent flowers etc. Linnaeus continued in the attempts started by his predecessors. He was convinced that 'there is no other plant function for which Nature would have such constant organs as for reproduction', and he devoted his attention to carpels and stamens, regarding them as the most important parts of flowers. Linnaeus' system was artificial and based on comparisons between certain parts of the plants. He founded his original classification on the number, arrangement and position of stamens and carpels. He divided plants into 24 classes, the classes into orders, orders into genera and genera into species. His findings were compiled in several treatises; *Systema naturae* (The System of Nature, 1735) in which he briefly described in Latin all known plants and animals; *Genera plantarum* (The Genera of Plants, 1737) and *Species plantarum* (The Species of Plants, 1753), in which he described 7,300 species and used for the first time the binomial nomenclature (the use of the two Latin names). Botanical nomenclature still uses *Species plantarum* as the basis for naming new plants. When describing a new species or variety, it is necessary for a botanist to go back to the original herbarium in which the species was described for the first time. The oldest documents still in use date soon after 1753, when the *Species plantarum* was first published. Sometimes several authors have given different names to the same species or conversely have given the same Latin name to different species. Such a confusing situation is solved by the principle of priority, that is the oldest given name is kept and the others become synonyms. When different species have been given the same name, the later species is renamed.

The system created by Linnaeus greatly facilitated scientific work. Linnaeus also made the botanical nomenclature more accurate and enriched it by new terms. He invented some of them and adapted and explained others in detail. The thousand or so terms introduced by Linnaeus include: perianth (sepals and petals), corolla (petals), ovary, nectary, filament, anther, receptacle and many others.

Linnaeus' binomial system was simple and efficient but the actual classification he devised was inaccurate. It failed to demonstrate the relationships between plants, it merely helped to classify them. Linnaeus himself was aware that his system was not ideal; he grouped plants like barberry (*Berberis*) and reeds together because they had the same number of stamens (*Berberis* is a dicotyledonous plant and reeds are monocotyledons); carrots and flax were grouped together because both have flowers growing in umbels. In fact they belong to different families. On the other hand, species of the same genus but with a different number of stamens were separated, for instance Pepperwort (*Lepidium campestre*) has six stamens and *L. ruderale* has two stamens, and would be separated according to Linnaeus' system. Nevertheless the new system was an enormous aid to plant identification in Linnaeus' time and his binomial nomenclature has been used for more than 200 years.

The scientific name of a genus, species or other taxon is followed by the name of the author who gave it the name and published the description. The name is often abbreviated (L. = Linnaeus). The author who changes the name of a plant adds his name and puts the name of his predecessor into brackets: *Potentilla erecta* (L.) Rauschel.

The species is the basic classification unit or taxon. Every species belongs to a genus, the genus to a family and the family is part of an order. Other superior taxa are classes, divisions, phyla, subkingdoms and kingdoms. The species is subdivided into subspecies, varieties and forms. Taxa higher than the species have only one name and their hierarchical value is expressed by a Latin name with a particular ending for each group. Scientific nomenclature is an international means of communication in science and in related practical disciplines like forestry, agriculture, pharmacology etc.

Before Linnaeus' time, plants either had vernacular names or they were described in Latin, for example anemone with blackish drooping flowers was *Pulsatilla florae nutans nigricans*. It is now *Pulsatilla nigricans*. Similarly the small forest carnation with a single flower was *Caryophyllus sylvestris humilis flore unico* and is now called *Dianthus arenarius*. It is not easy to give a plant a characteristic and fitting name. Many plants were named after Linnaeus' friends or famous botanists, for instance *Rudbeckia* was named after Prof. Rudbeck, Professor of Botany in Uppsala where Linnaeus worked as an assistant. *Gentiana clusii* was named after Charles de l'Ecluse (Carolus Clusius). One plant, the Twinflower, was named after Linnaeus himself as *Linnaea borealis*.

The scientific name is often the Latin or Greek version of an important feature of the plant. When introducing new names, Linnaeus was most often inspired by the shape of the leaves, flowers or fruits; for instance the name *Medicago falcata* (Sickle Medick, a herb with sickle-shaped fruits) is derived from the Latin *falcatus*, meaning sickle-shaped. The flower of an orchid, Lady's Slipper (*Cypripedium calceolus*), resembles a slipper (Lat. *calceolus*). The leaf of *Hepatica nobilis* is shaped like liver (Gk. *heparatos* = liver). The three leaflets of the leaves of the clovers gave rise to the name *Trifolium*. The genus *Dracocephalum* has labiate flowers resembling a gaping dragon's mouth (Lat. *dracocephalus* = like a dragon's head). The greyish-white pappus of hairs on the fruits of *Senecio* (groundsels and ragworts) resemble

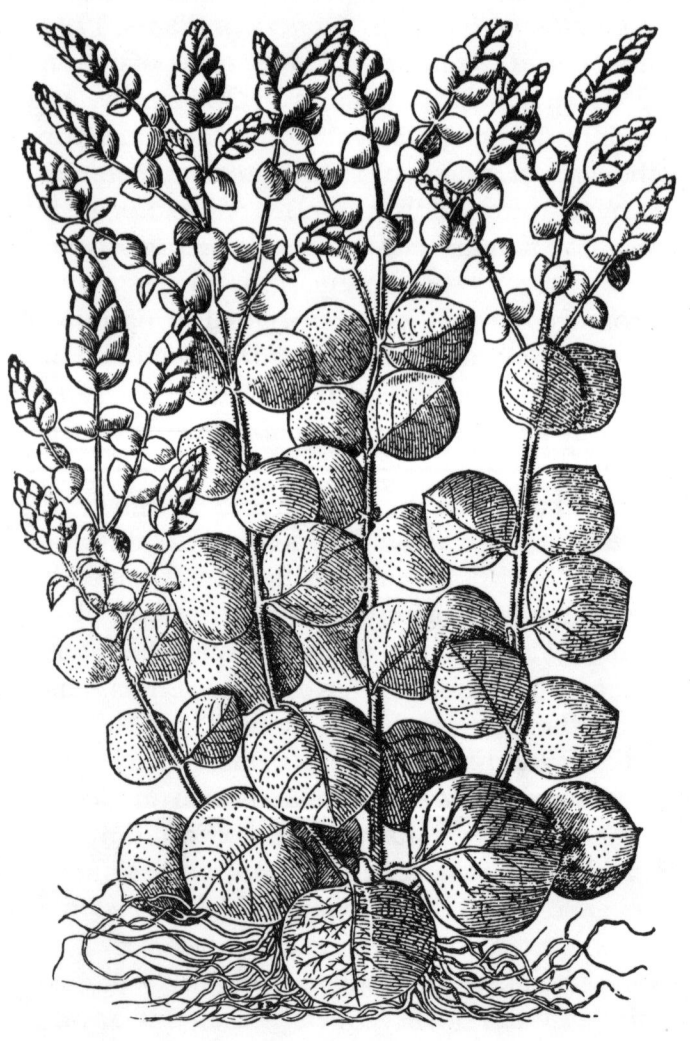

A sheet from Matthioli's Herbarium (16th century)

the grey hair of old people. The stems of the milk-thistles, genus *Lactuca,* exude a milky juice when broken (Lat. *lacteus* = milk). The names of some spiny plants come from the Latin *spina,* meaning spine or thorn (*Prunus spinosa*) while the names of others come from the Latin *germanica,* named after the German people and expressing Linnaeus' attitude to what he considered the aggressive attitude of these people.

Some plants are named after their habitat or their country of origin. Examples include the grass *Ammophila arenaria* found on sand-dunes (*arena* = sand, *ammophila* = sand-loving). Plants with the species name *sylvestris* are woodland plants (Lat. *silva* = wood), those with the species name *pratense* grow in meadows (Lat. *pratum* = meadow), those with the species name *maritima* are found near the sea (Lat. *mare* = sea). The origin of the oldest fodder, Lucerne, is still preserved in its scientific generic name, *Medicago*. It grew in the ancient oriental country of Media, which in the 8th to the 6th centuries B. C. formed the centre of the Median Empire (now the northwestern part of Iran).

Some plants are named for their utility value. Sugar Cane (*Saccharum officinarum*) contains sugar in its pulp (Lat. *saccharum* = sugar). The generic name of Soapwort, *Saponaria,* is derived from the Greek word, *sapon,* which means soap. Some names describe goddesses or heroes from Roman or Greek mythology. The beautiful name of the Greek goddess of the rainbow, Iris, was given to the baroque flowers of the irises. Adonis was part of a Roman legend, in which the jealous god Mars sent a wild boar to kill Adonis, but Venus transformed him into a bright red-flowered plant, the Pheasant's Eye (*Adonis aestivalis*). Paris, the son of the Trojan King Priam, kidnapped most beautiful woman in the world, Helen, with the help of Aphrodite and in so doing he started the Trojan wars. His name has been given to the forest plant Herb Paris (*Paris quadrifolia*). There are many mythological stories related to the violets. One of them is the Greek legend in which Phoebus, the god of the sun, chased Atlas' beautiful daughter with his rays. Zeus heard her pleading for help and turned her into a violet growing in the shade. The Latin name *Viola* has been translated into similar names for this genus in many European languages (French violette, English violet, German veilchen, Dutch viooltje, Polish fiolek, Czech fialka, Spanish violeta).

Folk Lore
Ancient and Modern

The names of many plants are derived from their place in folk lore, either in connection with magic and superstition or with their use in folk medicine. For many hundreds of years certain plants have been regarded as magical. Before the advent of Christianity, Druids revered the oak as a sacred tree together with the mistletoe which sometimes grew on it. This parasitic plant was used as a medicinal plant by the Druids, presumably to treat epilepsy and other nervous disorders for this is how it is sometimes used today.

Some plants were magical symbols of the changing of the seasons and of the seasonal festivals. The dark of the year or the winter solstice was a dangerous time, when the gods had to be propitiated to ensure the return of the sun and the new growth of the crops. Mistletoe, ivy and holly, all still green and in berry at this time, were used to decorate peasant huts and castles from the time of the Druids onwards, as a protection against the evil spirits which were particularly active during the long nights. Hawthorn and Rowan trees were key elements in the May Eve and May Day celebrations; both were in flower at the time and were used to ward off witches and other evil spirits that were roused into life by the coming of summer. Hawthorn hedges and Rowan trees were planted around dwellings to protect them against evil. Trees seem to have played a more significant role in magic than have the smaller herbaceous plants, presumably because they were large, easily recognisable features of the landscape, whose blossoms and berries transformed the colours of the land.

Of the smaller magic plants, some owed their magic properties to the fairies or brownies with which they were associated. Herb Robert (*Geranium robertianum*) may owe its name to its reddened leaves and beak-like fruits which recalled the Robin Redbreast, a lucky bird if well-treated but unlucky if disturbed, which was associated with the brownie called Robin Goodfellow. Many plants are given local fairy names including Fairy Gloves for the Foxglove (*Digitalis purpurea*), Fairy's Thimbles and Fairy Bells for the Harebell (*Campanula rotundifolia*) and Fairy's Brush for Teasel (*Dipsacus fullonum*) amongst many others.

Other plants owed their magic properties to the fortunate numbers associated with them. Clovers (*Trifolium* species) for instance, were already lucky with their trifoliate leaves for three was a lucky number; a rare four-leaved clover was doubly fortunate since such variants of common plants, like four-leaved clovers and white heathers, could be used as amulets or talismans to ward off evil. Nine was also a magic number, being a multiple of three, and dew was a magical substance, so that a plant with nine-lobed leaves forming a shallow cup which caught the dew was doubly magic. Such a one was the Lady's Mantle (*Alchemilla vulgaris*), and the dew trapped in its leaves was given to cows and sheep in poor health because, so it was conjectured, they had been shot by the arrows of the fairies and brownies; this legend was particularly common in Scotland and Ireland.

Some plants undoubtedly owed their magic virtues to the very real effect they had when used in folk medicine, and many were an extremely important source of effective medicines. Some, like foxgloves and poppies, are still used today, the active ingredients being extracted from their leaves, seeds or roots and made into tablets. These are plants with highly potent medicinal qualities, whose action on the human body is immediately evident. In primitive medicine they were used to treat symptoms, even though the people had no real understanding of the origin of the disease which gave rise to the symptoms, nor of the compounds in the plants which cured them. No wonder it seemed like magic. Now it is known that foxglove leaves contain digitalis, which regulates heart beat and reduces the water retention in the body following heart attack, while poppy capsules contain opium from which is derived the painkiller, morphine. Both plants are poisonous in large quantities.

Poisonous Plants

Poisonous plants play an important role in folk lore. It was important that adults and children alike knew which plants were edible and which were poisonous — especially which berries and roots could be used as food and which had to be avoided. It is still just as important today that children are taught to distinguish the poisonous plants from the harmless ones. Often the members of a whole plant family contain similar chemicals which make them noxious; included amongst the poisonous families are the Ranunculaceae (buttercups), Euphorbiaceae (spurges) and the Solanaceae (nightshades).

Buttercups (*Ranunculus*), hellebores (*Helleborus*), anemones (*Anemone*) and Traveller's Joy (*Clematis vitalba*) all contain irritant poisons which are at their most concentrated just before flowering. The plants may only be poisonous in a green state; if eaten fresh and raw buttercups can blister the mouth and cause intestinal inflammation. For obvious reasons these plants pose a much greater threat to grazing livestock than to people but most animals avoid them. The poison is destroyed by drying so that buttercups growing in hayfields pose no threat to their sheep and cattle. Hellebores and Monkshood (*Aconitum napellus*), on the other hand, are much more lethal and retain their poisons after drying.

Many members of the Umbelliferae are poisonous, probably the most infamous example being Hemlock (*Conium maculatum*). Well known to the Greeks, its poisonous properties were also familiar to the Saxons and have become part of folk lore. It is particularly dangerous in that it resembles Wild Parsley (*Petroselinum crispum*) and Wild Parsnip (*Pastinaca sativa*) and may be gathered in mistake for these edible plants; it can be distinguished from them by the purple spots on its smooth stems and by its unpleasant mousy odour, quite unlike the distinctive scents of parsley and parsnip. In folk medicine Hemlock was used as an antidote to strychnine poisoning or in the treatment of tetanus and rabies. This is because its sedative, paralysing effect, so deadly under normal circumstances, was an effective method of counteracting the excitability and irritation of the nervous system induced by this poison or these infections. It was difficult, however, to estimate the dose needed, and victims could be killed by the cure if they did not die of the disease.

Several other members of the Umbelliferae are poisonous, including Water Hemlock (*Cicuta virosa*) and the water dropworts (*Oenanthe*). These plants grow on pond edges and in ditches and are most likely to cause poisoning to livestock when their roots are left lying on the banks after ditches have been dredged.

The members of the family Solanaceae are notorious in folk lore and include the nightshades (*Solanum* and *Atropa*) and Henbane (*Hyoscyamus niger*) as well as food plants like potatoes and tomatoes (also species of *Solanum*) and tobacco (*Nicotiana*). They all contain deadly alkaloids although, of course, this fact was not recognised until modern times; only the effects of their poisons were known, not the cause. Deadly Nightshade (*Atropa belladonna*), Henbane and Thorn-apple (*Datura stramonium*) contain mostly hyoscyamine and atropine. These cause severe illness in animals and men — even three berries of Deadly Nightshade may kill a child. Young animals and children are most at risk, being attracted by the berries and most susceptible to the poison. Symptoms include dilation of the pupils of the eyes, loud heartbeats, delirium, coma and death. The hyoscyamine in Henbane is used in modern medicine as a sedative and as a preventative of spastic contractions of the intestines and bladder; it is also used to allay nervous hysteria and asthma.

The other nightshades, potatoes and tomatoes (all members of the genus *Solanum*) contain solanine. The poison is present in the green parts of the potato and tomato plants, which is why tomatoes and potatoes are safe to eat and why green tomatoes and potatoes and sprouted potatoes are best avoided. The leaves and stems may cause severe anaemia and prostration if eaten in any quantity, and in other members of the genus, like Woody Nightshade (*Solanum dulcamara*), the whole plant is poisonous including the berries and roots, causing similar symptoms. Tobacco contains another alkaloid, nicotine, which is equally as poisonous as the others, especially in the pure state when extracted from the leaves. It can then be absorbed through the skin (it does not have to be eaten) and causes sweating, convulsions and death. It has been used for the treatment of warble fly in cattle and horses, also for mange and lice, but the dosage has to be carefully controlled. Tobacco leaves from ornamental plants can cause poisoning and death in livestock.

Another family of toxic plants is the spurge family, the Euphorbiaceae, a large family which includes many tropical trees and shrubs but which is represented in northern temperate regions only by the spurges (*Euphorbia*) and the mercuries (*Mercurialis*). Spurges are familiar weedy plants with acrid milky juice in stems and leaves which may blister the skin if it comes into contact with it. In folk medicine the juice from certain spurge species was used to burn off warts, although care had to be taken not to let it come into contact with the surrounding skin. Beggars are said to have used the juice to promote ulcers and sores on their bodies so as to gain sympathy and money from those who saw them.

Some poisonous plants are invaluable medicinal plants if their active ingredients are used in small quantities. For instance Foxgloves (*Digitalis purpurea*) are widely grown as a source of the alkaloid digitalis, which regulates the action of the heart and stimulates the kidneys to excrete the excess water, so often retained by patients with heart problems. But if eaten by children or livestock this plant is very poisonous causing changes in the pulse rate. Fortunately poisoning is very rare as the leaves are extremely bitter.

One of the factors which has brought folk medicine into disrepute has been the failure to take notice of its practitioners' insistence, that plants must be harvested at certain times of the day and month, and often under specific weather conditions. Sceptics have frequently ignored these restrictions, picked the plants at any time and then have found that the medical results were poor; they are then confirmed in their scepticism of all folk medicine. The harvesting of the Foxglove plants has shed some interesting light on this aspect of folk medicine for it has now been demonstrated beyond doubt that the activity and content of the alkaloids in the leaves varies considerably. They are at their highest when the flowering is about two-thirds over. First-year plants and early second-year plants contain very little digitalis and upper stem leaves contain less than lower stem or basal leaves. The leaves must be picked dry and the alkaloids extracted as soon as possible after picking, or the leaves must be carefully dried. If care is not taken, mildewing or overheating of the leaves during drying may result. It has also been demonstrated that alkaloid activity varies with the colour of the flowers. Foxglove blooms range in colour from white to rose and purple. Plants with purple flowers yield the highest amounts of digitalis, those with rose-coloured flowers the lowest — only half the amount of the purple-flowered forms. Perhaps herbalists are right after all to insist that time of year, weather conditions and form of plant are important in herbal medicine.

Herbs, Spices, Vitamins and Minerals

Just as important in folk lore and herb medicine as the potent drug plants, are the many species that exert much more subtle effects on the human body. Many such herbal plants, like garlic and onion (both members of the genus *Allium*), are used almost every day in cooking to flavour food; both are also invaluable aids to digestion. Garlic (*Allium sativum*) has additional properties in that it has been used extensively as an antiseptic, to cure sores and to prevent infection. In view of its undoubted antiseptic properties, the use of garlic to prevent the spread of epidemics may be less of an old wives' tale than might be thought.

Many herbs used in cooking also aid digestion, as well as adding flavour to soups, casseroles and sauces. Amongst these are the peppers, several members of the mint family including marjoram and oregano which stimulate bile secretion, and sage which relieves intestinal spasms; members of the carrot family, including dill, coriander and parsley stimulate stomach action and relieve flatulence. Other herbs, like the mints, fennel and thyme relieve sore throats, while parsley, rosemary and watercress act as diuretics and stimulate the kidneys; sage helps to relieve inflammation.

Herbs are used mainly in the cooking of meats, whereas spices are more often used in baking, in making breads, cakes and biscuits. They are often hotter than herbs and are frequently in the form of seeds and nuts, herbs being chiefly shredded leaves. Spices like nutmegs, mace and cinnamon are similar in their action on the body to the digestive herbs, relieving flatulence and stimulating digestion. Cloves and allspice also act as digestive aids but cloves, like garlic, also have effective antiseptic properties — oil of cloves in particular is a powerful antiseptic which can be used externally.

For hundreds of years people have known that a lack of certain foods in their diet could cause the onset of some uncomfortable symptoms. It is difficult to realise that until modern times fresh fruit and vegetables were difficult to obtain in the late winter months and many people suffered from scurvy — their gums bled, they bruised easily and they had pains in their joints. There were several remedies recommended, all based on plants rich in Vitamin C; although the people were unaware of the presence of Vitamin C they knew that these plants cured the symptoms. Amongst the species involved were the scurvy grasses (*Cochlearia*), one of which was grown in herb gardens and others which were gathered in the estuarine marshes and on the rocky coasts where they grow wild. Fresh leaves were pounded to express the juice, which was mixed with that of Watercress (*Rorippa nasturtium-aquaticum*) and imported Seville oranges to make a spring tonic. Plants that stayed green in winter, or overwintering annuals that germinated in autumn, were a source of vitamins and used as a substitute for fresh garden vegetables. These included Watercress, nettles (*Urtica*), Winter Cress (*Barbarea vulgaris*) and Brooklime (*Veronica beccabunga*) which were used in salads; Parsley (*Petroselinum crispum*), which was used both in salads and to flavour soups and sauces, is still one of the best sources of Vitamin C. Another plant grown in autumn and winter was Spinach (*Spinacia oleracea*), introduced to Europe in the 15th century and a species exceptionally rich in Vitamin C as well as in iron and other minerals; it must have greatly improved the health of the people who used it as a winter vegetable. Before the introduction of spinach, two other plants — Good King Henry (*Chenopodium bonus-henricus*) and Fat Hen (*C. album*) — were used as similar pot-herbs but were probably less rich in vitamins and minerals (although they do contain Vitamin C). They are still eaten today in some parts of the country, the leaves tasting like spinach and the shoots like asparagus.

Although green vegetables were scarce in winter, roots from overwintering perennials or biennials were still available unless the ground was deeply covered in snow or frozen hard. Wild Carrot (*Daucus carota*) roots are much thinner than those of the cultivated varieties but are still rich in Vitamin A and some of the B vitamins, as are the roots of the Dandelion (*Taraxacum officinale*), which can be eaten raw or boiled, like those of the carrot.

Wound Plants

Before the discovery of antibiotics in the 1940's, wounds, sores and boils as well as respiratory and other infections were far more dangerous than they are today. A small localised infection could lead to generalised septicaemia, high fever and death. Many plants, like Garlic and cloves, contain antiseptic chemicals and were widely used in poultices and dressings to help cleanse infections of the skin and green wounds. Chickweed (*Stellaria media*) is one such plant and can still be useful, formed into a poultice, for treating leg ulcers for instance. Common St John's Wort (*Hypericum perforatum*) is also used to help heal cuts and bruises and several members of the daisy family, like Yarrow (*Achillea millefolium*) and Wild Chamomile (*Matricaria chamomilla*) are also effective. Other members of the daisy family provide treatments for respiratory infections, Coltsfoot (*Tussilago farfara*) is still used in proprietary cough medicines and Feverfew (*Tanacetum parthenium*) was used for hundreds of years to reduce body temperature. The effects of these plants are associated with the presence in their leaves of many different essential oils, a varied collection of organic chemicals whose medical action is poorly understood. Some act as bactericides, others act as sedatives and others reduce temperature.

Many species of plants have been used by man through the centuries and the spread of these plants throughout Europe, and sometimes through much of the world, can often be traced directly to their use as herbal medicines or as fruits and vegetables. Such plants are very rarely threatened by extinction, for their wide distributions often enable them to survive, even when their original habitats are destroyed by modern agricultural techniques or by urban development. However, other plant species, more dependent on true wilderness conditions and of man, or so attractive that they have been greatly overcollected, have been less fortunate and many are today facing the very real danger of extinction.

Conservation

Until relatively recently, much of the effort of conservation has been aimed at preserving endangered species; birds and mammals have perhaps received a disproportionate share of attention and individual animals have been cared for in zoos, sometimes to be reintroduced into the wild in nature reserves but more often spending their lives in a very abnormal way. Plants and invertebrates have received less attention, being much less likely to be missed when they disappear. Today, however, scientists and naturalists are concerned less with the extinction of individual species, than with the wholesale destruction of habitats, such as the felling of the South American forests or, on a smaller scale, the 'reclamation' of saltmarshes for urban development. This kind of habitat destruction leads to the extinction of all the species present simultaneously and the sudden change in vegetation cover may even lead to long-term changes in local weather patterns.

Modern agricultural techniques and an ever increasing demand for housing developments are placing an intolerable strain on the few natural and semi-natural areas left in Britain today. Conservationists fear that in ten years' time our wildlife will exist only in small scattered nature reserves and many of the rarer and wilderness-dependent species will be extinct.

Huge areas of monoculture, like the wheat fields now so familiar in our countryside, maintained by artificial fertilisers and kept pest- and weed-free by increasing doses of pesticides and herbicides, are a poor substitute for the natural diverse communities with their roots in a soil teeming with microscopic life and a multitude of plant and animal species. The natural habitat is self-sustaining. It has a high level of redundancy built into the system and its potential pests are in a natural balance with host organisms and predators. It is such systems that are threatened by the use of artificial fertilizers for they destroy vast numbers of the microscopic soil organisms which keep the soil healthy and aerated, while pesticides and herbicides destroy the natural balance of predators and prey, with the result that pests multiply unchecked.

Some farmers are now attempting to return to organically-based methods in which they put back into the land the equivalent of what has been taken out. Some startling results have been achieved with these methods; high yields of pest-free crops have been achieved and they have a better flavour and food value than crops grown in the artificial systems. Such organic systems go a long way towards restoring species diversity for, in the absence of harmful chemicals, predators return and the soil organisms multiply. Organic farming methods, combined with the retention of hedgerows and woodland copses together with less emphasis on meadowland drainage schemes, would go a long way towards restoring our wildlife heritage. Some people would argue that such methods would result in the production of less food. Conservationists would reply that they would result in fewer butter mountains, milk or rapeseed oil lakes and in less dumping of unwanted tons of tomatoes or other crops, for which the taxpayers have already subsidised the farmers.

In 1981, the Wildlife and Countryside Act was passed by Parliament. Under this law, over 60 species of plants and many more species of animals are now protected and may not be subjected to any disturbance. With respect to wild plants, the law now states that these protected species may not be picked at all or seeds taken, while other wild plants may not be uprooted except in certain situations and circumstances. It is, in fact, illegal to dig up *any* plant for transplanting to a garden or for any other purpose, except on your own land. The law also encourages people not to pick flowers to the extent that there are not enough left for the plant to set seed. This sounds sufficiently protective in theory, but in practice if each of a thousand visitors to a wood picked one primrose (a not unlikely event in a wood close to a road), then even though the spirit of the law had been respected, the primroses would still die out within a few years since they need renewal from seed relatively frequently. It is better not to pick any flowers at all; taking them home as images on the film of your camera is a more satisfying and lasting way of continuing to enjoy them.

The government agency responsible for nature conservation is the Nature Conservancy Council (NCC). This body has the power to designate areas with special wildlife interest as Sites of Special Scientific Interest (SSSI). Unfortunately many conservationists think that the law does not go far enough in this respect for an SSSI is not protected by law in any real way — if a farmer wishes to clear a piece of woodland with such a designation there is nothing to stop him. He must, however, inform the NCC of his intention and an agreement may be reached, in which the NCC compensates the farmer for the profit he would have made if he had converted the SSSI into a commercially viable crop-growing area or grassland ley, for example.

A real contradiction may occur when a farmer receives an EEC improvement grant, to drain an unimproved piece of meadowland, for example. The term 'unimproved' is often used to describe a piece of land which has been undisturbed for centuries and this very lack of disturbance usually means that it is rich in wild flowers, rare grasses, insects and birds. The EEC will often pay a farmer to destroy the habitat while the NCC may pay him to leave it alone.

Many people contrast the situation, in law, of an SSSI with that of a protected building. They argue that the cases are similar, both have a historical value that cannot be measured in monetary terms and neither can be replaced. Buildings are subject to planning permission and council regulations, and cannot be changed even by the owners without permission. SSSI's have no such protection and are therefore far more vulnerable to human interference.

In many countries large wilderness areas have been set aside as National Parks to function as wildlife areas, but these parks are coming under increasing pressure from urban populations in search of open air and wide open spaces. The Parks are in danger of being viewed merely as recreational areas for people and, in consequence, the plant and animal life, as part of the scenery, will be subjected to trampling and destruction by too many cars and feet. Plant communities can absorb only a certain amount of such treatment and the animal community depends on healthy vegetation as much as it does on lack of disturbance.

There are many organisations in this country concerned about the ever-accelerating rate of destruction of natural and semi-natural habitats by their replacement with large expanses of grassland leys, arable land and urban sprawl.

They include organisations like the Royal Society for Nature Conservation and its affiliated County Trusts, the Royal Society for the Protection of Birds, the Nature Conservancy, the National Trust and the Forestry Commission amongst others. One method that organisations are using with increasing success is the acquisition of large and small areas of land throughout the country, so that habitats like woodland, heathland and downland are preserved in nature reserves. There is also much concern about wetlands – marshes, fens and water meadows. The EEC policy with respect to grants for land drainage has greatly increased the rate of disappearance of such habitats and small wetland areas cannot easily be preserved when the surrounding land is drained, for the water table often drops and the preserve becomes too dry for the species it was set up to protect. Many ordinary people are involved in the running of the reserves; they are largely managed by volunteers who undertake scrub clearance where necessary and who regularly survey the reserve to make sure that any endangered species are doing well.

Another important role played by the conservation bodies is education, for one of the problems that conservationists face is ignorance. Many people think that the urge to preserve animals and plants is a sentimental one, and that sentiment has no place in the modern world. Land use is part of big business and is geared to the profit motive; therefore, since organic farming techniques and environmental conservation are more expensive in the short-term than monoculture development maintained by the use of artificial fertilizers and pesticides, then the conservationist techniques are considered a poor alternative. What is happening in many parts of the world today is that soil structure is breaking down with the disappearance of its organic humus, soil erosion is increasing and a final and total loss of fertility will ensue if the soil is lost. A natural environment is covered with vegetation at all times, in the form of trees, grasses and decaying remains which cover the soil and bind it together. In organic farming, even though the soil is exposed at certain times of the year, it still contains enough humus to bind and stabilise it. Education is the only method of combating the ignorance which leads to faulty farming techniques. The Henry Doubleday Association is particularly concerned with organic farming practises; it runs film shows, sends out newsletters and, by increasing the membership, attempts to make more people aware of the need for nature conservation. Grass roots organisations like these are an essential prerequisite to the task of persuading many farmers, developers, businessmen, politicians and the media that maintenance of the diversity of the natural world is essential, not sentimental.

There are many ways in which the individual can help to conserve wild plants and animals. There are over a million acres of town and country gardens in Britain, a very large area which could be the focus for a new conservation effort, to offset the habitat destruction and species loss in the agricultural countryside. Gardens vary greatly in size from the tiny paved front yard of the urban terrace to the grassy expanse and large flowerbeds of the country house. But both can be used to encourage wildlife. One important factor essential to the establishment of a wildlife-rich garden is the planting of at least some native species, for many endangered birds and insects do not feed on foreign species. Many people today are planting shrubs, as these provide good ground cover, good foliage and a minimum of work. Conservation-conscious gardeners may choose many attractive shrubs and their varieties from the native species, including the *Prunus* species, Rowans and Whitebeams (*Sorbus* species), dogwood (*Cornus* and its varieties) and the heathers (*Calluna* and *Erica* species). Herbaceous flowering plants that have native representatives in our flora include the cranesbills (*Geranium* species), sages (*Salvia*) and marjoram (*Origanum*), primroses and cowslips (*Primula* species), stonecrops (*Sedum*) and avens (*Geum*). There are also a few annuals like the forget-me-nots (*Myosotis*) and the cultivated varieties of pansies (*Viola* species) that do well. Many of these plants are commonly grown in gardens, but others, like the many different cranesbills for instance, are less well known and well worth growing. In addition there are many cultivated and foreign shrubs and herbaceous plants that provide pollen, nectar and berries for insects and birds; the more highly hybridized a plant is, however, the less likely it is to produce pollen or nectar. True species plants, therefore, are of more use in a conservation garden than highly bred hybrids. Many seedsmen and nurseries carry a range of plants native to our country and it should be from these sources, *not* the wild, that you acquire your stock.

A problem familiar to many bee-keepers is the phenomenon known as the June gap — there is a time in early summer when the spring flowering plants are over and the summer-flowering plants are not yet in bloom. Adult insects, bees, butterflies and hoverflies that are flying at that time can suffer badly from lack of food, especially if the weather is cool and wet, for they need the sugar-rich nectar to provide energy. There are several nectar-rich plants that can be grown to cover the June gap, amongst them lupins (*Lupinus* species) and *Limnanthes douglasii.*

A good way to gather the information you need to ensure that at least some plants are in flower in a garden throughout the year is to watch neighbouring gardens and record the succession. In addition to these garden species, there are many wild plants which can be given space in the garden, in odd corners or in prominent positions. Amongst these are Foxgloves (*Digitalis purpurea*), Primroses (*Primula vulgaris*), Snowdrops (*Galanthus nivalis*) and violets (*Viola* species). Violets are particularly useful as they provide food for several species of butterfly larvae.

One of the reasons why many present-day gardens do not contribute to conservation is that they are tidy sterile extensions of the living room. Flower beds are large expanses of bare earth, punctuated by highly-bred sterile varieties of foreign plants or twig-like hybrid roses growing in rose-sick soil. The whole 'garden' is maintained by artificial fertilizers and by pesticides which poison any native plants and insects that are borne in on the wind, and dismissed as weeds or pests. No normal balance of nature is possible because predators have been destroyed. The process is carried to the ultimate in the lawn which is grown from highly bred varieties of grass, weed-free and made to look like a carpet, not a natural living area of vegetation.

Discarding notions of tidiness, ignoring bitten leaves and tolerating plants other than grasses in the lawn may be difficult at first, but these are essential first steps in restoring real life to a garden. Artificial fertilizers, herbicides and insecticides have to be abandoned, other than a few quickly biodegradable ones like soapy water or pyrethrum. But even these should be used only as a last resort — perhaps in the early years when insects like greenfly and blackfly are still liable to reach pest proportions due to the lack of predators. A compost heap is essential and liberal top dressings of compost, together with the sparing use of organic fertilizers like bonemeal or blood, fish and bone will help to restore soil life. The soil will not need digging as this will destroy the structure that you are so carefully rebuilding.

A variety of habitats can be provided, even in a small garden. A hedge planted from a variety of native small trees, such as Hawthorn (*Crataegus monogyna*), Beech (*Fagus sylvatica*) and cherries (*Prunus* species), will provide nesting places and food plants for a variety of birds and insects and will also provide more year-round interest than a single species hedge. Conifers can also be included as they form valuable cover in the winter when other shrubs and trees have lost their leaves.

A portion of the lawn sown with meadowland seeds and left uncut until late June or July (the normal hay-making season) so that the flowering plants can set seed, will give pleasure to the garden owner and food for caterpillars and other insects; their numbers are kept in check by predatory insects and birds which feed on them. Meadowland flower seeds are available from many seed firms, but only some of these mixes are made up from native species, so a careful check of the species list is necessary.

A pond and/or marshy area is more work to make and maintain but is well worthwhile, attracting frogs and toads, as well as insects such as pond-skaters and dragonflies. Dragonflies and damselflies, in particular, are to be encouraged for they are active predators on insects like mosquitoes and greenflies. Native fish, such as minnows, feed on mosquito larvae and other undesirable pond species. A natural-looking pond with a muddy bottom can be made by using heavy-duty polythene to line the hole and then covering it completely with earth. The marsh is then simply a shallow extension of the pond. Fringe plants, such as Yellow Flag (*Iris pseudacorus*), Purple Loosestrife (*Lythrum salicaria*) and Marsh Marigold (*Caltha palustris*) can be planted around the edges and in the marsh.

None of these areas need be large — it is the variety of habitat which encourages diversity. However, they do need to be large enough to support viable populations of native species if the gardens around are the normal suburban kind. A series of wildlife gardens where neighbours have worked together could establish a really valuable nature reserve.

The Plants

Over 450 species of flowering plants found in the British Isles are depicted and described in the following pages. Many of them are common native plants, others are rare or introduced; some have interesting names, others have a fascinating history in herb lore; some are deadly poisonous, others are edible. Altogether they represent a varied and interesting cross section of the British flora.

To simplify the task of identification, the plants are divided into nine groups, based on their habitat preference. Each plant is placed in its most usual habitat group, but plants do not respect man-made concepts and many grow in several different situations – woodland as well as hedgerows, or moist meadows as well as waterside, for example. Others are more particular and grow only in the habitat under which they have been grouped here. Where a plant may well be found in a habitat (or habitats) other than the one in which it is featured in this book, that is indicated in the fact panel at the foot of each description (see overleaf). The nine habitats are denoted by symbols that occupy the top outer corner of every page. The habitats and their symbols are:

is characteristically found on wasteland, and that is the habitat under which it is featured (see page 39); it is also found on roadsides and in hedgerows, however, as well as in moist grassland, and is therefore listed in the 'other section' index which appears on the introductory page of its 'secondary' habitats.

Within each section the plants are arranged according to a formal botanical sequence based on flower structure. This begins with the dicotyledonous families, starting with the Ranunculaceae (the buttercup family) in which the flowers have free petals and many free stamens and carpels, progressing through families like the Geraniaceae (the cranesbill family) with free petals and a reduced number of stamens and carpels, and the Scrophulariaceae (the snapdragon family) in which the flowers have fused petals and carpels, to the Compositae (the daisy family) which have multi-floreted flower heads. The sequence is completed by the families of monocotyledonous plants that include the lilies, irises and orchids. This type of arrangement is found in most wild flower books.

Accompanying the illustration of each plant is a short text which gives a brief description,

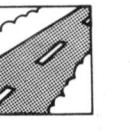

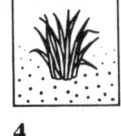

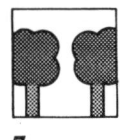
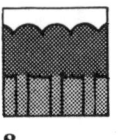

1   2   3   4   5   6   7   8   9

1	*Wasteland*	4	*Dry grassland*	7	*Open woodland*
2	*Roadsides and hedgerows*	5	*Arable land*	8	*Shady woodland*
3	*Moist grassland*	6	*Water and waterside*	9	*Moors and heaths*

On the reverse of the title page of each habitat section is an alphabetical index of the common names of the plants that are described within that section. The second index on the page is a list of all the plants that could also be found in that habitat but are featured in another section elsewhere in the book. For example, Silverweed

including any major distinguishing features and interesting details such as the derivation of its name, its place in herb lore and its distribution in Europe. Much additional information is given in the fact panel which appears at the bottom of each text. A full explanation of the various elements in a fact panel is given overleaf.

Synonyms Included here are any outdated scientific names that may still be found in other books but have now been discarded by most botanists, either because the plant has now been placed in a different genus to the one in which it was originally included, or because it has been discovered that an earlier name exists, the older name taking precedence.

Other names Some plants are known by more than one common name. Often the use of the different names is restricted to different parts of the country.

Family name Representatives of about 120 families of the 200 or so known to exist, occur in Britain. Designation to a family depends chiefly on flower structure, particularly that of the female reproductive parts.

Flowering period The shaded area depicts the months of the year during which the plant can be found in flower. This can be very variable, however, depending on annual climatic variation (spring comes earlier in some years than in others), or latitude (a plant in the south of England flowers earlier than its counterpart in the north of Scotland).

Family	**Labiatae**
Synonym	*Nepeta glechoma*
Other names	**Alehoof**
Status	**Common**
Distribution	**Except in far north**
Height	**20—40 cm**

J F M A M J J A S O N D

Height This often varies considerably and often depends on the quality of the habitat in which the plant is growing. Usually a plant is short and compact in an open, sunny place, growing taller and more lax in shady situations.

Other habitats Any habitat symbols appearing here indicate that the plant can also be found in those habitats. Some plants are more tolerant than others and may be found with equal regularity and in equal abundance in more than one habitat. In such cases, featuring them in this book in one of their habitat sections rather than another is a more or less arbitrary decision. Other plants, however, may be more commonly found in one particular habitat among the several from which they might have been recorded, and that is the one under which they are featured in this book.

Distribution A statement of the plant's regional occurrence. Where this is described as **throughout Britain,** the statement should be taken to include England, Scotland, Wales and Ireland (strictly, the British Isles). Most of the distribution statements are self-explanatory. The term **scattered** is used of a species that is widely distributed but nowhere common, while **occasional** is mainly used to describe introduced species that are regarded as casuals, occurring in isolated places where a few seeds have managed to germinate and survive.

Status A statement of the plant's abundance and its standing as a member of the British flora. A **common** plant is one that is widespread throughout its distribution area in high enough numbers to be familiar to those who know the area. It may, however, be small and easily missed, or usually found amongst many other plants in the dense growth of hedgerows in high summer; or it may be dowdy with dull coloured flowers. For these and other reasons the beginner may be unfamiliar with some of the commonest of wild plants. **Very common** and **abundant** species are known to most people, and include plants such as Daisy and Dandelion. A **frequent** plant is one that is found in many parts of the country but not in such high numbers as a common plant. A plant that is **locally common** is one that is widespread and familiar in certain areas but not in others; a plant that grows only on acid soils, for example, may be common in places where the soil is suitable but absent elsewhere. A plant designated simply as **local** is usually even more restricted in its habitat requirements and is often not common, even where the habitat is ideally suitable. **Rare** plants are even less likely to be encountered, and are often protected.

Native species are those that occur naturally in the British Isles. Others are known to have been **introduced** at some time, often from Asia or North America. Many introduced plants have arrived by chance — as seeds in grain shipments, or with the mud on tourists' shoes, for example — and have never become properly established in Britain; they are then known as **casuals**. Occasionally an introduced plant thrives in the wild, spreads widely and becomes established alongside the native species; it is then known as a **naturalized** plant. Many plants, introduced to be grown in gardens, depend on the owner's care and attention to keep them alive, and therefore remain confined. A few, however, have a limited capability of seeding themselves into surrounding areas; these are the ones that are termed **garden escapes,** but they usually lack the vigour and adaptability to establish themselves permanently in the wild.

Species featured in this section

Species featured in another section

Lesser Tufted Vetch
Vicia villosa

This is an annual plant with hairy quadrangular stems and compound leaves formed of many opposite oblong leaflets. The leaves end in branched tendrils which cling to other plants. Long one-sided racemes, with up to 30 blue-violet flowers, are borne in leaf axils and from the flowers develop smooth pods, each containing 8 round seeds. A single plant produces up to several hundred seeds which germinate in the autumn. This cultivated plant is often grown for fodder and may be found as an escape in corn fields and waste ground. It is native to the Mediterranean, western Asia and northern Africa and was introduced to more northern areas of Europe.

Family	**Leguminosae**
Other names	**Fodder Vetch**
Status	**Not infrequent**
Distribution	**Occasional**
Height	**30—120 cm**

J F M A M J J A S O N D

Silverweed
Potentilla anserina

An attractive perennial plant of sand dunes, road-sides and waste places, especially in damper spots, Silverweed grows throughout the Northern Hemisphere. Creeping stems bear compound leaves with 7—12 large leaflets alternating with smaller ones. The leaves are covered with silver silky hairs, at least on the lower surface, a feature that gives the plant its very descriptive name. Yellow flowers with five petals and sepals are borne singly on long flower-stalks growing from the leaf axils. They open only in sunlight, closing at night and in dull weather. This plant was once cultivated for its root which was eaten as we now eat potatoes, and it was also used in herbal remedies for mouth ulcers and other internal disorders.

Family	**Rosaceae**
Status	**Common**
Distribution	**Throughout Britain**
Height	**15—50 cm**

J F M A M J J A S O N D

Lupin

Lupinus polyphyllus

This robust plant originated in the Pacific region of North America where it is grown as cattle fodder or ploughed into fields as organic fertiliser. As well as a perennial taproot the plant has numerous secondary roots bearing nodules, and nitrogen-fixing bacteria living in these nodules enrich the soil with nitrogen. Lupin is also used for stabilising soil on railway embankments and roadside slopes, since its numerous roots hold the sloping ground in place. The plant has long-stalked rounded leaves with 13−15 elongated leaflets and dense erect racemes of blue or blue-white pea-like flowers. Cultivated plants have flowers in a variety of pastel hues.

Family	**Leguminosae**	
Status	**A garden escape**	
Distribution	**Occasional**	J F M A M J J A S O N D
Height	**100−150 cm**	

Hop Trefoil

Trifolium campestre

This is a low-growing herb with weak branched stems and compound leaves, each with three leaflets of which the central one has a longer stalk than the other two. Small heads of 20−50 tiny yellow flowers grow on long stalks in the axils of the leaves. They are followed by round clusters of light brown single-seeded pods, each enclosed by the persistent fused petals which become dry, brown and withered and probably help in the dispersal of the fruits by wind. The fruits look like a bunch of hops and so the plant is called Hop Trefoil. This small plant grows in dry sandy areas, dry grassland and on roadsides in warmer regions of Europe and east Africa.

Family	**Leguminosae**	
Synonym	***T. procumbens***	
Status	**Relatively common**	J F M A M J J A S O N D
Distribution	**Except in the north**	
Height	**15−30 cm**	

Golden Trefoil

Trifolium aureum

This plant has stouter and more erect stems than the similar Hop Trefoil. The flower-head is up to 1 cm wide and consists of 20—50 tiny golden-yellow flowers, turning brown from the bottom upwards as the flowers wither. Dry petals and sepals persist around the ripening fruits, which are one-seeded pods, and help in their dispersal by wind. The leaves have three leaflets like Hop Trefoil, but all three leaflets have stalks of approximately the same length in this species, and so the two plants can be distinguished from each other. Golden Trefoil is a sun-loving plant of acid grassland, fields and rocky slopes, growing throughout Europe except in the north.

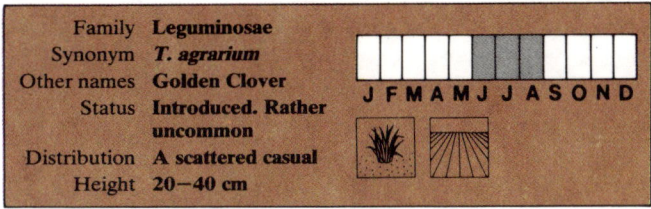

Family	Leguminosae
Synonym	*T. agrarium*
Other names	Golden Clover
Status	Introduced. Rather uncommon
Distribution	A scattered casual
Height	20—40 cm

J F M A M J J A S O N D

Common Melilot

Melilotus officinalis

This is a robust perennial plant of the warmer areas of Europe and Asia. The branched stem bears slender flower stalks with many yellow flowers, followed by small ovoid pods. A single plant is capable of producing up to several thousand seeds which over-winter in the ground before they germinate. The dense root system, which enables the plant to draw water and nutrients from deep in the soil, makes it a suitable plant for the reclamation of sandy soils. It often grows in waste places, especially in railway cuttings and on sloping roadsides. The foliage, which smells strongly of new-mown hay, is used in herbal teas for treating cramps and insomnia and the leaves are used to aid the healing of wounds.

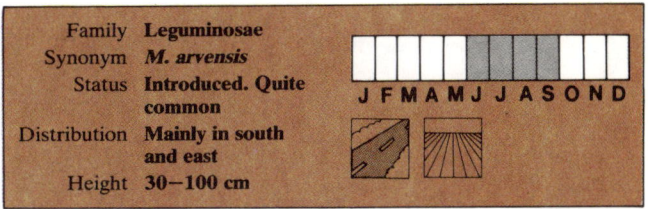

Family	Leguminosae
Synonym	*M. arvensis*
Status	Introduced. Quite common
Distribution	Mainly in south and east
Height	30—100 cm

J F M A M J J A S O N D

Treacle Mustard

Erysimum cheiranthoides

A tall annual or overwintering field weed, first forming a basal rosette of narrow lance-shaped leaves, from which grow erect flowering stems while the basal leaves wither. The tiny yellow flowers are borne in large erect inflorescences, opening from the bottom upwards, while the whole inflorescence lengthens as the lower flowers die and the fruits form. The fruits are long and slender and contain a single row of seeds. This plant is one of some hundred species of the genus inhabiting the Northern Hemisphere; it has probably been introduced into Britain where it grows in lowland fields and waste places.

Family	Cruciferae
Status	Locally common
Distribution	Mainly in south and east
Height	20—60 cm

J F M A M J J A S O N D

White Melilot

Melilotus alba

This robust herb resembles the yellow-flowered Common Melilot, differing mainly in the colour of its flowers and in the type of habitat in which it is found. Both melilots grow in fields, waste places and on railway embankments and roadsides but White Melilot prefers stony or heavy clay soils. Both species are biennials. The erect branched stem bears compound leaves, each with three oval toothed leaflets. Long erect racemes of white flowers grow from leaf axils. White Melilot smells of coumarin (new-mown hay), especially during drying, and it is sometimes an unwanted weed of hay fields as too much coumarin can harm cattle fed on such hay.

Family	Leguminosae
Status	Introduced. Fairly common
Distribution	Mainly in south and east
Height	30—120 cm

J F M A M J J A S O N D

Horse-radish
Armoracia rusticana

The rich inflorescence of pure white flowers appears at the end of spring growing from a ground rosette of long-stalked leaves. The tough, pointed, glossy basal leaves have markedly toothed edges, a feature that differentiates a non-flowering Horse-radish from the superficially similar Broad-leaved Dock. The smaller stem leaves have no stalks. This species originally grew wild on the banks of rivers and streams in southeastern Europe and western Asia. Escapes from cultivation have contributed to its present distribution in Europe, North and South America, Japan and New Zealand. The long, thick, pungent root used as a condiment is only found in cultivated plants. The pungent smell and taste of the root is due to mustard oil and it also contains Vitamin C in large quantities.

Family	Cruciferae
Synonym	*Cochlearia armoracia*
Status	Widely naturalized
Distribution	Mainly in midlands, south and east
Height	60–140 cm

J F M A M J J A S O N D

Hoary Alison
Berteroa incana

This plant has a greyish appearance, caused by the many star-shaped hairs covering the stem and lance-shaped leaves. At the beginning of summer, the flowers, formed by four white deeply divided petals, start opening from the bottom upwards of the inflorescence, so that above the ripening fruits masses of new flowers open in succession. The fruits are oval and grey-felted and contain many seeds. This plant is an annual, biennial or perennial weed of wasteland and cultivated ground particularly in the warmer parts of eastern Europe and western Asia. It is found as a casual in scattered localities in Britain, usually in arable fields or waste ground.

Family	Cruciferae
Synonym	*Alyssum incanum*
Status	Introduced
Distribution	Scattered
Height	30–65 cm

J F M A M J J A S O N D

Perfoliate Penny-cress
Thlaspi perfoliatum

This small annual or overwintering plant begins to flower in early spring and is in full bloom by April and May. It has a basal rosette of stalked leaves and one or more flowering stalks with smooth leaves and many tiny white flowers. The flowers open from the bottom of the inflorescence upwards and the following fruits are small, broadly heart-shaped and winged. This plant is a native of Europe, north Africa and Asia and has been introduced to North America and Britain. Here it is a rare casual, growing only on limestone wasteland in four counties in central southern England, although the Field Penny-cress, *Thlaspi arvense,* is more common.

Family	Cruciferae	
Status	Rare	
Distribution	Central southern England	
Height	10—25 cm	

J F M A M J J A S O N D

Narrow-leaved Pepperwort
Lepidium ruderale

This small annual or biennial plant has a basal rosette of long-stalked divided leaves from which grows an erect branched stem with finely divided leaves; the whole plant has a rather unpleasant smell. Tiny greenish flowers are borne in long racemes, opening from the bottom of the inflorescence upwards. The flowers have no petals and are followed by heart-shaped winged fruits with many seeds. This pepperwort grows throughout Europe but is only common in southern and eastern England in the British Isles. It grows in open areas in wasteland and on roadsides, in railway sidings and short grassland, especially near the sea.

Family	Cruciferae	
Status	Locally common	
Distribution	Central and south-eastern England	
Height	10—35 cm	

J F M A M J J A S O N D

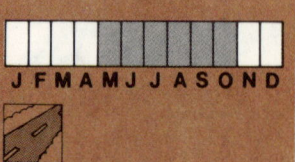

Shepherd's Purse

Capsella bursa-pastoris

This annual plant is a common weed of cultivated as well as waste land, gardens and roadsides and has a worldwide distribution. The small white flowers, sometimes lacking the petals, can be seen at almost any time of year. The triangular flat fruit is reminiscent of a purse and gives the plant both its common and its Latin name. The branched stem grows from a ground rosette of deeply lobed leaves. Upper leaves are attached directly to the stem by their bases. Shepherd's Purse has been used in herb lore for centuries to make herbal teas and infusions which help to stop bleeding from cuts and nose-bleeds and after childbirth. The young leaves can be used in salads.

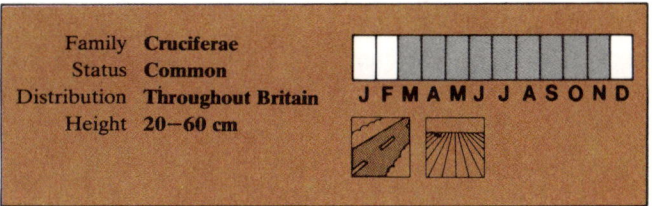

Family	Cruciferae
Status	Common
Distribution	Throughout Britain
Height	20—60 cm

J F M A M J J A S O N D

Field Pansy

Viola arvensis

This is a common weed of fields and wasteland. It usually occurs together with the similar Wild Pansy (*Viola tricolor*). They are not only similar but also closely related and often indistinguishable. The Field Pansy has creamy yellow flowers, sometimes with a faint violet tinge, especially on the upper and side petals. The flowers of the Wild Pansy are much more violet in colour and its petals are markedly longer than the sepals, whereas in the Field Pansy the petals and sepals are approximately the same length. Both pansies have been used in herbal medicine, particularly in the treatment of asthma and eczema and some rheumatic conditions.

Family	Violaceae
Status	Fairly common
Distribution	Throughout Britain
Height	5—20 cm

J F M A M J J A S O N D

Small-flowered Mallow
Malva pusilla

The branched feeble stems of this species bear long-stalked rounded leaves similar to those of Dwarf Mallow. The flowers, however, are smaller, white or pink and much more inconspicuous, the petals never appearing much beyond the sepals. From two to six flowers grow on long flower-stalks from the axils of the leaves. The tiny disc-like fruits are enveloped in the persisting calyx as in the preceding species, but they differ in being rather wrinkled. This annual plant shares the same habitats as Dwarf Mallow, growing in dry waste places throughout Europe. It has been introduced in scattered localities throughout Britain and is particularly likely to be found on coastal foreshores.

Family	**Malvaceae**	
Status	**Introduced, locally common**	
Distribution	**Scattered except in far north**	
Height	**10—35 cm**	

J F M A M J J A S O N D

Dwarf Mallow
Malva neglecta

An annual plant with densely hairy, more or less prostrate, stems and long-stalked rounded leaves. The flowers grow in few-flowered racemes from the leaf axils and are whitish or pale lilac in colour with darker lilac veins. The sepals are only half the length of the petals but are persistent and almost completely envelope the disc-like fruits, composed of up to 15 segments arranged around a central column — the well-known 'cheeses'. Dwarf Mallow grows in waste places, on roadsides and near the sea. It is much more common in southern England than in the north, and in southern Europe than in northern Europe. It is used as a herb flavouring for casseroles in Egypt.

Family	**Malvaceae**	
Other names	**Wayside Mallow**	
Status	**Locally common**	
Distribution	**Mainly in south and east**	
Height	**10—40 cm**	

J F M A M J J A S O N D

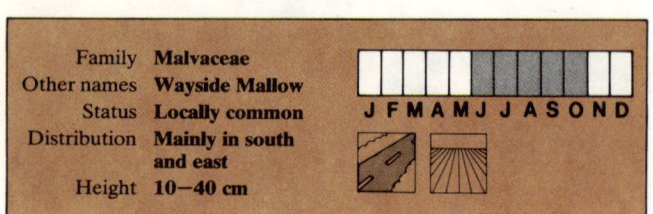

Ground Elder

Aegopodium podagraria

This is a notorious stubborn garden weed, capable of producing an indestructible network of thin branched underground stems in hedgerows, gardens and wasteland. Any small parts of these stems left in the ground by the gardener soon produce new plants which quickly form dense growths. The perennial rootstock sends forth attractive compound leaves and several hollow grooved stems bearing dense umbels of white flowers. The fruits resemble caraway fruits but the seeds lack the spicy smell and have a sharp bitter taste. The name Goutweed and Latin name *podagraria* are both derived from the former use of this plant, in compresses for the treatment of rheumatism and gout.

Family	Umbelliferae
Other names	Bishop's Weed, Goutweed, Herb Gerard
Status	Common
Distribution	Throughout Britain
Height	50—90 cm

J F M A M J J A S O N D

Caraway

Carum carvi

This aromatic meadow plant has been cultivated since time immemorial, although it also grows in waste places and on roadsides in the wild. It has an erect branching stem with long-stalked deeply divided compound leaves and terminal umbels of white flowers which are followed by oblong fruits containing the caraway seeds. These have a distinctive spicy smell and taste and they are used in baking bread, biscuits and cakes and in making the liqueur called Kümmel. The healing properties of the plant were known in ancient times and it was mentioned by Pliny the Elder and Dioscorides, well-known Roman and Greek physicians. Caraway stimulates the appetite and improves the digestion, it relieves flatulence and alleviates colic.

Family	Umbelliferae
Status	Rather rare
Distribution	Scattered throughout Britain
Height	30—80 cm

J F M A M J J A S O N D

Falcate Hare's Ear
Bupleurum falcatum

This species belongs to the only genus of the family Umbelliferae with undivided entire leaves which may, in some species, resemble hare's ears. The leaves in this species are lance-shaped, often sickle-shaped, the lower leaves are attached to the hollow stem by their narrowing stalk-like bases. The upper leaves are stalkless and all have 3—7 veins. The yellow flowers are borne in small umbels and are followed by flattened fruits. This plant is found scattered throughout Europe and Asia, on sunny slopes particularly in limestone areas.

Family	Umbelliferae
Status	Very rare
Distribution	Eastern Essex
Height	20—100 cm

J F M A M J J A S O N D

Stinging Nettle
Urtica dioica

This common plant of wasteland, roadsides and gardens is completely covered with hollow stinging hairs containing formic acid. The brittle end of the hair breaks on contact and the contents are ejected on to the skin, causing a painful rash. The plant possesses a perennial underground network of tough yellow roots from which grow the coarse stems bearing opposite toothed leaves. The dangling sprays of green petal-less flowers grow from leaf axils and there are male and female flowers on separate plants. Nettles are surprisingly useful as a vegetable, rather like spinach when cooked, and rich in vitamins and minerals.

Family	Urticaceae
Status	Common
Distribution	Throughout Britain
Height	50—150 cm

J F M A M J J A S O N D

Petty Spurge

Euphorbia peplus

The small, broadly circular leaves are characteristic of this small plant and unlike other spurges, the leaves just below the flowers are almost the same in shape as the other leaves. The stem is erect, smooth and green and often branches immediately low above the ground. It is hollow and filled with a poisonous milky white sap, a feature of all spurges. Tiny yellowish flowers are arranged in complex inflorescences in which the bracts (the 'leaves' beneath the flowers) look like green petals. The fruit is a capsule. Petty Spurge is an abundant weed in gardens and waste places and is one of several annual spurges which are almost cosmopolitan in their distributions.

Family	Euphorbiaceae
Status	Common
Distribution	Throughout Britain
Height	15—50 cm

J F M A M J J A S O N D

Annual Mercury

Mercurialis annua

This annual weed is related to spurges but does not possess the milky sap of those plants. A cosmopolitan species, it is most abundant in warmer regions of Europe and is only locally common in southern areas of Britain where it grows in wasteland, cultivated fields and gardens. It emits an unpleasant smell when rubbed. Although poisonous, the foliage was formerly used as a medicinal drug or cooked like spinach. The tall erect stem is quadrangular with opposite leaves and male and female flowers are borne on separate plants, the male flowers in long-stalked spikes, the female ones in stalkless spikes. Both grow from the leaf axils. The closely related Dog's Mercury grows in shady woodland.

Family	Euphorbiaceae
Status	Local
Distribution	Mainly in south and east
Height	20—50 cm

J F M A M J J A S O N D

Persicaria

Polygonum persicaria

This robust species has swollen reddish stems and dark crescent-shaped spots on the upper side of its long lance-shaped leaves. Membranous leaf-sheaths, which clasp the stem where the leaf-stalks are attached, are characteristic of this and all other members of the genus *Polygonum* and are important identification features. The leaf-sheaths in Persicaria firmly clasp the stem and are shortly hairy with long hairs along the edges. The tiny flowers with pale pink or white petals are arranged in short erect spikes, growing on long leafy side stalks. This almost cosmopolitan weed grows in waste places, cultivated ground and beside ponds.

Family	**Polygonaceae**	
Other names	**Red Shank,**	
	Willow Weed	J F M A M J J A S O N D
Status	**Common**	
Distribution	**Throughout Britain**	
Height	**20—70 cm**	

Knotgrass

Polygonum aviculare

A very resilient plant, Knotgrass tolerates even heavy trampling on paths, in cracks between paving stones and on roadside verges. This cosmopolitan species grows anywhere from seashores and lowlands to mountains. The prostrate clumps are formed by slender branched stems and the small whitish or pinkish flowers are borne in the leaf axils. It is a highly variable species; four races are distinguished according to the prostration of the stem and the shape of the leaves. Knotgrass has been used in herbal medicine especially in an ointment for the treatment of ulcers and sores and to stop bleeding, also to alleviate rheumatism and arthritis.

Family	**Polygonaceae**	
Status	**Common**	
Distribution	**Throughout Britain**	J F M A M J J A S O N D
Height	**10—45 cm**	

Common Chickweed
Stellaria media

One of a group of plants of worldwide distribution which often flower even in winter. It grows in all types of soil, preferring damp, humus-rich sites from lowlands to mountains and is often found in gardens, waste ground and fields. It has many adventitious roots growing from the brittle prostrate stems which break easily; pieces left in the ground soon root again and start to grow. This particular chickweed can be identified by the single line of hairs which grow along the stem. The flowers are small and white, growing in the leaf axils and producing thousands of seeds. The leaves are bright green, rich in vitamins and minerals and used in salads.

Family	Caryophyllaceae
Status	Abundant
Distribution	Throughout Britain
Height	10—40 cm

J F M A M J J A S O N D

Pale Persicaria
Polygonum lapathifolium

This is a highly variable annual species which closely resembles Persicaria and grows in similar habitats. It has branched, often red-spotted, stems and the long lance-shaped leaves lack the dark patches of the former species and are paler beneath. Small dot-like glands are present on the under surfaces of the leaves. The leaf sheaths in Pale Persicaria have smooth or only shortly hairy edges. The flowers are pink or greenish-white in cylindrical spikes and the fruits are small and dry and enveloped in the dried brownish petals.

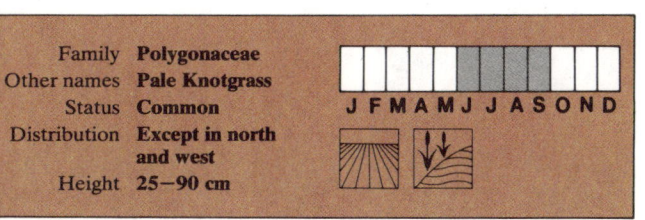

Family	Polygonaceae
Other names	Pale Knotgrass
Status	Common
Distribution	Except in north and west
Height	25—90 cm

J F M A M J J A S O N D

Jagged Chickweed
Holosteum umbellatum

This plant has ashy grey erect stems with 2−3 pairs of leaves, terminated by a cluster of minute white flowers on long stalks. The flower stalks lengthen and droop after flowering and straighten again when the fruits ripen. Fertile plants bear ovoid capsules which are longer than the persistent sepals. A single plant may produce up to several hundred seeds. Jagged Chickweed grows throughout Europe except in the far north, in fields, stony ground and waste places, flowering soon after the snow has melted and dying towards the end of spring. In Britain it is most likely to be found on walls or roofs but it is very rare.

Family	**Caryophyllaceae**	
Other names	**Umbellate Stitchwort**	
Status	**Very rare**	
Distribution	**Southern England**	
Height	**5−20 cm**	

J F M A M J J A S O N D

Smooth Rupture-wort
Herniaria glabra

The minute yellow-green plants of this species form neat circular clumps of prostrate stems, closely pressed to the dry sandy ground in which it grows. The branched stem and leaves are smooth or finely hairy, as are the sepals. The flowers are very small, with white petals reduced to filaments, and they are packed in dense clusters growing in the axils of the leaves on alternate sides of the stem. Smooth Rupture-wort has been used in herbal medicine to stimulate the kidneys and reduce dropsy. Both the scientific generic name and the common name refer to the fact that the plant was used to treat hernias, especially in children, in mediaeval times.

Family	**Caryophyllaceae**	
Status	**Rare**	
Distribution	**Scattered in England**	
Height	**5−15 cm**	

J F M A M J J A S O N D

Wild Amaranth

Amaranthus retroflexus

Most members of the family Amaranthaceae are native to the tropics and subtropics. The temperate zone is the home of only a few resilient species which are rarely more than impermanent casuals. Wild Amaranth is one of these. This annual plant was introduced to Europe from America in the 18th century. Since then it has become an unpleasantly prickly weed of arable land particularly where root and field crops are grown, although it is rare in Britain. The greenish flowers are packed in dense spikes, the whole spike made prickly by the coarse spiny bracteoles (leaf-like structures beneath the flowers) which are twice the length of the flowers. A single plant produces up to several hundred thousand seeds. These are tiny and easily dispersed by wind and water.

Family	**Amaranthaceae**	J F M A M J J A S O N D
Other names	**Reflexed Amaranth**	
Status	**A rare casual**	
Distribution	**Occasionally found in Britain**	
Height	**20—100 cm**	

Fat Hen

Chenopodium album

This robust, up to 2 metres high, representative of the genus *Chenopodium* can be found growing throughout the world. It is a densely branched and highly variable annual herb. The whole plant is whitish-mealy, particularly when young and covered in characteristic bladder-like hairs. The minute flowers are arranged in clusters, these in turn forming large loose inflorescences. The petals are whitish-green at first, becoming dry later and enveloping the fruits. One plant produces up to several hundred or thousand fruits which may remain dormant for many years. The plant is thus capable of rapidly colonising bare ground or wasteland such as compost heaps or rubbish tips, usually near human dwellings.

Family	**Chenopodiaceae**	J F M A M J J A S O N D
Other names	**White Goosefoot, Allgood**	
Status	**Very common**	
Distribution	**Throughout Britain**	
Height	**20—100 cm**	

Shining Orache

Atriplex nitens

Tall branched stems are densely covered with hairs and the broadly arrow-shaped leaves are glossy dark green above, greyish-mealy below. Clusters of tiny green male and female flowers are arranged in dense inflorescences which droop when the fruits ripen; the female flowers and the fruits look as if they are enclosed in green shells. This plant is native to the warmer regions of Europe and Asia and has been introduced to the more northern areas where it grows near human habitation, especially on rubbish heaps and in waste places.

Family	Chenopodiaceae	
Status	Rare	
Distribution	Occasional	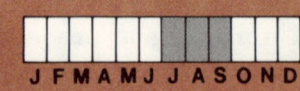
Height	60—150 cm	J F M A M J J A S O N D

Good King Henry

Chenopodium bonus-henricus

This species grows in nitrogen-rich soils around human habitation, particularly in farmyards, on road sides and in fields and meadows. It has large leaves, shaped like spear-heads with curled edges, and tall tapering inflorescences growing from the upper leaf axils. The flowers are like those of Fat Hen, but Good King Henry is a perennial plant, unlike the other members of the genus *Chenopodium*. Its leaves can be used as a green vegetable, like spinach, but it is said to be rather insipid in flavour. It was used in folk medicine for treating coughs and to improve the digestion. The name of the plant is unrelated to King Henry ('King' was probably added later) but the plant was called Good Henry to distinguish it from another, but poisonous, plant called Bad Henry.

Family	Chenopodiaceae	
Other names	Allgood, Mercury	
Status	Common	J F M A M J J A S O N D
Distribution	Throughout Britain	
Height	20—60 cm	

Bugloss

Anchusa officinalis

This is a conspicuous hairy, medium-tall herb bearing dense one-sided flower clusters in the leaf axils. The flowers are borne on very short stalks, purplish when opening, the colour deepening to a velvety deep blue-violet. The funnel-shaped flower has five rounded petals. The leafy flower cluster lengthens as the fruits, dotted nutlets, are forming. This sun-loving plant grows throughout many parts of Europe but is a rare casual in Britain, where it is replaced by another bugloss, *A. arvensis*. In folk medicine it was used in the preparation of cough syrups. The name *Anchusa* means paint and is a reference to the reddish dye obtained from the roots of the related Alkanet, *A. tinctoria,* which is used to stain wood the colour of rosewood or mahogany.

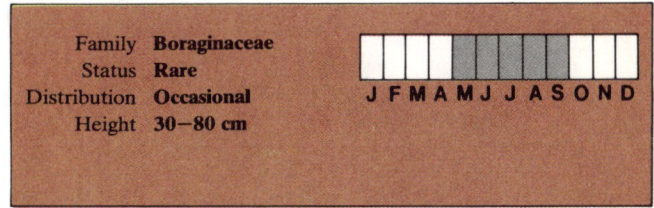

Family	**Boraginaceae**
Status	**Rare**
Distribution	**Occasional**
Height	**30—80 cm**

J F M A M J J A S O N D

Common Orache

Atriplex patula

This annual herb is particularly abundant in waste lands and cultivated ground, on roadsides and near the sea, where it grows together with Hastate Orache (*Atriplex hastata*). The stem is much branched and the lowermost leaves are diamond-shaped, wider at the bottom than at the top. The upper lance-shaped leaves narrow towards the plant's top, the uppermost ones being almost linear. The female flowers, and later the dry fruits, grow from leaf axils in green diamond-shaped sheaths, each with 1—2 teeth on the sides. Common Orache is much smaller than *A. nitens* and its leaves are mealy both above and below. It can be used as a spinach-like vegetable.

Family	**Chenopodiaceae**
Other names	**Iron-root**
Status	**Common**
Distribution	**Throughout Britain**
Height	**30—100 cm**

J F M A M J J A S O N D

White Deadnettle
Lamium album

This brittle herb, with its quadrangular hollow stems and large deeply toothed leaves, is reminiscent of the Stinging Nettle. It grows in woodlands, hedgerows and gardens. The honey-scented flowers are creamy white and grow in several whorls in the axils of the coarse opposite leaves. They produce large amounts of nectar which can only be reached by long-tongued bumble-bees; the bees pollinate the flowers in their efforts to reach the nectar. Unlike the leaves of Stinging Nettles, those of this species have no stinging hairs and so the plant was given the name, Deadnettle, because of its inability to sting. In folk medicine this plant has long been used in the treatment of a variety of internal disorders, sore throats and open wounds.

Family	**Labiatae**
Status	**Common**
Distribution	**Throughout Britain except the north**
Height	**20–50 cm**

J F M A M J J A S O N D

Motherwort
Leonurus cardiaca

This coarsely hairy plant has the quadrangular hairy stems typical of the family to which it belongs, and spikes of pale pink flowers growing in whorls in the axils of the leaves. Its leaves are distinctive, being palmately lobed with up to seven pointed toothed lobes. Motherwort is a native of Asia, extensively naturalized in Europe but relatively rare in Britain. It grows in hedgebanks and waste places and has been used for hundreds of years in folk medicine as a heart and nerve tonic. The name Motherwort comes from its use in alleviating various female complaints including painful uterine contractions and the side effects of menopause.

Family	**Labiatae**
Status	**Rare**
Distribution	**Scattered, mainly in England**
Height	**30–100 cm**

J F M A M J J A S O N D

Field Hempnettle

Galeopsis ladanum

This hempnettle has branched, softly downy stems. The opposite lance-shaped leaves have broad bases and hooded purple flowers grow in the leaf axils. Both the stem and the sepals of the flowers are dotted with glands and the sepals have stiff whitish hairs. This plant grows all over Europe and Siberia in fields and forest clearings where the soil is limy, but is a rare casual in Britain where it may occasionally be found on cultivated land or in waste places. It can be distinguished from the Common Hempnettle, *G. tetrahit,* by the fact that, in this latter species, the stems are swollen just below the leaf-bases.

Family	Labiatae
Status	Rare
Distribution	Occasional
Height	10—80 cm

J F M A M J J A S O N D

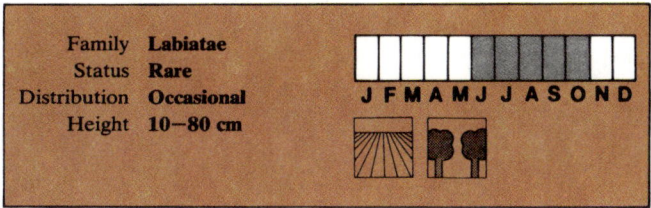

Whorled Clary

Salvia verticillata

This hairy, unpleasantly scented plant has basal rosettes of oval toothed leaves, from which grow branched upright flower stalks. The basal leaves usually die before the flowers open and the leafless flower spikes grow in the axils of hairy heart-shaped leaves. The spikes are formed by dense whorls of pale violet, rarely white, flowers. There are 15—30 flowers in a whorl, each with two stamens protruding from the two-lipped flowers, which droop after pollination. From its original home, southeastern Europe and Asia Minor, this perennial plant has spread to most of Europe. It grows in sunny grassy places and in wasteland.

Family	Labiatae
Status	Local
Distribution	Scattered, mainly in England
Height	30—60 cm

J F M A M J J A S O N D

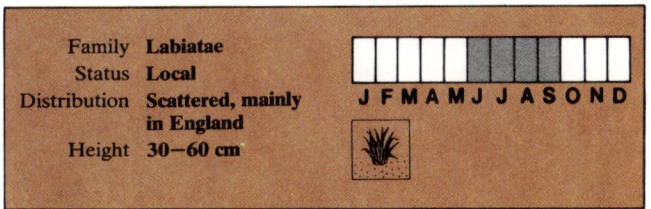

Henbane

Hyoscyamus niger

This is a low-growing, densely leafy, very glandular plant covered in sticky hairs. The relatively large flowers have glandular-hairy sepals and the petals are hairy on the outside, dingy yellow in colour with marked purple veins. Violet-coloured anthers are borne on hairy filaments. The fruit, a capsule shaped like a jug with a lid, is enclosed in persistent sepals. Each capsule contains some 200 tiny oval seeds and a single plant produces about 50 capsules. This plant is found mainly in sandy ground, especially in farmyards and wasteland, often in coastal areas. It is deadly poisonous, containing the alkaloids hyoscyamine, atropine and scopolamine which affect the nervous system and which are used in sleeping tablets and pain killers.

Family	Solanaceae
Status	Local
Distribution	Mainly in southern areas
Height	20—80 cm

J F M A M J J A S O N D

Common Vervain

Verbena officinalis

In late summer this plant bears slender spikes of tiny pale violet or white flowers, each with a tubular two-lipped corolla. The tough quadrangular branched stem bears divided opposite leaves. Common Vervain is an old medicinal plant used in a variety of herbal treatments. Its name, Vervain, is derived from an old Celtic word meaning 'to drive away the stone', illustrating its use in the treatment of kidney stones. It was used by both the ancient Egyptians and Romans as an altar herb, especially as a symbol of the goddess Isis and also as an amulet to protect them from harm. Vervain grows on roadsides and waste ground, especially on calcareous soils.

Family	Verbenaceae
Other names	Herb of Grace
Status	Locally common
Distribution	Mainly in south and east
Height	30—80 cm

J F M A M J J A S O N D

White Mullein

Verbascum lychnitis

This is a tall biennial plant with a rosette of lance-shaped leaves in the first year and a tall flower-spike in the second. The leaves are dark green above and powdery white beneath, with roughly scalloped edges. The candelabra-like flower spikes are covered with white powder and usually only a few of the many flowers are open at any one time. The petals may be white or yellow but British plants almost all have white flowers, yellow-flowered forms being only found in Somerset. The flowers are tubular, with short tubes and five widely opened petals. White Mullein is distributed throughout Europe, preferring dry banks and grassy slopes on limy soil.

Family	Scrophulariaceae
Status	Very local
Distribution	Mostly in southeast
Height	60—120 cm

J F M A M J J A S O N D

Thorn Apple

Datura stramonium

Scientists are not quite sure whether this plant is native to subtropical North America or to the regions of the Caspian and Black Seas, but all agree that it has become cosmopolitan in its distribution in the warmer regions of all the continents. It reached Europe via Spain after 1500 and it is still cultivated for its healing properties, in many European countries. The drug obtained from the leaves contains the poisonous alkaloids hyoscyamine, atropine and scopolamine, which have the same effects as described for Henbane. Thorn Apple is a robust leafy plant with large white or purple bell-shaped flowers opening in the evening. It grows in waste places and arable land.

Family	Solanaceae
Other names	Jimson Weed
Status	An uncommon introduction
Distribution	Scattered, rare in north
Height	30—120 cm

J F M A M J J A S O N D

Cleavers

Galium aparine

The weak stems of this species are prostrate or climbing, up to 2 metres long, markedly quadrangular and covered with many hooked hairs. The tough hairs cover not only the stem edges but also the margins and undersides of the whorls of leaves. The branching habit of the plant and its scratchy surface enable it to climb successfully along surrounding vegetation. The rounded fruits are always found in pairs and their hooked bristles cling to animal hairs and man's clothes and are thus dispersed. This capacity is even reflected in the plant's scientific specific name (the Greek *aparein* means to cling). It is distributed throughout most of Europe where it grows almost anywhere from seashores to mountains, hedgerows and waste ground.

Family	Rubiaceae
Other names	Goosegrass
Status	Common
Distribution	Throughout Britain
Height	60—200 cm

J F M A M J J A S O N D

Creeping Bellflower

Campanula rapunculoides

This handsome blue-violet bellflower is usually a garden or field weed which has been introduced into Britain from Europe. Densely branched tuberous roots contribute to the spread of the plant in cultivated ground and this is assisted by the seeds, up to several thousand of which are produced by a single plant. The seeds are tiny and retain their viability for several years, thus contributing to the plant's nuisance value as a weed. This robust bellflower with its one-sided racemes of purple flowers is sometimes mistaken for the similar Bats-in-the-Belfry (*C. trachelium*) in which, however, the flowers are hairy and grow from all sides of the flower-stalk.

Family	Campanulaceae
Other names	Creeping Campanula
Status	Locally introduced
Distribution	Throughout Britain
Height	30—80 cm

J F M A M J J A S O N D

Grim the Collier

Hieracium aurantiacum

This hawkweed originated in the alpine meadows of European mountains but has become extensively naturalized in lowland areas and can be an aggressive weed. It is sometimes grown in gardens, in flower borders and larger rock gardens, mostly in northern areas of Britain. The hollow hairy stem grows from a basal rosette of simple leaves and bears 2—12 flower-heads with orange-red to brick-red florets which are followed by hairy fruits. This is one of the few members of the genus, *Hieracium,* which can easily be distinguished; most of them are yellow-flowered and very difficult to tell apart. This species is protected in some countries.

Family	**Compositae**
Other names	**Fox and Cubs, Orange Hawkweed**
Status	**A garden escape**
Distribution	**Mainly in northern areas**
Height	**20—50 cm**

J F M A M J J A S O N D

Prickly Lettuce

Lactuca serriola

This biennial or overwintering plant has a stiff erect stem which exudes milky juice when cut. The prickly stem leaves are all held vertically in the north-south plane when the plant is fully exposed to the sun, hence its name Compass Plant. The few flower-heads are pale yellow, often tinged with mauve and formed of ray florets only. They are followed by hairy fruits like parachutes. Prickly Lettuce grows in waste places, on sunny banks and on walls in lowland and mountain areas and is sometimes found on sand dunes, especially once they have become stabilised.

Family	**Compositae**
Other names	**Compass Plant**
Status	**Local**
Distribution	**South and east**
Height	**60—120 cm**

J F M A M J J A S O N D

Common Dandelion
Taraxacum officinale

This common plant has basal rosettes of deeply toothed leaves and several hollow flower-stalks, all containing milky juice. The solitary bright yellow flower-heads are followed by greyish-white spheres — 'clocks', formed by the fruits and their hairy 'parachutes'. These small parachutes are easily carried by the wind when the fruits have ripened. Dandelion has been used as a medicine to treat gall-bladder and stomach disorders since time immemorial. The bitter root is still collected, roasted and used as a substitute for coffee. Young leaves are made into vitamin-rich salads and flower-heads are made into dandelion wine.

Family	Compositae
Status	Abundant
Distribution	Throughout Britain
Height	10—50 cm

J F M A M J J A S O N D

Smooth Sowthistle
Sonchus oleraceus

Smooth Sowthistle is an annual plant with an upright hollow stem filled with milky juice and large toothed leaves which lightly clasp the stem. Its close relative, the Spiny Sowthistle (*S. asper*) has spiny-edged leaves which closely clasp the stem. The many small flower-heads are enclosed in overlapping rows of bracts and are formed of yellow ray florets only, the outermost of which are tinged with mauve. They are followed by greyish-white balls of parachuted fruits. This plant is a common annual weed of cultivated ground, roadsides and wasteland throughout much of Europe. It is a favourite food of rabbits and pigs; the young leaves in particular are rich in minerals and Vitamin C and can be used in salads, although a little prickly.

Family	Compositae
Other name	Smooth Milkthistle
Status	Common
Distribution	Throughout Britain
Height	30—100 cm

J F M A M J J A S O N D

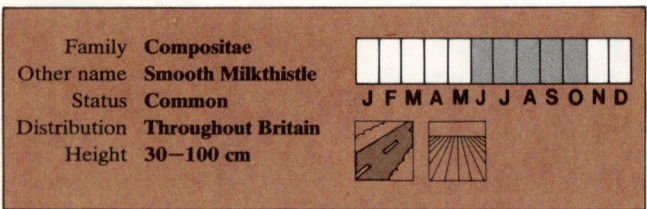

Stinking Mayweed
Anthemis cotula

This plant emits an unpleasant smell when rubbed, unlike the related Chamomile (*Chamaemelum nobile*) or the Corn Chamomile (*Anthemis arvensis*), which are both pleasantly aromatic. All three species have finely divided feathery leaves and solitary flower-heads. The flowers have central yellow disk florets and white ray florets, numbering 10−13 in Stinking Mayweed. The fruits of this plant do not have hairy parachutes. It is found in cultivated land and waste ground, together with several other similar white-flowered daisy-like plants which are difficult to distinguish from each other, most often on heavy soils. There is also a subspecies with prostrate stems which grows near the sea.

Family	**Compositae**	
Status	**Locally common**	
Distribution	**Rare in the north**	J F M A M J J A S O N D
Height	**15−50 cm**	

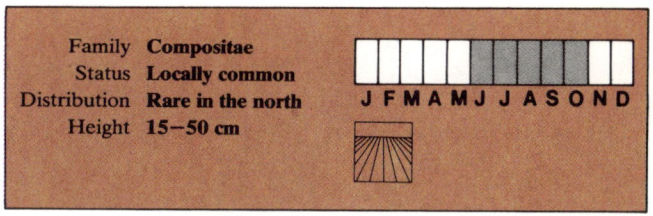

Yellow Chamomile
Anthemis tinctoria

This perennial plant has a simply branched stem and compound feathery ash-green leaves with greyish undersides. It has long-stalked decorative flower-heads formed of tiny golden-yellow tubular florets surrounded by a circle of golden-yellow toothed ray florets, unlike all the other members of this genus which have white ray florets. The plant is often grown in flower borders. At one time it was used in dyeing for it yields two natural yellow dyes from the flower-heads. It is a native of dry stony slopes of Europe and western Asia but has become naturalized in waste places and roadsides in many parts of Europe, where it has escaped from gardens.

Family	**Compositae**	
Status	**Locally introduced**	
Distribution	**Scattered throughout Britain**	J F M A M J J A S O N D
Height	**30−60 cm**	

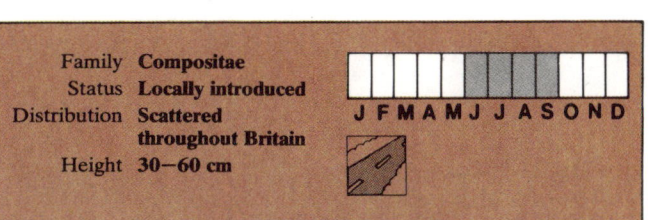

Pineapple Weed
Matricaria matricarioides

This small plant has spread from its original homes in North America and eastern Asia to all of the Northern Hemisphere. It reached Europe in the second half of the 19th century and has become a common wayside and wasteland plant of seashore, town and country. It can withstand any amount of trampling and may be found growing on paths as well as beside them, almost beaten into the ground and still flowering. It is an annual aromatic herb like its relative, Wild Chamomile (*M. recutita*), but it has no ray florets, so that the flower-heads are formed only by the greenish tubular flowers and look like small green domes. The plant bears many finely divided leaves.

Family	**Compositae**	
Other names	**Rayless Mayweed**	
Status	**Widely naturalized**	J F M A M J J A S O N D
Distribution	**Throughout Britain**	
Height	**5—30 cm**	

Feverfew
Tanacetum parthenium

This medium-high, densely branched and leafy plant attracts attention by its distinctive aroma. The stems are erect, bearing many soft, much dissected leaves and terminated by clusters of flower-heads. These are small with yellow tubular florets in the centre and white ray florets around the outside of each head. Feverfew was once cultivated and used in herb lore for the treatment of fevers (hence its common name) and as a wormicide. It is still grown in its double form as a garden plant, particularly the variety known as 'White Bonnet'. It grows in wasteland, on roadsides and in hedgerows and on stony slopes throughout Europe.

Family	**Compositae**	
Synonym	***Chrysanthemum parthenium***	
Status	**Common, probably introduced**	J F M A M J J A S O N D
Distribution	**Throughout Britain**	
Height	**30—60 cm**	

Tansy

Tanacetum vulgare

This plant has creeping underground stems from which grow stiffly erect flower-stalks, clothed with finely divided, aromatic, dark green leaves. The flower-heads are borne in flat clusters at the tops of these stems. Each flower-head consists of many yellow tubular disk florets arranged into a disc-like shape and lacking the petal-like ray florets. Tansy grows in waste places, on roadsides and in hedgerows throughout Europe. It was used in herb medicine to cure worms in children and as a flavouring in cakes and puddings. A bunch of dried plants is said to act as an insect repellent.

Family	**Compositae**	
Synonym	***Chrysanthemum vulgare***	J F M A M J J A S O N D
Status	**Common**	
Distribution	**Throughout Britain**	
Height	**60–120 cm**	

Wormwood

Artemisia absinthium

This sun-loving perennial plant grows in dry waste places and grasslands throughout Europe. It is almost like a shrub with a branched, more or less woody, base from which grow many erect silvery-grey stems each year. These bear divided silvery hairy leaves and long drooping sprays of tiny round, silvery-yellow flower-heads which have only tubular disk florets. Wormwood has been used in herbal medicine as a tonic, to promote digestion by stimulating the flow of digestive juices and to increase the appetite. At one time it was the principal flavouring in the liqueur absinthe, but its use has been discontinued, since wormwood is poisonous when dissolved in alcohol.

Family	**Compositae**	
Status	**Locally common**	J F M A M J J A S O N D
Distribution	**Rarer in the north**	
Height	**60–120 cm**	

Groundsel

Senecio vulgaris

This common garden and wasteland plant is native to Europe, northern Africa and Asia. The plant spreads easily by means of its small fruits equipped with simple, white ephemeral hairs. A single specimen can produce up to several thousand fruits in one year. The growing season of this hardy species lasts almost the whole year; it is capable of flowering even in mild winters. The flower-heads are small and hidden in enclosing bracts and there are no ray florets. Groundsel is a favourite food of rabbits and the seeds are eaten by birds. It was formerly used in folk medicine in a variety of ways, especially to stop bleeding in nose bleeds and menstruation.

Family	Compositae
Status	Abundant
Distribution	Throughout Britain
Height	10—30 cm

J F M A M J J A S O N D

Gallant Soldier

Galinsoga parviflora

This South American plant first appeared in Europe in the 18th century and was named after Dr. Galinsoga, keeper of the Botanical Gardens of Madrid. The English name, Gallant Soldier, is a corruption of the Latin. The plant is found mostly around London where it grows in cultivated and waste ground; in Europe it is more widespread, particularly in vineyards, gardens and sandy fields. It is a small annual species with a branched stem and simple opposite leaves bearing stalked clusters of flower-heads in their axils. The small flower-heads are formed mainly of yellow disk florets with a few white ray florets.

Family	Compositae
Other names	Joey Hooker
Status	Locally common
Distribution	Mainly in southeast England
Height	10—60 cm

J F M A M J J A S O N D

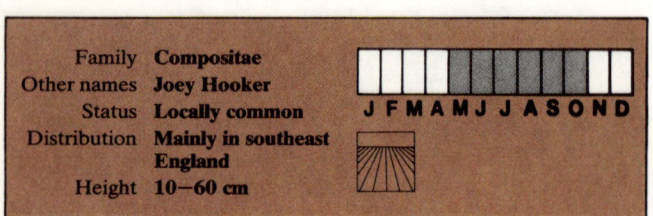

Canadian Fleabane
Erigeron canadensis

This cosmopolitan species has been introduced to Europe from North America. Its spread since its introduction in the 17th century is due to its liking for newly disturbed ground and, as it followed the building of the railways in the 19th century, so now it grows on the verges of new motorways. It is also found on wasteland, sand dunes, walls and cultivated ground. It is an annual plant with an erect branched stem, densely covered with narrowly lance-shaped leaves, and bearing many flower-heads in dense clusters. Each flower-head has many central tubular disk florets and several outer rows of ray florets. Both are yellow white.

Family	Compositae
Synonym	*Conyza canadensis*
Status	Local
Distribution	Mainly in south and east
Height	30—80 cm

J F M A M J J A S O N D

Stinking Groundsel
Senecio viscosus

This is an annual, aggressively spreading weed, which grows on railway banks, in wet places along tracks and in waste ground. It forms extensive colonies in forest clearings and is also found on sea-shores. The whole plant is covered by sticky glandular hairs, hence its common name. The tiny yellow flower-heads are borne in large complex clusters and are formed from dull yellow disk florets and yellow ray florets, these latter soon curling up and withering. After flowering the heads are followed by grey-white spheres formed of many hairy fruits, which blow in the wind and disperse the plant.

Family	Compositae
Status	Locally common
Distribution	Rare in Scotland and Ireland
Height	15—50 cm

J F M A M J J A S O N D

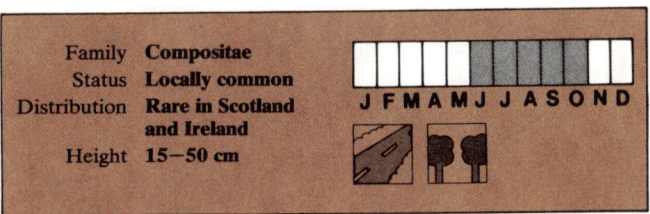

Coltsfoot
Tussilago farfara

The bright yellow heads of this widely distributed species open in early spring. The hollow scaly flowering stems bear flower-heads with golden yellow disk florets and similarly coloured ray florets. The large rounded leaves appear after flowering; they grow from long creeping underground stems and are up to 50 cm long. Young leaves are white-felted both above and below, mature leaves only on the underside. This species is native to Europe, northern Africa and northern Asia. It grows on waste ground, roadsides and rocky ground and on sand dunes. Both flowers and leaves yield a drug used as a remedy for coughs and the healing of wounds.

Family	**Compositae**	
Status	**Abundant**	
Distribution	**Throughout Britain**	J F M A M J J A S O N D
Height	**7—20 cm**	

Downy Burdock
Arctium tomentosum

This is a tall stout biennial herb of shrubby growth. The stems are longitudinally grooved, reddish and felted so that they look as if they are covered in cobwebs. The large heart-shaped leaves are similarly greyish-felted on the under surfaces. The spherical flower-heads with purple disk florets have very cottony bracts, the outer ones being equipped with hooks and the inner ones hookless. Ripe fruits cling by the hooks to clothing and the fur of animals. This species together with the related Great Burdock and Lesser Burdock are used in herb medicine — they are rich in Vitamin C and are also used as blood tonics. Downy Burdock is widespread in Europe and western Asia in heavy soils but is a rare casual in Britain.

Family	**Compositae**	
Other names	**Felted Burdock**	
Status	**Very rare**	J F M A M J J A S O N D
Distribution	**Occasional**	
Height	**80—150 cm**	

Lesser Burdock

Arctium minus

This robust biennial plant is bushy in habit with undivided leaves and it differs from the related Downy Burdock in that its flower-heads are smaller, the size of a hazel-nut, and the bracts are slightly cottony when young, later becoming smooth and hairless. The flowers are reddish-purple in colour. Its fruits are equipped with hooked bracts which cling to clothing or fur. This burdock grows in a wide variety of habitats including wasteland, hedgerows and open woodland, in both lowlands and uplands. Herb medicine seems to make no distinction between this species and Great Burdock (*A. lappa*) and the dried roots of 'burdock' were powdered and recommended to ward against the onset of colds and 'flu.

Family	**Compositae**	
Status	**Common**	
Distribution	**Throughout Britain**	J F M A M J J A S O N D
Height	**50—100 cm**	

Spear Thistle

Cirsium vulgare

At first sight it is difficult to distinguish the prickly plants of this genus, *Cirsium,* from the thistles of the other common genus, *Carduus.* The only safe distinguishing feature is the hairy fruit, for in the genus *Carduus* the hairs are simple, whereas in *Cirsium* species they are feathery. A basal rosette of spiny leaves, with cottony under surfaces, produces a tall stem in its second year. This stem has narrow spiny wings and bears heads of purple flowers. Stem leaves clasp the stem, and the leaf segments end in pale yellow spines. Spear Thistle is a common plant of waste places, fields and roadsides where it often grows in colonies. It occurs from lowlands to mountains in Europe and western Asia.

Family	**Compositae**	
Synonym	***Carduus lanceolatus***	
Status	**Common**	J F M A M J J A S O N D
Distribution	**Throughout Britain**	
Height	**60—120 cm**	

Cocklebur

Xanthium strumarium

This Eurasian sun-loving species rapidly colonises new areas by means of animals, which disperse the hooked fruits attached to their hair or skin. The branched plant bears lobed leaves and separate male and female flower-heads. The ovoid female heads grow in the axils of the large lower leaves. The male flowers are in spherical heads on the upper part of the stem. The similar Spiny Cocklebur (*X. spinosum*), native to South America and naturalized in Europe, has yellow spines on the stem under the leaves. Flowering upper parts of the stem of the Cocklebur are used in herbal medicine as an antiseptic and to stop bleeding.

Family	**Compositae**	
Status	**Introduced**	
Distribution	**Occasional**	
Height	**30—120 cm**	J F M A M J J A S O N D

Globe Thistle

Echinops sphaerocephalus

This plant resembles the true thistles of the genus *Carduus* in its overall appearance. The quadrangular white-felted and sparsely branched stem is terminated by compound, perfectly round prickly flower-heads composed of tiny, one-flowered heads of pale grey-blue, five-petalled flowers. The sphere becomes even more prickly after flowering, until the fruits have ripened and the fruiting head has disintegrated. The prickly character is reflected in the scientific generic name; *echinos* means 'hedgehog' in Greek. This European plant comes from the Mediterranean and is grown in flower borders in more northerly areas; it grows in dry stony ground in the wild and in similar places in wasteland and gardens.

Family	**Compositae**	
Status	**A garden escape**	
Distribution	**Occasional**	
Height	**60—120 cm**	J F M A M J J A S O N D

Species featured
in this section

Species featured
in another section

Creeping Cinquefoil
Potentilla reptans

Creeping Cinquefoil is a plant of low habit, with creeping stems, up to 100 cm long. They spread rapidly and root easily, sending out at intervals a few five-lobed palmate leaves, with eared stipules joined to the leaf-stalks. The solitary yellow flowers are borne on long stalks and their petals are twice as long as the sepals. An epicalyx of sepal-like structures is situated beneath the calyx (the sepals) and grows up after flowering to surround the many small dry fruits. Creeping Cinquefoil grows on wasteland and in gardens as well as on roadsides and in hedgerows, usually in open grassy places, in basic or neutral soils.

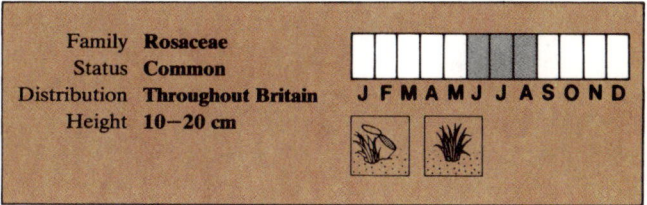

Family	Rosaceae
Status	Common
Distribution	Throughout Britain
Height	10—20 cm

J F M A M J J A S O N D

Common Agrimony
Agrimonia eupatoria

This fragrant perennial herb has a basal rosette of divided leaves in the spring. The leaves are highly distinctive with large opposite leaflets alternating with smaller ones, all closely covered with grey hairs on the under surfaces. From this rosette grow erect flowering spikes in summer, with many small yellow flowers followed by distinctive fruits. Each has a ring of small hooked spines on the top, an aid to dispersal by passing animals. Agrimony is used in herb medicine as a gargle and as a herb tea; it is said to be of benefit as a general tonic and in the treatment of ulcers. It grows in hedgebanks, on the edges of fields and in other similar places throughout much of Europe.

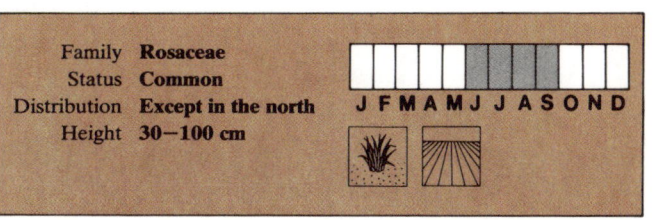

Family	Rosaceae
Status	Common
Distribution	Except in the north
Height	30—100 cm

J F M A M J J A S O N D

Bush Vetch

Vicia sepium

A trailing perennial plant with weak quadrangular stems and large compound leaves with 5—9 pairs of leaflets. The leaves are terminated by branched tendrils which curl around surrounding plants, to which the vetch clings. Flowers are pale purple in colour and borne in racemes of up to six blooms, growing from the leaf axils. They are followed by long beaked pods, containing up to ten seeds; these pods turn black when they are ripe and split open, twisting at the same time and expelling the seeds. This plant is common throughout Europe in grassy places and hedgerows.

Family	Leguminosae
Status	Common
Distribution	Throughout Britain
Height	30—60 cm

J F M A M J J A S O N D

Alsike Clover

Trifolium hybridum

This perennial clover is a trailing plant with rather weak stems and the typical clover leaves, each with three leaflets. However, unlike White Clover (*T. repens*) which it resembles, it has no white bands on the leaflets and its leaf stipules have long pointed tips. The flowers of Alsike Clover are pinkish white, in round heads growing on long stalks in the leaf axils. This plant is cultivated throughout Europe as fodder for cattle and to enrich the soil, for its roots have the nodules, containing nitrogen-fixing bacteria, found in all leguminous plants. It is also present in moist grassland and on roadsides.

Family	Leguminosae
Status	Widely naturalized
Distribution	Except in the north and west
Height	30—50 cm

J F M A M J J A S O N D

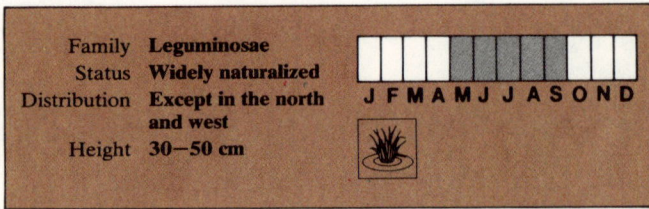

Birdsfoot Trefoil

Lotus corniculatus

This undemanding yellow-flowered perennial grows in short dry grassland, on roadsides and in waste places throughout Europe from lowlands to mountain areas. As a hardy drought-resistant plant, it is grown with grasses and clovers in pastures and meadows. Its weak stems bear leaves with five leaflets, but the lowermost pair of leaflets are stalkless and resemble stipules. Whorls of three to six yellow flowers grow on long flower-stalks from the axils of the leaves. The fruits are multi-seeded pods which crack sharply after ripening; the valves twist and eject small globular seeds away from the parent plant.

Family	**Leguminosae**
Other names	**Bacon and Eggs, Lady's Fingers**
Status	**Common**
Distribution	**Throughout Britain**
Height	**5—40 cm**

J F M A M J J A S O N D

Spiny Restharrow

Ononis spinosa

This spiny, almost semi-shrubby perennial plant has much-branched erect stems. Each stem has two lines of hairs running along its length, a feature which distinguishes it from the other Restharrow species, *O. repens,* in which the spineless stems are hairy all around. Spiny Restharrow has small few-flowered clusters of pink pea-like flowers growing in the leaf axils of short thorny twigs. The small oval single-seeded pods are covered by fine hairs and enclosed in the persistent enlarged sepals. It is a characteristic plant of rough grassland in many parts of Europe except the far north and mountainous regions. The roots were used in folk medicine in the treatment of several disorders, but particularly to alleviate inflammation of the kidneys and bladder.

Family	**Leguminosae**
Status	**Scattered**
Distribution	**Mainly in south and east**
Height	**30—60 cm**

J F M A M J J A S O N D

Greater Celandine
Chelidonium majus

This perennial herb is particularly likely to be found in hedgerows near towns and houses throughout Europe and Asia. It has smooth yellow-green divided leaves in a basal rosette and erect flowering stalks, with small clusters of yellow four-petalled flowers. These are followed by characteristic long seed-pods which look as if they are divided into sections. The seeds are attractive to ants which disperse them by carrying them off. The whole plant contains a caustic orange sap which was used in herb medicine to burn off warts and corns. This sap is rich in powerful opiate-like alkaloids which can be used to stimulate the activity of heart and liver.

Family	Papaveraceae
Status	Frequent
Distribution	Except in the north
Height	30—70 cm

J F M A M J J A S O N D

Evening Primrose
Oenothera biennis

This tall biennial plant is native to North America, from whence it has been introduced to other continents of the Northern Hemisphere. It grows alongside roads and railway tracks, on sunny banks and sand dunes and in waste places. The large glossy yellow flowers open at night and attract moths, nocturnal pollinators, with their subtle fragrance. Each flower lasts for one night only. The fruit is a capsule with many small seeds. Evening Primrose has an edible sweet-tasting root, sometimes eaten in salads, and the leaves and stems are used in herb medicine in the treatment of intestinal disorders and as a sedative.

Family	Onagraceae
Status	Commonly naturalized
Distribution	Mainly in south and east
Height	50—250 cm

J F M A M J J A S O N D

Winter Cress

Barbarea vulgaris

This biennial or perennial plant has a rosette of compound basal leaves which resemble those of watercress. From this grow several branched inflorescences, on which the leaves are simple and toothed with bases clasping the stem. The deep yellow four-petalled flowers are borne in large terminal clusters on the inflorescences, which lengthen as the narrow erect fruits ripen. This European plant grows throughout the Northern Hemisphere in hedgerows, on stream banks and in other damp places. It remains green throughout the winter, hence the name Winter Cress, for its leaves are rich in Vitamin C and can be used in winter salads.

Family	**Cruciferae**
Synonym	***Erysimum barbarea***
Other names	**Yellow Rocket**
Status	**Common**
Distribution	**Mainly in the south**
Height	**30—90 cm**

J F M A M J J A S O N D

Tower Mustard

Turritis glabra

This tall slender biennial plant has a basal rosette of oblong, sometimes toothed, leaves covered by soft hairs. These die before the flowers open. The leafy inflorescence which appears in the second year, has leaves of a different type — smooth and untoothed and clasping the stem. The inflorescence consists of a terminal cluster of yellowish blossoms, followed by long thin fruits, and the whole stalk lengthens as the fruits ripen. The fruits are at least three times as long as wide and have two rows of seeds. Tower Mustard is common in warm places with stony or calcareous soils, such as sunny banks, cliffs, roadside verges and waste places throughout the Northern Hemisphere.

Family	**Cruciferae**
Synonym	***Arabis glabra***
Status	**Local**
Distribution	**Scattered in England**
Height	**60—120 cm**

J F M A M J J A S O N D

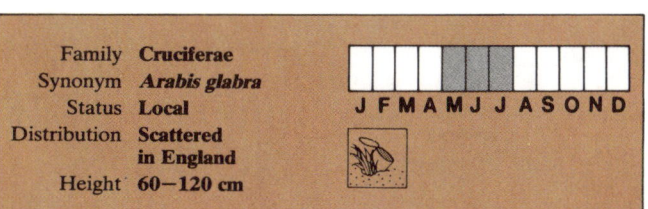

Jack-by-the-Hedge
Alliaria officinalis

This is a common biennial or perennial plant found in hedgerows, woodland edges and alongside walls throughout Europe and Asia. It has large coarse, heart-shaped basal leaves growing in a rosette and tall inflorescences. These bear similar leaves and a lengthening cluster of white flowers followed by erect narrow fruits. The whole plant gives off the scent of garlic when rubbed, hence its common names. This is an old culinary plant recommended in old England for flavouring fish or roast meat. It was also used in herb medicine for treating ulcers and sores, as a gargle to alleviate sore throats and tonsillitis and as a spring tonic, after a long winter without fresh vegetables.

Family	**Cruciferae**	
Synonym	*Sisymbrium alliaria*	
Other names	**Garlic Mustard, Hedge Garlic**	
Status	**Common**	
Distribution	**Except in the north**	
Height	**20—100 cm**	

J F M A M J J A S O N D

Pepperwort
Lepidium campestre

A medium-high greyly hairy annual or biennial herbaceous plant, with a basal rosette of spoon-shaped leaves. The stem leaves are simple and arrow-shaped with their bases embracing the stem. The flowers are small and white in a dense erect inflorescence and are followed by broad, flat, notched fruits on long stalks. Pepperwort is a sun loving European species, often spreading from its natural habitats on dry grassland to secondary man-influenced sites such as roadsides and waste ground. It ranges from lowlands to the subalpine zone. It is related to the Garden Cress (*L. sativum*) and can be distinguished from that species by the shape of the leaves.

Family	**Cruciferae**	
Status	**Not uncommon**	
Distribution	**Mainly in south and east**	
Height	**20—60 cm**	

J F M A M J J A S O N D

Common Mallow

Malva sylvestris

A common perennial plant with large rounded lobed leaves and many erect stems. Large pink flowers grow in clusters in the leaf axils and are followed by the highly characteristic fruits which look like round segmented cheeses – hence its common name Cheese Flower. Mallow grows in hedgerows and waste places throughout Europe. Like other mallows this plant is an old food plant, eaten as a vegetable since Roman times. It was also used in herb medicine to alleviate inflammations of throat and intestines. The whole plant is full of a mucilaginous sap which was used in soothing ointments. A similar sap from the Marsh Mallow (*Althaea officinalis*) is still used in the pharmaceutical and confectionery industries.

Family	**Malvaceae**	
Other names	**Cheese Flower**	
Status	**Not uncommon**	
Distribution	**Except in north and west**	
Height	**30–100 cm**	

J F M A M J J A S O N D

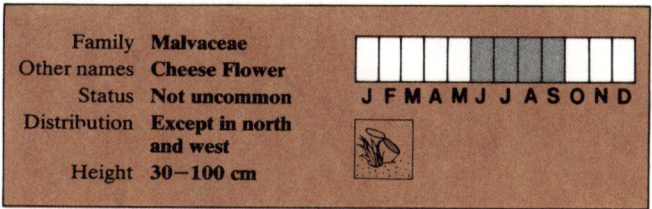

Mountain Cranesbill

Geranium pyrenaicum

Mountain Cranesbill grows in hedgerows and on field edges of western Europe and may spread extensively, particularly in orchards and gardens or waste places in warmer areas. It is a biennial or perennial herb. Its erect stem has a few long hairs and bears rounded, palmately lobed leaves. Several pairs of bluish-red flowers are borne on long stalks. Each flower has five separate notched petals which are much longer than the sepals. The beaked fruits separate at maturity and split open from the central column into five independent, twisted one-seeded sections. These become attached to animals' hair by means of the hooked beaks and are dispersed.

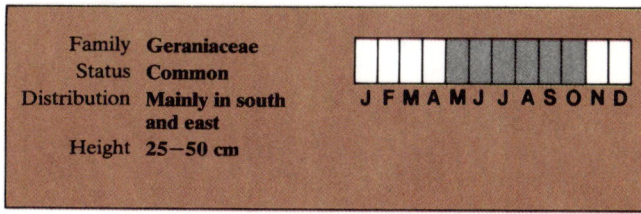

Family	**Geraniaceae**	
Status	**Common**	
Distribution	**Mainly in south and east**	
Height	**25–50 cm**	

J F M A M J J A S O N D

Wild Parsnip

Pastinaca sativa

Wild Parsnip grows in meadow plant communities and on grassy roadsides throughout Europe, especially on calcareous soils. It is a tall biennial plant with a deeply grooved angular stem and divided glossy leaves. The yellow flowers are borne in compound umbels on the tops of the flowering stems and are followed by rounded fruits, each with a narrow wing on either side. These can be used in soups, casseroles etc. and have a flavour rather similar to dill. The whole plant has a very distinctive smell. Wild Parsnip is the wild form of Parsnip, the roots of which are eaten as a vegetable. The plant has been used in herb medicine for hundreds of years particularly in the treatment of kidney disorders.

Family	**Umbelliferae**
Synonym	*Peucedanum sativum*
Status	**Locally common**
Distribution	**Mainly in south and east**
Height	**30—100 cm**

J F M A M J J A S O N D

Herb Robert

Geranium robertianum

This glandular plant has a branched stem often flushed with red and clothed with erect hairs. It is distinguished from other species of its genus by its markedly unpleasant scent and its divided triangular leaves (the leaves of the others are more lobed and rounded in outline). Several pairs of flowers grow in the axils of leaves on long flowering stalks. The pink petals have white lengthwise streaks and they are twice as long as the sepals. The styles are fused into a beak and the ripe beaked fruit splits into five one-seeded sections. A Eurasian species, common in damp shady locations such as hedge banks and shady walls or rocks. In folk medicine the fresh flowering stems were applied to blisters and wounds.

Family	**Geraniaceae**
Status	**Common**
Distribution	**Throughout Britain**
Height	**20—40 cm**

J F M A M J J A S O N D

Cow Parsley
Anthriscus sylvestris

This robust plant is abundant alongside woodland paths, in hedgerows, waste places and on roadsides. It occurs throughout Eurasia extending from lowlands to the subalpine zone. It is a biennial plant with an erect hollow stem bearing divided toothed leaves. It blooms in early summer, when the road verges and hedgerows almost disappear beneath its lacy white flowers, giving it the name Queen Anne's Lace. The flowers are borne in compound umbels and are followed by smooth oblong fruits. It is very similar to several other common hedgerow umbellifers from which it is most easily distinguished by its flowering time in early summer (the others mostly flower later).

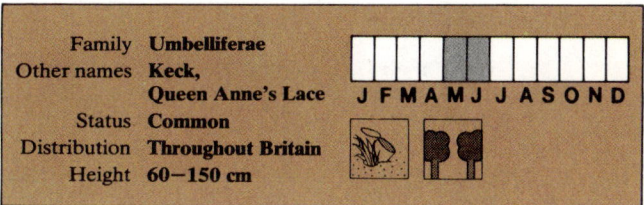

		J F M A M J J A S O N D
Family	**Umbelliferae**	
Other names	**Keck,**	
	Queen Anne's Lace	
Status	**Common**	
Distribution	**Throughout Britain**	
Height	**60—150 cm**	

Rough Chervil
Chaerophyllum temulum

This annual or biennial umbelliferous plant is poisonous. It contains the toxic substance, chaerophyllin, which dulls the senses of animals that have consumed it (Lat. *temulentum* = intoxicated). Like Hemlock (*Conium maculatum*), this species has a red-spotted stem, entirely hairy and thickened below the leaf-bases. The leaves are finely divided and pale green in colour. White flowers are borne in compound umbels, followed by smooth, oblong fruits. The root is thin and easily drawn out from the ground. Rough Chervil is a sun-loving species frequenting grassy places and hedgerows throughout much of Europe.

		J F M A M J J A S O N D
Family	**Umbelliferae**	
Status	**Common**	
Distribution	**Except in Scotland**	
	and Ireland	
Height	**30—120 cm**	

Hop
Humulus lupulus

The wild Hop grows in thickets, along fences and forest margins. The cultivated form is an important commercial crop, the female cone-like fruits yielding the raw material for the production of beer. The drug obtained from hop cones exerts a soothing action on the nerves and stimulates the appetite. Young shoots can be eaten in salads. Hop plants produce two types of flowers on separate plants; male plants bear anther flowers in clusters and female plants bear pistillate flowers in short spikes, changing into cones. Hop is a perennial vine-like plant in which the twisting climbing stems always twist in a clockwise direction.

Family	**Cannabiaceae**
Status	**Locally common and cultivated**
Distribution	**Mainly in south and east**
Height	**200—600 cm**

J F M A M J J A S O N D

White Campion
Silene alba

This campion is found in hedgerows and waste places throughout Europe, Asia and northern Africa. Clumps of flowering and non-flowering shoots bear opposite, soft, lance-shaped leaves. They are sticky and glandular and bear white flowers in small clusters. There are two kinds of flowers which usually open in the afternoon, to be pollinated by moths. The slender male flowers have the stamens while the female flowers are larger with five long styles projecting beyond the petals. After flowering the pale green sepals become swollen, with toothed margins. They are persistent and enclose the capsule which, on ripening, releases a number of small kidney-shaped seeds.

Family	**Caryophyllaceae**
Synonym	***Melandrium album***
Status	**Common**
Distribution	**Except in western Ireland**
Height	**30—100 cm**

J F M A M J J A S O N D

Bladder Campion
Silene vulgaris

This is a common plant of roadsides and dry grassy places, ranging from lowlands to mountains in Europe and Siberia and with several different varieties according to habitat and elevation. It is a perennial with smooth erect shoots and large terminal clusters of white flowers. Each flower has five deeply notched petals and five greenish-red sepals joined into a bladder-like tube. This persists after flowering and encloses the fruit. Bladder Campion can be distinguished from White Campion by these bladder-like sepals and from Sea Campion (*S. maritima*) by its erect growth. (The Sea Campion forms a flat cushion of fleshy blue-green leaves and grows usually near the sea.)

Family	Caryophyllaceae		
Synonym	*S. cucubalus*		
Status	Common		
Distribution	Rarer in north and west		
Height	15—50 cm		

Soapwort
Saponaria officinalis

Soapwort grows in hedgerows and wayside places in central and southern Europe and western Siberia, often near towns and villages. It is a perennial with a creeping underground stem from which grow erect flowering shoots. These have deep green opposite leaves and terminal clusters of 5—7 scented flowers in the axils of the leaves. The flower has reddish sepals joined into a tube and five long pink petals. The whole plant contains saponin, a poison which is mainly concentrated in the root. This substance foams in water and the flowers are sometimes used to wash fine silk and wool. Soapwort is also used as a drug to cure internal inflammations.

Family	Caryophyllaceae		
Other name	Bouncing Bett		
Status	Locally common		
Distribution	Mainly in south and east		
Height	30—70 cm		

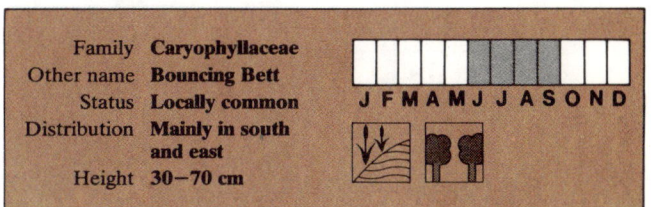

Procumbent Pearlwort

Sagina procumbens

Procumbent Pearlwort is a minute clump-forming perennial with a basal leaf rosette and stems rooting on contact with the soil. It grows wild in lawns, roadside verges and other grassy places from lowlands to mountains throughout the Northern Hemisphere. It is sometimes planted in crevices between paving stones in garden paths, because it tolerates trampling, but it more often grows as a weed. The tiny whitish flowers are borne continuously from late spring to early autumn, on thin flowering stalks which project above the yellow-green cushions of long linear leaves. The flowering stalks droop after flowering but become erect again when the fruits — capsules — are formed.

Family	Caryophyllaceae	J F M A M J J A S O N D
Status	Common	
Distribution	Throughout Britain	
Height	2—15 cm	

Common Mouse-ear Chickweed

Cerastium fontanum

This small perennial plant has a clump of trailing ascending stems, of which some are flowering while others are sterile leafy shoots. The flowers are inconspicuous, with five white petals cleft to one third of their length, approximately as long as the sepals. The flowering stalks are erect but spread horizontally after flowering. The whole plant is densely covered with short hairs including the undersides of the sepals. The leaves are oblong and stalkless, the upper bracts beneath the flowers are membranous along the edges. Mouse-ear Chickweed is a cosmopolitan species occurring in lowlands, mountains and coastal regions in all kinds of habitats.

Family	Caryophyllaceae	J F M A M J J A S O N D
Synonym	*C. vulgatum*	
Status	Common	
Distribution	Throughout Britain	
Height	5—50 cm	

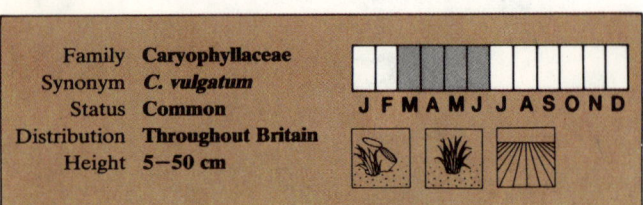

Larger Bindweed
Calystegia sepium

This herbaceous perennial plant often twines around branches of bushes and trees to a great height or festoons wooden or wire fences. It always twines in an anti-clockwise direction. It has large spearhead-shaped leaves which seem to completely cover the stems. In the axils of these leaves grow large bell-shaped white or pink flowers which open only during the day. The sepals and later the fruiting capsules are enclosed in two large bracts. This plant has deeply penetrating underground stems which make it one of the most difficult weeds to eradicate when it is growing in the wrong place. It was used in herb medicine as a laxative and purgative.

Family	**Convolvulaceae**
Other names	**Bellbine**
Status	**Common**
Distribution	**Throughout Britain**
Height	**100—300 cm**

J F M A M J J A S O N D

Birthwort
Aristolochia clematitis

This poisonous, unpleasantly scented, perennial plant has a creeping underground stem and many erect shoots with large heart-shaped leaves. The flowers grow in whorls in the axils of the leaves. Each one is dull yellow and tubular in shape, with an enlarged bulb-like swelling at the base and is followed by a pear-shaped fruiting capsule. Birthwort was introduced to Britain from central Europe and was cultivated as a medicinal herb. It was, and still can be, used in the treatment of rheumatism and gout and as a stimulant to speed up childbirth. It grows in hedgerows and waste places.

Family	**Aristolochiaceae**
Status	**Locally naturalized**
Distribution	**Mainly in eastern England**
Height	**30—70 cm**

J F M A M J J A S O N D

Large Dodder

Cuscuta europaea

This plant is unusual since it lacks chlorophyll and leads a parasitic way of life. It obtains its food from other plants, to which it clings by many thin twining reddish stems. The usual hosts are Stinging Nettle or Hops and the dodder attaches itself to these plants by special suckers. The leaves are reduced to small scales and the tubular flowers are pale pink or white, borne in dense clusters along the stem. Fruiting capsules follow the flowers. The plant is an annual and seedlings germinate in the usual way, then the young stem turns in a circle until it finds a host. Once contact is established, the roots die and the dodder relies on its suckers penetrating the host for food.

Family	**Convolvulaceae**
Status	**Rare**
Distribution	**South and east England**
Height	**30–150 cm**

J F M A M J J A S O N D

Lungwort

Pulmonaria officinalis

A common spring-flowering plant of European woods, often grown in gardens in several cultivated varieties. The inflorescences appear before the leaves and bear one-sided clusters of pink flowers which later turn blue. These are followed by rosettes of large coarse leaves which are often white-spotted, supposedly resembling the spotty texture of lungs, hence the common name. Similar plants lacking the white spots are classed as a subspecies or independent species (*P. obscura*). Lungwort is an old medicinal plant used in the treatment of coughs and lung infections but it is probable that its reputation was based on its resemblance to lungs rather than on its effectiveness.

Family	**Boraginaceae**
Other names	**Soldiers and Sailors, Jerusalem Cowslip**
Status	**Locally naturalized**
Distribution	**Mainly in southern England**
Height	**10–30 cm**

J F M A M J J A S O N D

Spotted Deadnettle

Lamium maculatum

Erect quadrangular stems grow from running underground and aerial stems. These are covered by pointed, heart-shaped, opposite leaves which are often marked by large white blotches in the garden forms; both stems and leaves are often flushed with red as are the flower spikes. These consist of whorls of pinkish-purple flowers growing in the axils of the leaves. The flowers are two-lipped with a violet pattern on the lower lip, and each one produces four small fruits — nutlets. This perennial species grows in shady mixed European woods from lowlands to mountains. It has been introduced to Britain as a garden plant and is sometimes found growing as an escape.

Family	**Labiatae**
Status	**Garden escape**
Distribution	**Occasional**
Height	**15—60 cm**

J F M A M J J A S O N D

Black Horehound

Ballota nigra

This foul-smelling relative of the deadnettles forms a clump of shoots with softly grey, hairy leaves. From the axils of the opposite, rounded and wrinkled leaves grow whorls of dull scarlet, two-lipped, hairy flowers each with a white pattern on the central lobe of the lower lip. The woolly sepals have bristly bracts on the underside and persist after flowering to enclose the four nutlets, which can be seen at the bottom of the sepal tube. Outside the flowering period, Black Horehound resembles White Deadnettle (*Lamium album*) but the latter species lacks the foul scent of the Horehound. Both grow in similar places on roadsides and in hedgerows.

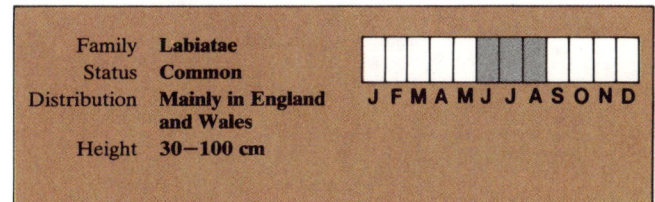

Family	**Labiatae**
Status	**Common**
Distribution	**Mainly in England and Wales**
Height	**30—100 cm**

J F M A M J J A S O N D

Wild Basil

Clinopodium vulgare

This is a straggling branched grey-green, perennial plant with square erect shoots growing from creeping rooting stems. The whole plant bears long soft hairs. From the axils of the upper oblong leaves grow pale purple flowers in dense terminal whorls composed of 10–20 blossoms. Wild Basil is a sun-loving plant which grows in dry hedgerows, in scrubland and woodland margins throughout Europe and Asia. It is somewhat aromatic, smelling rather like thyme, and has been used in herb medicine to make a tea which soothes acid indigestion. It can be used in herb sachets to sweeten the air of cupboards and in cooking, but it is not related to true culinary basils which are Asian members of the Labiatae.

Family	**Labiatae**
Other names	**Hedge Basil**
Status	**Common**
Distribution	**Rarer in the north**
Height	**30–60 cm**

J F M A M J J A S O N D

Ground Ivy

Glechoma hederacea

A creeping perennial with trailing and ascending stems, bearing rounded kidney-shaped leaves and whorls of blue-violet flowers in the leaf axils. The unbranched stems root at the nodes and produce new leaves and flowering stems. The flower is two-lipped with a larger patterned lower lip and a smaller straight upper lip. The sepals are covered with hairs and form a persistent tube with four nutlets at the bottom. This Eurasian species grows mainly in moist woods, hedgerows and waste places from lowlands to mountains. It is an old medicinal plant, recommended for use in the treatment of kidney and chest complaints. Before the introduction of hops it was used in their place in the making of beer.

Family	**Labiatae**
Synonym	*Nepeta glechoma*
Other names	**Alehoof**
Status	**Common**
Distribution	**Except in far north**
Height	**20–40 cm**

J F M A M J J A S O N D

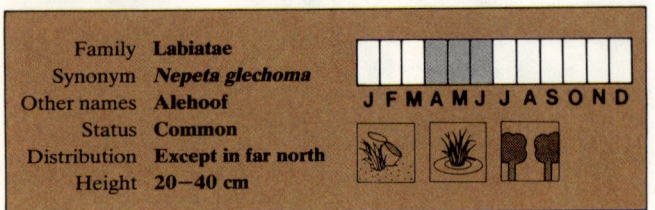

Horse-mint
Mentha longifolia

All parts of this robust perennial smell strongly of mint. It has many creeping underground stems from which grow a thicket of erect shoots. These have large opposite, lance-shaped leaves which have toothed margins and are usually hairy, at least on the lower surfaces. The small lilac-coloured flowers are borne in whorls in dense spikes, in the axils of the leaves. As the flowering season progresses, these spikes lengthen and the flower whorls are separated. Horse-mint grows in damp places on roadsides, in hedgerows and waste places in many parts of Europe. It is the most common species of mint grown in gardens, for use in mint sauce or mint jelly.

Family	**Labiatae**	
Synonym	***M. sylvestris***	
Status	**Local, probably introduced**	
Distribution	**Scattered**	
Height	**50–100 cm**	

J F M A M J J A S O N D

Wall Germander
Teucrium chamaedrys

Wall Germander is native to the Mediterranean, but also grows elsewhere in Europe, in warm lowland regions, particularly on sunny limestone rocks. It has been introduced to Britain as a garden plant and is sometimes found growing on old walls. It is a low-growing, delicately fragrant semi-shrub with ascending stems. The oval leaves are simple with rounded teeth and fine hairs, and they densely clothe the shoots. The flowers are one-lipped, with only the lower lip present, and they grow in terminal spikes made up of many six-flowered whorls. This medicinal herb is administered in gastric upsets and to stimulate the appetite.

Family	**Labiatae**	
Status	**Garden escape**	
Distribution	**Occasional**	
Height	**15–30 cm**	

J F M A M J J A S O N D

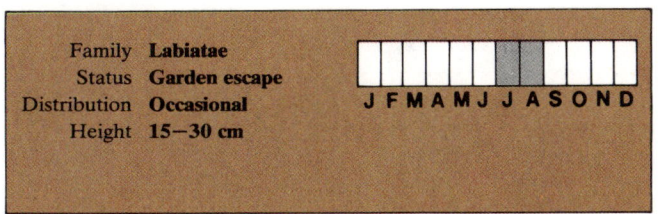

Cat-mint

Nepeta cataria

This is one of several different species of plants which are attractive to cats. It is strongly aromatic and has many branched erect shoots with opposite heart-shaped leaves. These leaves are toothed and white-felted on their lower surfaces. The flowers are borne in whorled spikes growing from the leaf axils of the upper leaves. They are two-lipped, with a flat upper lip and a spoon-shaped lower lip, white in colour with many purple spots. This plant grows throughout much of Europe and Asia in hedgerows and on roadsides, usually on calcareous soils, and is often grown in gardens. It is used in herb lore as a stimulant in the form of Cat-mint Tea and is said to help alleviate colds and fevers.

Family	**Labiatae**	
Other names	**Catnep**	
Status	**Local**	J F M A M J J A S O N D
Distribution	**Mostly in England**	
Height	**50—100 cm**	

Woody Nightshade

Solanum dulcamara

A climbing semi-shrub of hedgerows, woodland and waste ground inland, and also of shingle beaches and other coastal habitats. Its scrambling stems twine amongst the branches of other plants to a height of 3 metres. Stems become woody at the base and are covered by three-lobed leaves, each with a heart-shaped terminal leaflet. Opposite the leaves grow drooping clusters of dark violet flowers with golden-yellow cones of fused anthers in the centre of each. In autumn the plant bears clusters of glossy red berries. Bittersweet is poisonous containing two alkaloids, one sweet and the other bitter, hence the common name. The plant is used in medicine, since the drug extracted from it is used in the treatment of chronic skin problems and chest complaints.

Family	**Solanaceae**	
Other names	**Bittersweet**	
Status	**Common**	J F M A M J J A S O N D
Distribution	**Except the far north**	
Height	**30—250 cm**	

Dark Mullein
Verbascum nigrum

This biennial plant has a rosette of lance-shaped leaves in the first year, followed by a tall flowering spike in the second year. The leaves are thinly hairy as is the flower spike, unlike the related Aaron's Rod, *V. thapsus,* which is densely covered with white woolly hairs. The single flowering spike bears many yellow, purple-spotted flowers in which the stamen filaments are clothed with scarlet hairs — a good distinguishing feature. The fruits are spherical capsules covered by star-shaped hairs. This plant grows on sunny banks, beside roads and in open places, usually on calcareous soils, throughout many parts of Europe.

Family	**Scrophulariaceae**
Status	**Locally common**
Distribution	**Mainly in southern England**
Height	**50—120 cm**

J F M A M J J A S O N D

Germander Speedwell
Veronica chamaedrys

One of the most widely distributed species of its genus, Germander Speedwell is a low-growing herb with two distinct rows of hairs on the little-branched stem. These weak stems bear toothed stalkless leaves, with their bases closely pressed to the stem and growing opposite to each other. From the axils of these leaves grow long-stalked clusters of brilliant blue flowers. In each flower the petals are joined to form a tube and at the centre of the flower there is a white eye, hence its other common name. This is a familiar weed of gardens, waste places, woods and hedgerows growing throughout Europe and much of Asia from lowlands to mountains. This speedwell was used in herb medicine, especially in the treatment of wounds and as a blood tonic.

Family	**Scrophulariaceae**
Other names	**Bird's Eye**
Status	**Common**
Distribution	**Throughout Britain**
Height	**15—25 cm**

J F M A M J J A S O N D

Ivy-leaved Toadflax
Cymbalaria muralis

This small plant thrives in unfavourable sites such as cracks in old walls or rocky crevices. The perennial, up to 50 cm long, hairless branched and trailing stem covers the wall and roots into the cracks and crevices. Rounded, kidney-shaped leaves are often purple on the underside and grow, on long leaf-stalks, at intervals along the stem. The distinctly spurred flowers, similar to those of Common Toadflax, are pale violet with a yellow convex part of the lower lip. The fruiting stalks with capsules turn away from the light. This sun-loving species is native to southern Europe but has been introduced to northern areas where it has become extensively naturalized.

Family	Scrophulariaceae	
Synonym	*Linaria cymbalaria*	
Status	Widely naturalized	J F M A M J J A S O N D
Distribution	Throughout Britain	
Height	30—60 cm	

Common Toadflax
Linaria vulgaris

Several erect shoots grow from a creeping underground stem. The shoots are covered with many linear leaves and terminated by dense spikes of flowers. The flowers are distinctive, like spurred snapdragons, and bright yellow with an orange centre. They are followed by ovoid capsules with many winged seeds. Toadflax grows in hedgebanks, waste places and sunny slopes throughout much of Europe. This is an old medicinal herb which is still used to some extent today, in the treatment of jaundice and other liver diseases, dropsy and skin sores and ulcers. Its name comes from its once common presence as a weed of flax and it was called 'Krotenflacks' in Germany; this was translated as Toadflax.

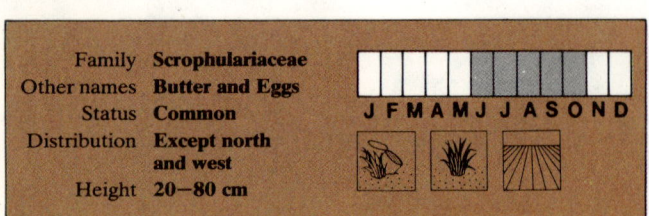

Family	Scrophulariaceae	
Other names	Butter and Eggs	
Status	Common	J F M A M J J A S O N D
Distribution	Except north and west	
Height	20—80 cm	

Dwarf Elder

Sambucus ebulus

Dwarf Elder is a Eurasian species found in damp soils in lowlands and mountains, often on roadsides and in waste places. Unlike the related woody elders (*S. nigra* and *S. racemosa*), Dwarf Elder is a herbaceous perennial, but it has similar compound opposite leaves with lance-shaped leaflets. The plant has an unpleasant aroma. The white flowers in dense flat clusters resemble those of Common Elder (*S. nigra*), but they are pinkish on the outside with purplish, later black anthers. The fruits are glossy black berries which serve as food for birds. Dwarf Elder tea is made from the leaves and is used in the treatment of dropsy and kidney and liver inflammations.

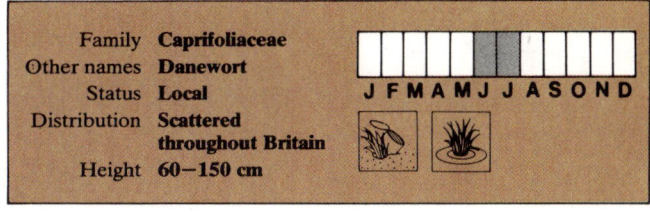

Family	Caprifoliaceae	J F M A M J J A S O N D
Other names	Danewort	
Status	Local	
Distribution	Scattered throughout Britain	
Height	60—150 cm	

Hedge Bedstraw

Galium mollugo

This perennial plant produces long creeping and branched underground stems, from which grow many ascending or climbing shoots with whorls of 4—8 linear leaves. The leaves all have forwardly pointing bristles on their edges so that they feel rough to the touch. The flowers are small and white and carried in clusters on side shoots growing from the axils of the leaves, the whole forming one large loose cluster. Hedge Bedstraw grows throughout Europe in hedgerows and grassy places, especially on calcareous soils. Like Lady's Bedstraw (*G. verum*), this plant can be used to curdle milk for cheese, and it was widely used for this purpose at one time, especially in Cheshire and parts of Tuscany.

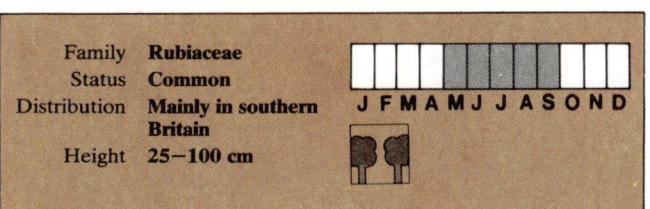

Family	Rubiaceae	J F M A M J J A S O N D
Status	Common	
Distribution	Mainly in southern Britain	
Height	25—100 cm	

Corn Salad

Valerianella locusta

This small tender annual herb is used as a salad plant, especially on the Continent. Young leaves of wild plants are collected or improved varieties are grown as vegetables. Being frost-resistant it is available even in winter. Erect branched stems bear long entire leaves and flat terminal clusters of small bluish blossoms. The fruits are three-lobed capsules containing a single seed in one cell, the other two cells being empty. Corn Salad grows in dry arable fields, hedgerows and open stony places inland and on sand dunes near the coast, throughout much of Europe except the extreme north, although it is never more than locally common.

Family	**Valerianaceae**
Synonym	***V. olitoria***
Other names	**Lamb's Lettuce**
Status	**Locally common**
Distribution	**Throughout most of Britain**
Height	**5–20 cm**

J F M A M J J A S O N D

Wild Teasel

Dipsacus fullonum

This biennial plant has a rosette of prickly leaves in the first year and an erect flower-stalk in the second. The edges of the stem, the margins of the opposite leaves and tough arched bracts beneath the flower-heads are all covered by short, prickly thorns. The small flowers together with prickly bracts, longer than the blossoms, are borne in large conical flower-heads. The flowers open successively from the centre of the heads both upwards and downwards and fruiting heads are used in dried flower arrangements. The common name 'Teazle' refers to the old use of the heads to raise the nap in newly woven cloth. Water collects in depressions in the leaves and was used as an eye wash and to cure warts, hence Venus' Basin as a common name.

Family	**Dipsacaceae**
Synonym	***D. sylvestris***
Other names	**Comb and Brush, Venus' Basin**
Status	**Locally common**
Distribution	**Mainly south and east**
Height	**70–150 cm**

J F M A M J J A S O N D

Wild Chicory
Cichorium intybus

From a rosette of deeply toothed basal leaves grow stiff, grooved stems bearing a succession of azure-blue flowers. These open regularly early in the morning and close after midday. The flower-heads are followed by dry fruits with a ring of tiny scales on the upper edge. This species is not the same as the cultivated Chicory or Endive (*C. endivia*), for the leaves of Wild Chicory are bitter to the taste. Nevertheless, leaves and roots are used in herb medicine to treat jaundice and to stimulate the appetite. The roots, like those of Dandelion, can be roasted and used as a coffee substitute. Chicory grows on roadsides and pastures throughout Europe, especially on calcareous soils.

Family	Compositae		J F M A M J J A S O N D
Other names	Wild Succory		
Status	Locally common		
Distribution	Except in the far north		
Height	30—150 cm		

Nipplewort
Lapsana communis

A medium-high weed with a branched taproot and numerous lateral roots. The plant forms a dense rosette of deeply divided leaves, each of which has a large diamond-shaped terminal leaflet. The erect stem is covered with small stalkless leaves and is terminated by a sparse cluster of small, stalked flower-heads which are composed of yellow ray florets. The plant produces up to several hundred dry fruits. Nipplewort is a European species naturalized in northern Africa, western Asia and North America. It grows in fields, gardens and waste grounds in the vicinity of human settlements. Its young leaves can be used as a vegetable.

Family	Compositae		J F M A M J J A S O N D
Status	Common		
Distribution	Throughout Britain		
Height	30—100 cm		

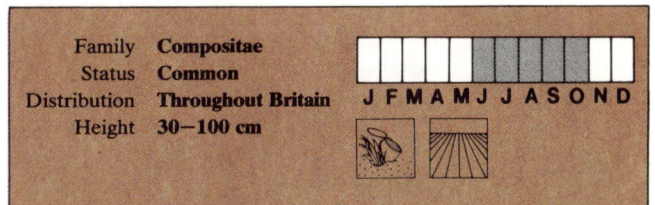

Hawkweed Ox-tongue

Picris hieracioides

Hawkweed Ox-tongue grows on waste ground and on grassy roadsides throughout much of Europe, especially on calcareous soils. It is a highly variable species forming several subspecies and may be biennial or perennial. The stout erect stem is grooved and bristly and bears many dandelion-like leaves, toothed and tapering towards the base or clasping the stem. It is terminated by a loose inflorescence of yellow flower-heads composed only of ray florets. These are succeeded by dry fruits each with a ring of cream-coloured feathery hairs which soon fall off. The leaves can be used as a vegetable or in salads.

Family	**Compositae**	
Synonym	*Helmintia echioides*	
Status	**Locally common**	J F M A M J J A S O N D
Distribution	**Mainly in south and east**	
Height	**30—70 cm**	

Wall Lettuce

Mycelis muralis

This tall perennial plant has an erect hollow stem and large, deeply toothed leaves with winged stalks. The lobes of these leaves are highly distinctive, looking rather like spear-heads or flattened diamonds. The flower-heads are borne in large loose inflorescences terminating the stem. Each head is small and yellow, made up of ray florets only and it produces a cluster of dry spindle-shaped fruits after flowering. Wall Lettuce grows on old walls, in ruined buildings, wasteland and woodland throughout Europe, especially on calcareous soils. It is particularly associated with beech woods where, if it is growing in deep shade, it may not flower. However, it is equally intolerant of strong sunlight.

Family	**Compositae**	
Status	**Locally scattered**	J F M A M J J A S O N D
Distribution	**Mainly in England and Wales**	
Height	**60—80 cm**	

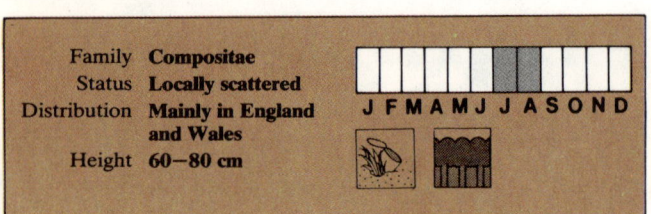

Yarrow
Achillea millefolium

Originally a Eurosiberian species, Yarrow has become naturalized over almost the whole world. It has tough creeping stems with many finely divided deep green leaves and flat much-branched clusters of small white flower-heads, which can be pinkish in acid soils. The fine foliage and the woolly stems give off a strong scent. This perennial herb is an old medicinal plant still used to stimulate digestion, improve blood circulation and alleviate coughs. As a gargle it cures inflammation of the gums and as a bath additive it speeds up the healing of wounds and helps cracked skin. It can be seen growing on almost any roadside verge or grassy place in Britain and Europe.

		J F M A M J J A S O N D
Family	**Compositae**	
Other names	**Milfoil**	
Status	**Very common**	
Distribution	**Throughout Britain**	
Height	**20—100 cm**	

Goat's Beard
Tragopogon orientalis

A Eurosiberian species distributed in the company of other Goat's Beards including the common British species *T. minor.* Many botanists consider that there is only one true species, *T. pratensis,* and that all the others are subspecies with overlapping distributions in Europe. *T. orientalis* has deep yellow ray florets, the outermost of which are longer than the involucral bracts; in *T. minor* the ray florets are only half the length of the bracts. All Goat's Beards are annual or perennial herbs with erect stems sheathed in linear leaves, and with solitary yellow flower-heads followed by 'clocks' of parachuted fruits. They grow on roadsides, in waste places and on sand dunes.

		J F M A M J J A S O N D
Family	**Compositae**	
Synonym	*T. pratensis*	
Other names	**Jack-go-to-bed-at-noon**	
Status	**Casual**	
Distribution	**Occasional**	
Height	**20—70 cm**	

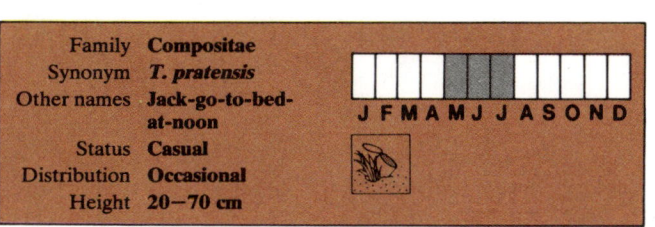

97

Scentless Mayweed
Tripleurospermum maritimum

An annual or perennial herb related to Chamomile, but with larger flower-heads and almost scentless. It has rather weak, branched stems clothed with very finely dissected deep green leaves. The flower-heads are borne singly or in small clusters and have white ray florets around the outside of the disk with tubular yellow disk florets in the centre. The flowers are followed by hairless dry three-ribbed fruits. There are several different subspecies, each occupying different habitats from coastal cliffs, foredunes and shingle beaches to arable land, wasteland and roadside verges, throughout the Northern Hemisphere.

Family	**Compositae**
Synonym	*Matricaria maritima*
Status	**Very common**
Distribution	**Throughout Britain**
Height	**20—50 cm**

J F M A M J J A S O N D

Mugwort
Artemisia vulgaris

This strangely scented perennial forms large leafy clumps with branched stems bearing divided leaves, smooth and green above and white-felted below. The upper part of the stem bears a series of long dense inflorescences in the axils of the leaves. These contain many small yellow flower-heads composed of tubular disk florets only. Several thousand hairless fruits ripen on a single plant. Mugwort ranks amongst the most ancient of herbs used in magic and medicine as a stimulant and nerve tonic, and as a flavouring in beer and other drinks. It grows in hedgerows, waste places, grasslands and roadside verges throughout much of the Northern Hemisphere.

Family	**Compositae**
Status	**Common**
Distribution	**Rarer in the north**
Height	**50—150 cm**

J F M A M J J A S O N D

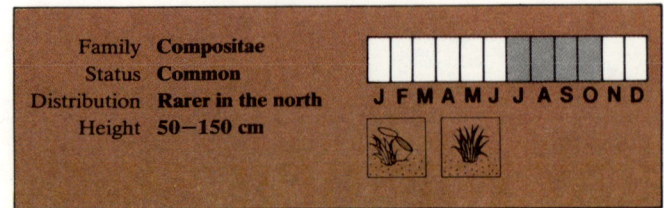

Ragwort

Senecio jacobaea

This common biennial or perennial plant forms a substantial clump of erect stems, which bear deep green divided leaves and which terminate in large flat clusters of yellow flower-heads. Each head has central tubular disk florets and a ring of outer ray florets, all bright yellow. They are followed by fruits, some of which have long hairs which soon fall off. Ragwort is a common sight on roadsides, wasteland and grazing land throughout Europe and may also be seen on dunes and shingle beaches. It has been used in herb medicine to treat eye and skin inflammations, ulcers, rheumatism and gout.

Family	Compositae	J F M A M J J A S O N D
Other names	Ragweed	
Status	Very common	
Distribution	Throughout Britain	
Height	30−100 cm	

Daisy

Bellis perennis

From the small mat-forming rosettes of paddle-shaped leaves grow the solitary flower-heads on long stems. The head has two types of florets, tubular yellow disk florets in the centre and white, red-flushed ray florets on the outside. The heads behave as single flowers: they are open by day in dry weather and close at night or in rain, hence the name 'Daisy' which is a shortened version of Day's Eye. The flowers also follow the sun. The florets are very hardy and can be found all year long. Daisies are familiar garden lawn weeds and grow in short grassland throughout Europe and Asia. Cultivated garden varieties have been developed from the wild form.

Family	Compositae	J F M A M J J A S O N D
Other names	Bairnwort	
Status	Very common	
Distribution	Throughout Britain	
Height	5−15 cm	

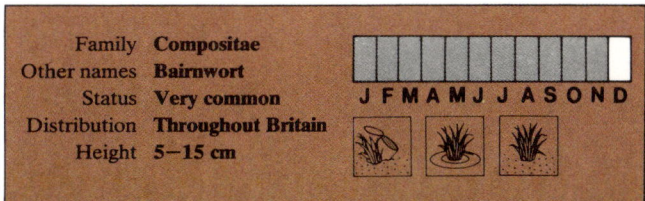

Musk Thistle

Carduus nutans

This robust ornamental biennial plant has an erect winged prickly stem which is sparsely branched. The prickly leaves are deep green in colour, with spine-tipped teeth and with bases clasping the stem. Each plant bears only a few solitary, large drooping flower-heads made up of many fragrant reddish-purple florets, and with thick hooked bracts beneath. The fruiting heads have many dry fruits with simple hairs (in contrast to the similar related thistles of the genus *Cirsium* in which the hairs are feathery). Musk Thistle grows on roadsides, fields and meadows, especially on calcareous soils, throughout much of Europe. It may also be found on sandy coasts in more northern areas.

Family	**Compositae**	
Status	**Not uncommon**	
Distribution	**Mainly in England**	J F M A M J J A S O N D
Height	**30—100 cm**	

Greater Knapweed

Centaurea scabiosa

A variable Eurosiberian perennial with several branched erect stems bearing many solitary purple flower-heads, larger than 2 cm and often up to 5 cm across. The sterile marginal florets are much longer than the disk florets and have funnel-shaped petals, deeply dissected into narrow lobes. The buds are distinctive, large and globular with many overlapping blackish-brown bracts and the flowers are followed by shortly hairy fruits. The stem leaves are usually divided with lance-shaped leaflets, dark green and coarse on both sides. Greater Knapweed grows on sunny slopes and grassland or on roadsides, especially on calcareous soils throughout Europe, Asia and North America.

Family	**Compositae**	
Status	**Common**	
Distribution	**Mainly in south and east**	J F M A M J J A S O N D
Height	**50—90 cm**	

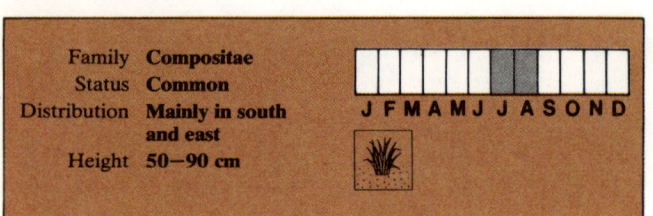

Species featured in this section

Species featured in another section

Meadow Buttercup

Ranunculus acris

This plant with glossy yellow flowers is a highly variable species, growing throughout Europe and Asia. It has a short thick creeping stem and a basal rosette of long-stalked lobed leaves with fine black markings. From this grows an erect stem with stalkless upper leaves and a few five-petalled flowers with many stamens and carpels; these are followed by rounded clusters of one-seeded green fruits. Many members of the family Ranunculaceae contain the poisonous alkaloid protoanemonine. It has an acrid taste (hence the name *acris*) and therefore this and other buttercups are avoided by grazing cattle. The poisonous effect is neutralized by drying, so hayfield buttercups are harmless.

Family	Ranunculaceae
Synonym	*R. acer*
Status	Very common
Distribution	Throughout Britain
Height	30—100 cm

J F M A M J J A S O N D

Creeping Buttercup

Ranunculus repens

A creeping plant with long runners, rooting where they touch the soil and forming many rosettes, so that a mat of plants eventually results. The hairy leaves have three deeply toothed leaflets. Flowers are borne in erect inflorescences in few-flowered clusters; they are typical buttercups — shiny yellow petals with many stamens, and they are followed by clusters of green one-seeded fruits. This is the most aggressive of the buttercups, a serious weed of farmland and gardens, where it prefers damp shady spots; it also grows on sand dunes. Cattle refuse to eat it because of its acrid taste and so it spreads when the plants around are eaten. It grows throughout Europe and Asia.

Family	Ranunculaceae
Status	Very common
Distribution	Throughout Britain
Height	15—40 cm

J F M A M J J A S O N D

Globe Flower

Trollius europaeus

A jewel of damp mountain woods and meadows usually growing in groups, throughout Europe. The stout erect stem bears large, long-stalked, palmately-lobed leaves and is usually terminated by several golden-yellow globular flowers formed of many petal-like sepals. These enclose the petals which are shorter than the sepals and transformed into funnel-shaped nectaries. The fruit is formed of a cluster of pods. The plant is very poisonous. The future existence of Globe Flower is threatened, not only by people attracted by the plant's showy flowers, but more seriously by the continuing disappearance of its natural habitats caused by large-scale drainage of damp meadows.

Family	Ranunculaceae
Status	Local
Distribution	Mountain areas in north and west
Height	30—60 cm

J F M A M J J A S O N D

Great Burnet

Sanguisorba officinalis

From thick branched underground stems grow rosettes of long compound leaves with up to 14 leaflets, and erect inflorescences. These bear many oblong heads of dull red flowers. The reddish colour comes from the sepals and the filaments of the stamens, there are no petals. The fruiting heads look very similar to the flowering heads, since the sepals remain to enclose the fruits. This is a well-known medicinal plant which was used to stop bleeding (*sanguisorba* means blood-absorbing), both internally and externally; it can still be used on burns and small wounds to promote healing. It grows in heavy ground, especially on clay soils, in damp grassland throughout much of Europe.

Family	Rosaceae
Synonym	*Poterium officinale*
Status	Locally common
Distribution	Mainly central Britain
Height	30—120 cm

J F M A M J J A S O N D

Meadow Vetchling
Lathyrus pratensis

This plant grows abundantly in meadows, open woods and hedgerows from lowlands to mountains. The feeble, scrambling or climbing stems are covered with soft hairs and bear distinctive leaves. Each leaf consists of a stem-like leaf-stalk, two blade-like leaflets and a terminal tendril by which it clings to other plants. Neither the stems nor the leaf-stalks are winged, unlike those of other members of the genus *Lathyrus*. The yellow pea-like flowers, in clusters of 10−12, are arranged in terminal racemes and are followed by pods with dark oval seeds. This plant grows throughout Europe, western Asia, Siberia and east Africa.

Family	**Leguminosae**	
Status	**Common**	
Distribution	**Throughout Britain**	J F M A M J J A S O N D
Height	**30−100 cm**	

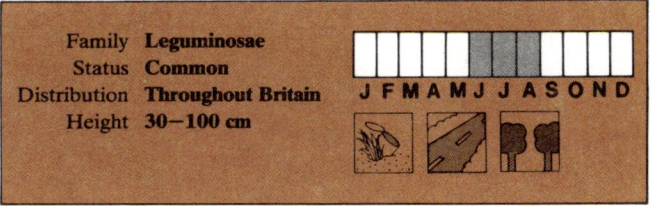

Tufted Vetch
Vicia cracca

A valuable fodder plant, this species grows in meadows both in lowlands and mountains throughout Europe. The angular scrambling, sparsely hairy stems climb by help of branched tendrils. The tendrils are found on the ends of the leaves which also bear 12 to 30 leaflets. In the leaf axils grow long-stalked ladder-like racemes of blue-purple pea-like flowers, which are followed by pods each containing up to 6 seeds. Numerous nodules on the branched roots contain the nitrogen-fixing bacteria (*Rhizobium*), which are capable of transforming nitrogen from the air into nitrogenous compounds, thus enriching the soil. This plant is more likely to be found in hayfields than on grazing land, since it does not tolerate trampling by cattle.

Family	**Leguminosae**	
Status	**Common**	
Distribution	**Throughout Britain**	J F M A M J J A S O N D
Height	**30−120 cm**	

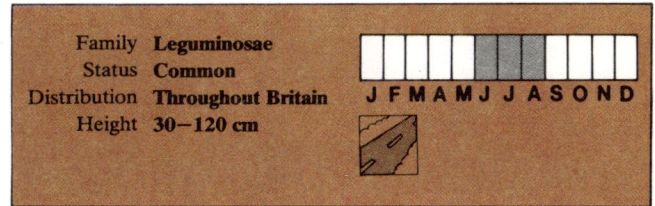

Dyer's Greenweed
Genista tinctoria

A dwarf spreading shrubby plant found growing in damp meadows and rough pastureland throughout central and southern Europe. In woodland margins and open woodland it may become taller and more woody and so more closely resemble the other brooms to which it is related. In its meadowland form it has many upright green stems, usually no more than 30–40 cm in height, with alternate simple bright green leaves and racemes of bright yellow pea-like flowers growing in the axils of the uppermost leaves. The flowers are followed by flattened hairless pods. Dyer's Greenweed, as its name suggests, has been widely used as a source of a good yellow dye which was obtained from the flowering tops and used to dye cloth. It is also used in herb medicine to treat rheumatism and as a diuretic.

Family	**Leguminosae**
Status	**Locally common**
Distribution	**England and Wales**
Height	**30–70 cm**

J F M A M J J A S O N D

Yellow Asparagus Pea
Tetragonolobus maritimus

This mat-forming plant has perennial, prostrate or ascending stems; the leaves have three leaflets and well defined stipules; there are one or two large, pale yellow, pea-like flowers growing on long stalks in the leaf axils. The flowers are followed by long pods with four narrow wings running along their length. The pods darken as they ripen and twist when they split open to release the seeds. This plant is related to Birdsfoot Trefoil and is sometimes placed in the same genus (*Lotus*). The common name refers to the fact that the large, unripe pods are used as a vegetable, like those of the related *T. purpureus* (Asparagus Pea) which is cultivated in Britain and southern Europe. It prefers heavy clay soils in meadows and marshlands.

Family	**Leguminosae**
Synonym	***Lotus siliquosus***
Status	**Rare introduction**
Distribution	**Mainly in central and eastern England**
Height	**10–30 cm**

J F M A M J J A S O N D

Meadow Cranesbill
Geranium pratense

This widely distributed species grows in lowland areas in the warmer parts of Europe and Asia. The robust branched stem grows from a short thick underground stem with numerous roots. The long-stalked, palmate basal leaves are arranged in a rosette, those on the stems are stalkless. The flower-stalks, drooping before and after flowering, are erect when the flowers open and again when the fruits ripen. Many glands can be seen on the upper half of the stem, the flower-stalks and the fruits. The wide open blue flowers grow in pairs and are followed by characteristic beaked fruits which disintegrate into five one-seeded segments, each with a long curved beak. These are dispersed by mammals, birds or water.

Family	Geraniaceae												
Status	Locally common
Distribution	Rare in Scotland and Ireland
Height	20—60 cm

J F M A M J J A S O N D

Cuckoo Flower
Cardamine pratensis

Scattered specimens of this plant decorate damp grassy places in springtime. It is distributed throughout the Northern Hemisphere from lowlands to mountains, in damp meadows and marshland. Several hollow, unbranched stems grow from a basal rosette of long-stalked, compound leaves. Each stem bears a sparse raceme of pale violet or white flowers, each with four dark-veined petals; these are followed by long seed-pods which open by valves from below, releasing the ripe, yellow-brown seeds. The plant also multiplies by vegetative means — by propagating buds formed on the underside of the basal leaves, particularly in damp situations. It is a foodplant for the caterpillars of the Orange-tip Butterfly. The young leaves make a good salad vegetable, they are rich in Vitamin C and can be eaten to prevent scurvy.

Family	Cruciferae
Other names	Lady's Smock
Status	Common
Distribution	Throughout Britain
Height	10—50 cm

J F M A M J J A S O N D

Hogweed
Heracleum sphondylium

When rubbed between the fingers this stout, conspicuous perennial gives off an unpleasant smell. The whole plant is bristly hairy, and the hollow stem bears markedly large leaf sheaths. All leaves are large, with three leaflets each in turn divided into three- to five-lobed segments, the bottom leaves having grooved stalks. The small, pure white or reddish flowers are borne in terminal compound umbels; the flowers on the outside of the umbel are largest with unequal-sized petals, those petals on the outer edge being the biggest. The flowers are followed by narrowly-winged, single-seeded fruits which are borne in pairs. At one time Hogweed was used as pig food, hence the common name. It grows in damp grassy places and hedgerows or on woodland edges throughout Europe.

Family	Umbelliferae
Other names	Cow Parsnip
Status	Common
Distribution	Throughout Britain
Height	80—150 cm

J F M A M J J A S O N D

Cambridge Parsley
Selinum carvifolia

This almost hairless plant has solid grooved stems with high, almost winged ridges on the stems. The finely-divided leaves grow in a basal rosette and on the stems, and smell of parsley. White flowers are borne in compound umbels and are followed by the typical umbellifer fruits — pairs of single-seeded dry fruits, suspended one on each side of a vertical stalk. The fruits of this parsley are flattened from side to side and winged so that they catch the wind, to be dispersed far from the parent. The plant grows in wet grassy places and marshes in northern and central Europe, but it is rare in Britain.

Family	Umbelliferae
Status	Rare
Distribution	East Anglia
Height	30—90 cm

J F M A M J J A S O N D

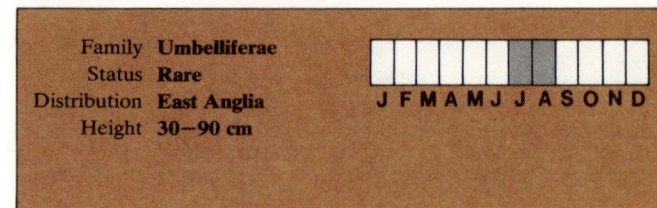

108

Hemlock

Conium maculatum

This robust biennial plant is native to the warm
lowlands of Europe and western Asia. The finely
divided leaves and the umbels of white flowers are
typical of the members of the family Umbelliferae but
this plant can be safely distinguished by the purplish
patches on the smooth ash-grey stem, which become
denser or even merge towards the roots. The whole
plant has a repulsive taste and smells of mice on
drying. All its parts contain a deadly poison — the
alkaloid coniine, which was given to people sen-
tenced to death in ancient Greece, the most famous
victim being Socrates. The fruits have the greatest
concentration of the poison, but are used in medicine
as an antidote to strychnine and to infections like
tetanus. The coniine acts to relax the muscles and
counteract the convulsions in these cases.

Family	Umbelliferae														
Status	Common														
Distribution	Rarer in the north and west	J	F	M	A	M	J	J	A	S	O	N	D
Height	80—180 cm														

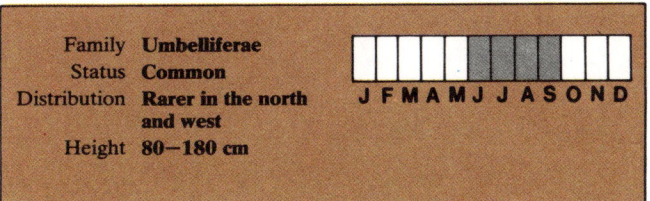

Snakeroot

Polygonum bistorta

From a thick perennial underground stem grow
clumps of large smooth lance-shaped leaves in spring,
together with slender erect flower-stalks. These bear
many terminal cylindrical flower spikes of tiny
bell-like flowers; they have no petals, only petal-like
sepals which are white or pink in colour and which
persist to surround the glossy brown single-seeded
fruits. Snakeroot is found in damp places in many
parts of central and northern Europe, especially in
wet, high altitude meadows where it may spread to
form a large colony. The leaves can be used as
a vegetable and the roots are used in herb medicine as
a good remedy for diarrhoea, haemorrhoids and
internal bleeding.

Family	Polygonaceae														
Other names	Bistort														
Status	Locally common	J	F	M	A	M	J	J	A	S	O	N	D
Distribution	Scattered in much of Britain														
Height	30—100 cm														

Ragged Robin

Lychnis flos-cuculi

This is one of the most characteristic plants of water meadows in early summer. Several stems form a spreading clump, the basal parts lying flat on the ground then turning upright to become leafy flowering shoots, with sticky lance-shaped leaves in opposite pairs. The flowers are borne in pairs in sparse clusters and are very distinctive, each with five divided 'ragged' petals, pink in colour or occasionally white. They are followed by toothed capsules with many seeds. Ragged Robin grows in wet meadows, fens and damp woodland throughout Europe and, although it is still relatively common, it is one of many wetland plants threatened by large-scale drainage plans.

Family	Caryophyllaceae
Status	Common
Distribution	Throughout Britain
Height	30—80 cm

J F M A M J J A S O N D

Sorrel

Rumex acetosa

From a clump of arrow-shaped leaves grow tall branched inflorescences. The leaves of the flowering shoots have characteristic membranous tubular stipules, called ochreae, and the numerous flowers are tiny and petal-less, greenish or reddish in colour, borne in many whorls along the stems. They are followed by many brownish fruits, each one enclosed in the persistent sepals which become greatly enlarged after flowering. Sorrel grows throughout the Northern Hemisphere. Its leaves are very acid to the taste and at one time it was used, like we use lemon, to flavour sauces eaten with meat or fish, and as a salad. It is rich in Vitamin C and is used to prevent scurvy and as a herb medicine to reduce fever.

Family	Polygonaceae
Other names	Sorrel Dock
Status	Common
Distribution	Throughout Britain
Height	30—100 cm

J F M A M J J A S O N D

Bugle
Ajuga reptans

This is a low-growing perennial plant with rosettes of leaves which produce long creeping leafy stolons, which soon intertwine to form a whole colony of plants with many tangled rosettes. The flowers, growing in the axils of opposite leaves in dense erect flower spikes, are usually blue but may be pink or white. The two-lipped flower has a well-defined lower lip, but the upper lip is reduced to two teeth. The sepals persist after flowering to surround the fruit, which consists of four nutlets. Bugle prefers damp heavy soils and shady spots, suffering from mildew in dry or sunny sites. It is a medicinal plant used to treat coughs and to stop bleeding.

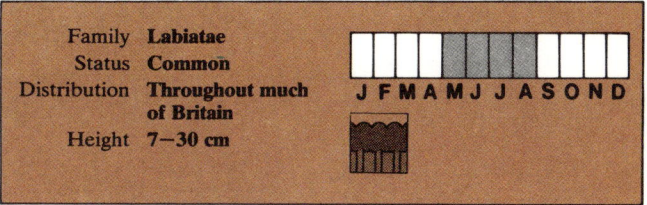

Family	**Labiatae**	J F M A M J J A S O N D
Status	**Common**	
Distribution	**Throughout much of Britain**	
Height	**7—30 cm**	

Creeping Jenny
Lysimachia nummularia

The fragile green creeping stems of this plant soon form thick rooted mats wherever the ground is damp enough to suit it, throughout much of Europe. The stems bear opposite rounded leaves, which are often dotted with red glands, and solitary star-shaped flowers grow on long flower-stalks from the axils of the leaves. They are bright yellow in colour and transform the green mat into yellow when the plant is in full bloom. This and a yellow-leaved form are often grown in gardens. It is an old medicinal plant used to treat rheumatism and skin diseases, as well as to speed healing of cuts and bruises and to treat internal bleeding.

Family	**Primulaceae**	J F M A M J J A S O N D
Other names	**Moneywort**	
Status	**Locally common**	
Distribution	**Mainly in south and east**	
Height	**10—50 cm**	

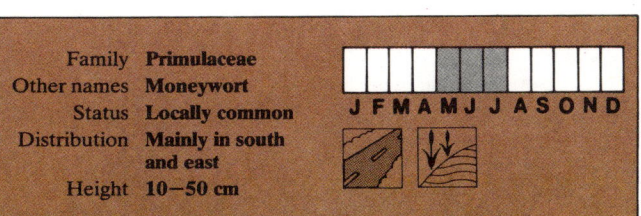

Yellow Rattle
Rhinanthus minor

This plant is unusual in that it is partially parasitic on other plants — its roots attach themselves to those of its hosts and withdraw water and mineral nutrients from them. It grows in wet meadows and marshes from lowlands to mountains in much of Europe and Asia. This annual plant has an erect black-spotted hairy stem with many opposite coarse toothed leaves. The hooded flowers are borne in the axils of the upper leaves; they have brown sepals fused together to form an inflated tube and yellow petals. The picturesque common name of the plant comes from the seed capsules which rattle in the wind when mature and dry. This species is very variable with several different subspecies in Britain and the Continent.

Family	Scrophulariaceae
Status	Locally common
Distribution	Throughout Britain
Height	15—40 cm

J F M A M J J A S O N D

Common Eyebright
Euphrasia officinalis

The eyebrights (*Euphrasia* spp.) are a very complex group of plants, often described as belonging to an aggregate species known as *E. officinalis*. One good reason for not describing the species individually is that many grow in very specialised habitats and have quite definite distributions, so that any species described would be unlikely to be the one found by any one person. In addition, they all look much alike so that a generalised description would fit most of them; the picture is further complicated by the fact that they often hybridise freely. In general, eyebrights are small, erect, slender or robust annual herbs with small leaves and distinctive flowers growing in the axils of the upper leaves. These are blue, violet or white, and two-lipped, the upper lip with two reflexed lobes and the lower lip with three lobes.

Family	Scrophulariaceae
Status	Common
Distribution	Species aggregate found throughout Britain
Height	5—25 cm

J F M A M J J A S O N D

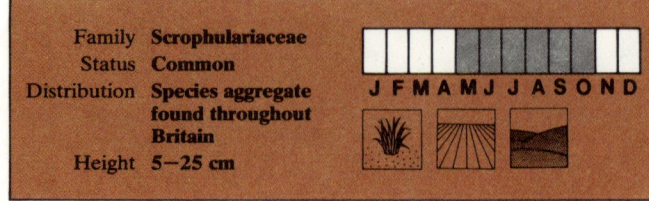

Meadow Eyebright
Euphrasia rostkoviana

This particular eyebright is found in wet meadows in Wales, parts of northern England and Ireland. Like the other eyebrights it is partially parasitic on the grasses with which it grows, taking nourishment by means of its roots which become attached to those of the host plants. It has slender weak stems with bright green leaves and large white, mauve-tinged flowers in the axils of the upper leaves. The flowers are followed by small, somewhat hairy, fruiting capsules. The name 'eyebright' comes from the way in which the plant is used in herb medicine, for an infusion of the herb can be used to bathe inflamed eyes, and to alleviate the discomfort of styes and conjunctivitis.

Family	**Scrophulariaceae**															
Status	**Very local**															
Distribution	**Scattered**	J	F	M	A	M	J	J	A	S	O	N	D			
Height	**5—30 cm**															

Common Valerian
Valeriana officinalis

This plant has a short thick rootstock from which grows a clump of compound leaves and an erect flowering stalk with several terminal heads of flowers. Each head is composed of many pink tubular flowers followed by many nut-like fruits. The sepals remain on the fruits after flowering and become feathery, acting as parachutes to aid dispersal. The whole plant is strangely scented, especially the roots, and very attractive to cats. Oil of Valerian is produced from these roots and is used in herb medicine as an effective treatment in nervous disorders, including St. Vitus' Dance, epilepsy and nervous tension. Valerian grows throughout much of Europe except the extreme north and south, in all sorts of grassy places and woodland clearings.

Family	**Valerianaceae**															
Other names	**Allheal**															
Status	**Common**	J	F	M	A	M	J	J	A	S	O	N	D			
Distribution	**Throughout Britain**															
Height	**70—150 cm**															

Cat's Ear
Hypochoeris radicata

This perennial meadow plant forms a basal rosette of wavy-edged leaves and several leafless flower-stalks covered only with tiny bracts. The sparsely branched, blue-green stems bear dark yellow flower-heads, about 2 cm long, and are thickened below the heads, thus differentiating this species from the similar Smooth Cat's Ear in which the flower-stalks are narrow. The florets are all of one type — strap-shaped and five-toothed on the tips. The single-seeded fruits have long beaks and feathery hairs to aid dispersal. Cat's Ear grows throughout Europe in many different grassland places including stable sand dunes and grassy tracks, as well as roadside verges and meadows.

Family	Compositae
Status	Common
Distribution	Throughout Britain
Height	15—60 cm

J F M A M J J A S O N D

Devil's-bit Scabious
Succisa pratensis

This perennial plant grows in wet meadows, damp woods and marshes throughout much of Europe. Spreading mats of narrow glossy leaves grow in spring followed by erect flowering stalks in summer. The flowers are arranged in semiglobular bluish-violet heads, simulating a single flower, and are followed by heads of single-seeded fruits. The curious common name refers to the short cylindrical black rootstock, which looks as if it had been bitten off, according to legend by the Devil, who resented the ability of this plant to cure all ills. It is still used in herb medicine in the treatment of internal inflammations, and as a gargle to alleviate sore throats and gums.

Family	Dipsacaceae
Status	Common
Distribution	Throughout Britain
Height	20—80 cm

J F M A M J J A S O N D

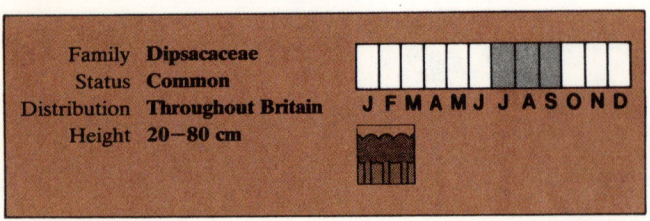

Sneezewort

Achillea ptarmica

In the summer months, Sneezewort is common in moist meadows and damp woodland, often growing near water. From perennial woody underground stems grow erect stems, densely covered with stalk-less lance-shaped serrated leaves and terminated by clustered flower-heads. Each head has outer white strap-shaped ray florets and central yellow tubular disk florets. Double-flowered forms (known as Bachelor's Buttons) are nowadays cultivated in gardens; these have only white florets and lack the central yellow ones. Sneezewort was used in the middle ages to cure colds and relieve stuffy heads (hence its common name) and to alleviate tooth-ache.

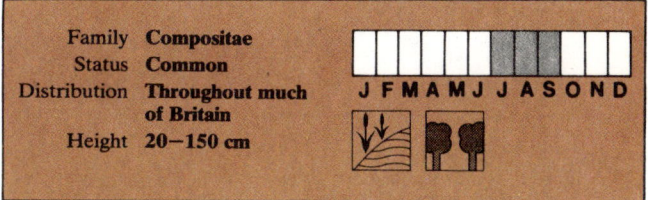

Family	**Compositae**
Status	**Common**
Distribution	**Throughout much of Britain**
Height	**20–150 cm**

J F M A M J J A S O N D

Rough Hawkbit

Leontodon hispidus

This common plant of late summer and autumn grows in meadows and on grassy slopes, especially on calcareous soils, from lowland to mountain areas in much of Europe and western Asia. It forms a rosette of lance-shaped leaves with toothed margins, and erect unbranched flower-stems with solitary yellow heads. It very much resembles a dandelion (*Tarax-acum*) but the flower-stalks are stiffer with less milky juice. The related *L. autumnalis* has leaves rather like those of an oak-tree in shape and branched flowering stems. Rough Hawkbit has two subspecies – one with hairy leaves and hairy involucral bracts (green sepal-like structures below the flower-heads), the other hairless. The single-seeded fruits have two rows of hairs to aid dispersal.

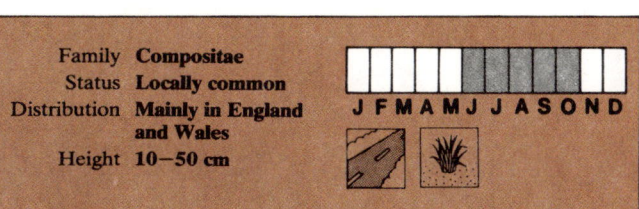

Family	**Compositae**
Status	**Locally common**
Distribution	**Mainly in England and Wales**
Height	**10–50 cm**

J F M A M J J A S O N D

Dwarf Scorzonera
Scorzonera humilis

Dwarf Scorzonera has a rosette of lance-shaped, ribwort-like leaves and simple erect stems, all growing from a scaly black rootstock and all filled with milky juice. The stems, leaves and involucral bracts beneath the flower-heads are woolly at first but lose their wool as they mature. The stem bears two or three leaves and a solitary, pale yellow flower-head composed of many strap-shaped ray florets. The single-seeded fruits bear several rows of dirty white hairs which aid dispersal. This feature may be used to distinguish it from the similar Goatsbeard which has only one line of hairs on the fruit. This plant grows in mountain areas in Europe but is found only in a few marshy meadows in two counties in England.

Family	**Compositae**
Status	**Rare**
Distribution	**Dorset and Warwickshire**
Height	**10—40 cm**

J F M A M J J A S O N D

Ox-eye Daisy
Chrysanthemum leucanthemum

This is a typical plant of wet and dry meadows in both lowland and mountain areas throughout Europe. It may form large colonies where it is not threatened by more vigorous species. The perennial rootstock produces a rosette of long-stalked, deeply divided leaves in early spring. At the end of May, solitary terminal heads open on a little-branched stem, with stalkless toothed leaves. The pure white ray florets of the flower-heads form a circle around the yellow disk of tubular florets. The involucre of bracts beneath the head is semi-globular, pale brown to black in colour. Ox-eye Daisy is often grown in the garden and is used in herb medicine to treat asthma, whooping cough and other irritations of the throat and chest.

Family	**Compositae**
Synonym	*Leucanthemum vulgare*
Other name	**Marguerite**
Status	**Common**
Distribution	**Throughout Britain**
Height	**20—100 cm**

J F M A M J J A S O N D

Willow-leaved Inula

Inula salicina

The whole of this plant is tough and hairless, with lance-shaped glossy leaves, the uppermost of which clasp the stem with heart-shaped bases. The stems bear one or a few terminal flower-heads; each head has central tubular disk florets and a row of outer strap-shaped ray florets, all yellow in colour. This Eurasian species is distributed from lowlands to submontane regions, mostly in heavy clay, often lime-rich, soils but it is also found in drier areas. In the British Isles this species of *Inula* is confined to a few marshy fens and loughsides in central Ireland.

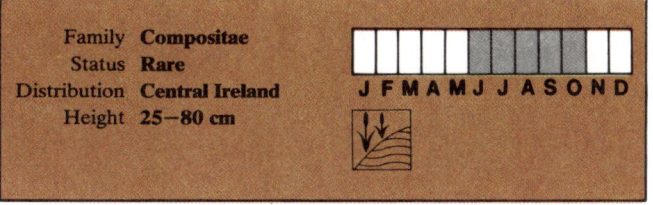

Family	**Compositae**
Status	**Rare**
Distribution	**Central Ireland**
Height	**25—80 cm**

J F M A M J J A S O N D

Marsh Thistle

Cirsium palustre

A biennial plant with a rosette of basal spiny-toothed lobed leaves in the first year and a tall erect spiny-winged stem, covered with leaves, in the second. The stem leaves are stalk-less with spiny-toothed margins and they clasp the stem with their bases. The flower-heads are borne in groups on short stalks at the top of the stem and are composed of purple, seldom pink or white, tubular disk florets. This plant is often wrongly identified as one of the *Carduus* species, but unlike the members of that genus, its fruits have feathery hairs instead of simple ones. Marsh Thistle is widespread in Europe and Asia, introduced in North America and prefers damp meadows and marshes both in lowlands and mountains, also growing in damp woods and hedgerows.

Family	**Compositae**
Synonym	***Carduus palustris***
Status	**Very common**
Distribution	**Throughout Britain**
Height	**50—150 cm**

J F M A M J J A S O N D

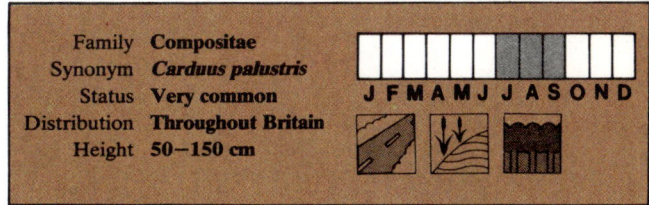

Autumn Crocus
Colchicum autumnale

Unlike the majority of 'bulbous' plants, this species produces its flowers in the autumn. They are like large, pale violet crocuses and are called Naked Ladies. They do indeed look naked since they appear without any foliage. The fruits and leaves grow in spring, the fruits just projecting above the soil. The leaves are large, lance-shaped and do not last long, once they have produced enough food to form a corm from which the autumn flowers will grow, they soon die down. Autumn Crocus grows, sometimes in large numbers when left undisturbed, in damp meadows and woodland on basic soils throughout central and southern Europe. The whole plant is deadly poisonous, particularly the seeds, which contain the poison colchicine. It is used in medicine in the treatment of rheumatism and gout.

Family	Liliaceae	
Other names	Meadow Saffron, Naked Ladies	
Status	Local	J F M A M J J A S O N D
Distribution	Mainly in southwest England and Wales	
Height	5—40 cm	

Melancholy Thistle
Cirsium heterophyllum

As suggested by the name *'heterophyllum'*, this thistle bears two types of leaves. The basal ones are attached to the stem by winged leaf-stalks, those in the middle and at the top of the stem are stalkless or even clasping the stem with heart-shaped bases. The top lance-shaped leaves are entire with finely spiny margins, the central ones are deeply toothed. The tall slender, little-branched stem and the undersides of the leaves are covered with white felt. Several red-violet flower-heads, measuring 3—5 cm across, are borne at the tops of the stems in late summer, followed by heads of single-seeded fruits with long white feathery hairs. This plant may form large colonies in damp alpine meadows, woodland clearings and fens. It is a small, supposedly sad-looking plant, hence the common name.

Family	Compositae	
Synonym	*Carduus heterophyllus*	
Status	Local	J F M A M J J A S O N D
Distribution	Scotland, northern England and Wales	
Height	50—100 cm	

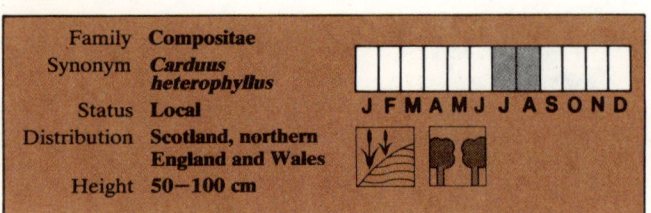

Spotted Orchid
Dactylorhiza maculata

Most members of the genus *Dactylorhiza* are very similar to each other, hard to distinguish and highly variable, producing many inter-species and inter-generic crosses. Two closely related species are *D. maculata* and *D. fuchsii,* both possessing leafless flower-stalks terminated by dense spikes of flowers. The flowers have wide three-lobed, pale yellow lower lips bearing a dark pattern of dots and lines. In *D. maculata* the central lobe is the shortest and smallest, in *D. fuchsii* it is narrow, pointed and longer than the lateral ones. Both species have blotched leaves. *D. maculata* grows in acid marshes and meadows while *D. fuchsii* grows in basic marshes, meadows and grassy slopes.

Family	**Orchidaceae**	J F M A M J J A S O N D
Synonym	*Dactylorchis maculata*	
Status	**Local**	
Distribution	**More common in north and west**	
Height	**10–70 cm**	

Fen Orchid
Dactylorhiza majalis

This is one of an interesting aggregate orchid species. There are four major species involved, differing mainly in their distributions, although hybrids occur when the species overlap. *D. praetermissa* grows mostly in more southerly counties; *D. purpurella* in the north; *D. traunsteineri* in Ireland, western Wales and southern England; and *D. majalis* in western Ireland and Scotland. They all grow in marshes or fens, usually in the rather rare fens with alkaline or calcium-rich water (acid water peat fens are the common ones), and in dune slacks, the damp areas occurring in the hollows of stable sand dunes. The orchids have a spirally arranged rosette of up to eight leaves, often without spots although this varies with species. The reddish-purple flowers are borne in dense terminal spikes on leafless flower-stalks.

Family	**Orchidaceae**	J F M A M J J A S O N D
Synonym	*Orchis occidentalis*	
Other names	**Marsh Orchid**	
Status	**Very local**	
Distribution	**Western Ireland and Scotland**	
Height	**20–100 cm**	

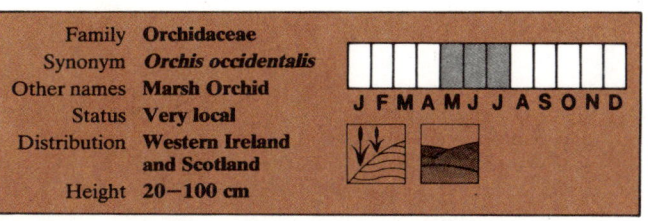

Fragrant Orchid

Gymnadenia conopsea

In a clump of pale green keeled leaves, the bottom ones are long and narrowly lance-shaped, the top ones smaller, bract-like. The dense flower spike grows at the top of the flower-stalk and bears up to 50 small, pink-violet flowers, occasionally red or even white. The flowers are very fragrant and give the plant its common name. The three upper petals are bent to form a hood, the lateral ones are spreading and the lower lip, broader than it is wide, has three lobes and a curved, slender spur which may be twice as long as the conspicuously twisted ovary. This is a highly variable species with several subspecies, growing on moist basic grassland or fens, especially in limestone areas, throughout Europe and Asia.

Family	**Orchidaceae**	
Synonym	***Orchis conopsea***	
Status	**Locally common**	
Distribution	**Throughout Britain**	J F M A M J J A S O N D
Height	**25—60 cm**	

Twayblade

Listera ovata

This is a low-growing perennial plant with a long, underground, creeping stem bearing scars from the previous years' growth; from their number one can tell the age of the plant. Two broadly oval, bluntly pointed, opposite leaves spread low above the ground. The grey-green flowers which are borne in a slender spike, have conspicuously elongated yellowish lower lips, forked into two segments and hanging vertically downwards; they have no spurs. After the flower has been pollinated by insects, a capsule is formed with a large number of tiny, light seeds. Twayblade grows in moist meadows and damp woodland on basic soils; it can also be found in wet areas in sand dunes (dune slacks). It grows throughout much of Europe.

Family	**Orchidaceae**	
Synonym	***Ophrys ovata***	
Status	**Common**	
Distribution	**Throughout Britain**	J F M A M J J A S O N D
Height	**20—50 cm**	

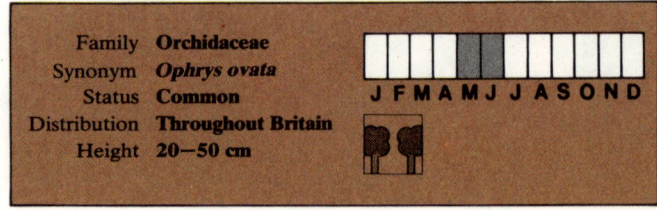

Species featured
in this section

Species featured
in another section

Lesser Meadow Rue
Thalictrum minus

This tall perennial herb has compound leaves growing on smooth or finely grooved stems which branch into many clusters of small flowers. These are drooping with short-lived petal-like sepals (there are no petals) and several conspicuous stamens with long filaments and long-pointed anthers. The flowers are followed by clusters of single-seeded fruits. Lesser Meadow Rue grows sporadically in dry grassy places of Europe and Asia from lowland to submontane elevations. There are several subspecies which differ in their environmental requirements, one growing on grassy slopes, shingle and rocky cliffs, another on sand dunes and yet another beside water.

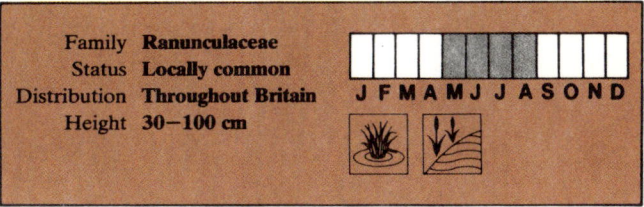

Family	Ranunculaceae
Status	Locally common
Distribution	Throughout Britain
Height	30–100 cm

J F M A M J J A S O N D

Bulbous Buttercup
Ranunculus bulbosus

A common European perennial of dry grassland, especially on calcareous soils, in lowland and mountain regions and also on sand dunes on the coasts. It is very similar to the other buttercups, with yellow flowers on erect stems and three-lobed leaves. An important distinguishing feature is the bulb-like enlargement of the base of the stem, giving the plant its name. Five-petalled yellow flowers grow on long stalks and have numerous anthers in the centres. The five hairy sepals that protect the flower bud become reflexed when the bud opens, another feature that distinguishes this buttercup from the others. The basal leaves are triangular in outline, with long leaf-stalks in contrast to the stem-leaves which are stalkless. The whole plant, like the other buttercups, is poisonous.

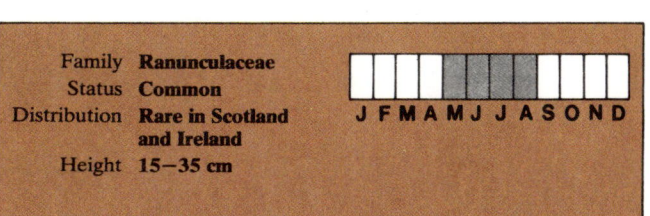

Family	Ranunculaceae
Status	Common
Distribution	Rare in Scotland and Ireland
Height	15–35 cm

J F M A M J J A S O N D

Wall Pepper

Sedum acre

A mat-forming plant with many creeping rooting stems, densely covered with bright green succulent leaves attached to the stems by wide bases. In the summer, short erect flowering stalks appear, terminated by clusters of yellow star-shaped flowers. The flowers may be so numerous that the normally green mat turns yellow. The flowers are followed by clusters of pods which open on the upper surfaces to release the seeds. This plant is well adapted to living on rocks, old walls and other dry places, including grassy slopes and sand dunes, especially on calcareous soils, and grows throughout Europe in such places. It has a sharp peppery taste and can cause skin blisters. At one time it was used as a cure for worms.

		J F M A M J J A S O N D
Family	**Crassulaceae**	
Other names	**Yellow or Biting Stonecrop**	
Status	**Common**	
Distribution	**Throughout much of Britain**	
Height	**5–10 cm**	

White Stonecrop

Sedum album

This is a low perennial plant with prostrate or ascending, often rooting stems. Two types of stems are formed; mat-forming creeping stems, densely covered with leaves and forming sparse tufts, and erect flower-bearing stems with fewer leaves. The leaves are dark green, fleshy and cylindrical in shape and attached to the stem by spurred bases. The clusters of pale white or pinkish star-shaped flowers open on hot summer days. Each flower has conspicuous stamens with red anthers and five ovaries which ripen into five many-seeded cylindrical pods; these open along their upper edges to release the seeds. Stonecrops are typical European succulents growing on rocks, mountain slopes and stony pastures in warmer regions and on walls and rock gardens in towns and villages.

		J F M A M J J A S O N D
Family	**Crassulaceae**	
Status	**Garden escape. Locally common**	
Distribution	**Scattered throughout Britain**	
Height	**8–20 cm**	

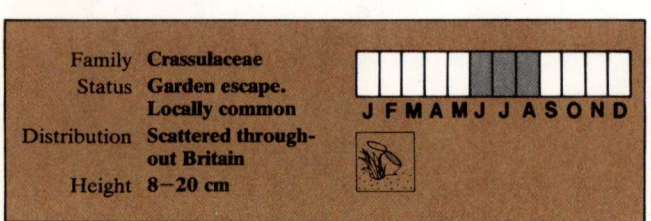

Meadow Saxifrage
Saxifraga granulata

This is an inconspicuous member of meadow communities with a slender unbranched sticky stem growing from a sparse ground rosette of hairy kidney-shaped lobed leaves. The plant spreads and overwinters by means of numerous brown bulbils which form in the axils of the basal leaves. The flowers, arranged in a sparse glandular cluster, are white with petals three times as long as the sepals. The fruit is a broadly ovoid, many-seeded capsule. Meadow Saxifrage occurs in dry, rather sparse grassland on sandy or stony soils throughout much of Europe. At one time it was used in herb medicine to treat gallstones — it was thought that if its roots could break up stony ground or walls, then it could break up the stones inside!

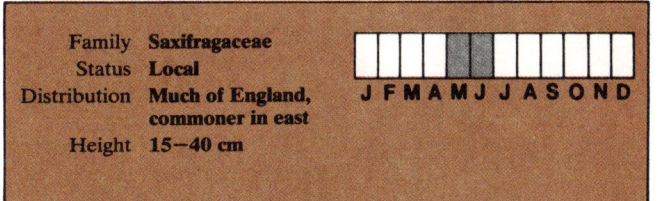

Family	Saxifragaceae
Status	Local
Distribution	Much of England, commoner in east
Height	15—40 cm

J F M A M J J A S O N D

Rose-root
Sedum rosea

This is a mountain plant of the subalpine and alpine regions, dispersed throughout the Northern Hemisphere in crevices, on stony slopes and rocky meadows. It differs from the two preceding species by having a thick fleshy rootstock which survives in the ground during periods of harsh high-mountain weather. From this rootstock grow several erect fleshy stems which branch at the top into densely packed terminal flower clusters bearing yellow or reddish flowers. The leaves are fleshy and flat, pointed at the tips and densely cover the stems. Some botanists classify Rose-root as belonging to an independent genus, *Rhodiola*, differing from *Sedum* by having four-petalled flowers and by bearing male and female flowers on separate plants. It is often grown in rock gardens.

Family	Crassulaceae
Synonyms	*Sedum rhodiola, Rhodiola rosea*
Other names	Midsummer Men
Status	Locally common
Distribution	Northern mountains of Britain
Height	10—35 cm

J F M A M J J A S O N D

Salad Burnet
Sanguisorba minor

This is a small drought-loving perennial plant, growing in dry grassland unlike the related Great Burnet (*S. officinalis*) which prefers wet meadows. The spherical flower-heads of Salad Burnet are greenish at first, later reddish with basal male flowers, hermaphrodite central flowers and the topmost flowers are female. The relatively small compound leaves have oval leaflets with toothed margins and very short leaf-stalks. Salad Burnet smells of cucumber and, as suggested by the common name, can be used in salads. It is an important food plant for sheep, since it grows on the sheep-grazed limestone and chalk downlands throughout central and southern Europe and it remains green in winter.

Family	**Rosaceae**
Synonym	***Poterium sanguisorba***
Status	**Locally common**
Distribution	**Throughout much of Britain**
Height	**15—50 cm**

J F M A M J J A S O N D

Common Lady's Mantle
Alchemilla vulgaris

This extremely variable species has large leaves arranged in folds in youth and later expanded into rounded, deeply lobed shallow 'funnels'. Large drops of water are exuded from the leaf margins and collect in the centre of the leaves, a process called guttation. This 'heavenly dew' was considered to have mystical properties and the leaves with their dew were used in mediaeval medicine to staunch bleeding and to treat infected wounds. The flowers are small and greenish-yellow, borne in large clusters. The seeds develop without pollination and many are formed so that the plant seeds itself prolifically in grassland and grassy verges, woodland and also on rocky areas, especially on lime-rich soils.

Family	**Rosaceae**
Status	**Locally common**
Distribution	**Throughout Britain, rare in north**
Height	**5—40 cm**

J F M A M J J A S O N D

Mountain Avens

Dryas octopetala

This decorative woody mountain plant forms low, spreading evergreen mats closely pressed to the ground. The short branches are covered with leathery, oak-like leaves which are deep green above and silvery below. In the summer months solitary eight-petalled white flowers are borne on long stalks; they resemble those of cinquefoils or wood anemones. After flowering the creeping shrubs are decorated by clusters of hairy white single-seeded fruits. Mountain Avens occurs in the wild mostly on limestone rocks, in cracks between stones and on screes at altitudes above 1,000 metres, sometimes colonising wide areas to form Dryas heaths. It is often grown in large rock gardens.

Family	Rosaceae		J F M A M J J A S O N D
Status	Local		
Distribution	Mountain areas of Britain		
Height	2—10 cm		

Spring Cinquefoil

Potentilla tabernaemontani

This is a semi-evergreen herb with many creeping underground and prostrate stems forming a dense mat. The sterile non-flowering shoots are long and rooting, with palmately lobed leaves formed of 5—7 hairy leaflets. Short upright flower-bearing stems grow from the axils of basal leaves and bear several flowers with bright butter-yellow petals which transform the bright green mats into bright yellow ones. The flowers are followed by clusters of dry one-seeded fruits. This plant is often grown in rock gardens. It grows in the wild at lower mountain elevations on sun-warmed rocks in many parts of Europe and is one of the first cinquefoils to flower.

Family	Rosaceae		J F M A M J J A S O N D
Synonym	*Potentilla verna*		
Status	Very local		
Distribution	Scattered in Britain		
Height	5—20 cm		

Hoary Cinquefoil
Potentilla argentea

This plant is characterized by the silvery white-felted undersides of the long-stalked palmate leaves which grow in a clump from the unbranched rootstock. The flowering stems have many stalkless divided leaves and relatively small five-petalled yellow flowers growing on short stalks in forked clusters. This Eurasian species grows on sunny grass-covered slopes and rocky ground in forest regions, and in woodland margins and clearings on shallow light sandy soils in lowland areas and hills. It does not form extensive colonies but tends to grow in isolated clumps on lime-free soil. It is sometimes grown in rock gardens.

Family	Rosaceae
Status	Local
Distribution	Central and southern England
Height	20—50 cm

J F M A M J J A S O N D

Sulphur Cinquefoil
Potentilla recta

Warm dry grasslands from lowlands to hills, particularly in eastern Europe and western Asia, form the home of this perennial plant. The rootstock produces a ground rosette of long-stalked palmate leaves each with 5—7 leaflets. Both the leaves and flower-stalks are clothed in long soft and shorter bristly hairs. Stout erect flowering stems grow from the ground rosette and bear clusters of large five-petalled, yellow, often sulphur-coloured flowers followed by clusters of dry single-seeded fruits. This plant is often grown in flower borders, where there are several different varieties with red or yellow flowers.

Family	Rosaceae
Status	A garden escape
Distribution	Mainly in southeast England
Height	30—70 cm

J F M A M J J A S O N D

Smooth Tare
Vicia tetrasperma

This annual or overwintering plant has feeble stems which climb over other plants with the help of unbranched tendrils. These grow at the ends of compound leaves composed of 3—4 pairs of long leaflets. Sparse clusters of violet flowers grow on long flower-stalks from the axils of the leaves, followed by hairless pods containing four round seeds. The similar Hairy Tare (*V. hirsuta*) has two-seeded, finely hairy pods and leaves with up to 8 pairs of leaflets, terminated by a long branched tendril. Smooth Tare is found throughout Europe and the Orient, growing in sunny open places in grassland where it is not shaded by other plants.

Family	Leguminosae	
Synonym	*V. gemella*	
Status	Locally common	
Distribution	Mainly in England and Wales	
Height	15—60 cm	

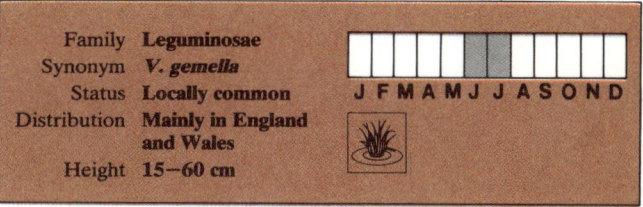

Dropwort
Filipendula vulgaris

Unlike the other *Filipendula* species, which grow in ditches and damp meadows, Dropwort is mostly found in dry grassland, on grassy slopes and downs on warm lime-rich soils, sometimes at mountain elevations but more often in lowlands and hills in Europe and Siberia. It is a perennial herb with tuberous roots, from which grows a clump of long compound leaves. Each leaf has up to 20 pairs of lance-shaped, deeply toothed leaflets alternating with stunted smaller leaflets. The few tough flowering stems are terminated by dense clusters of white pink-tinged six-petalled flowers smelling of bitter almonds. These are followed by clusters of small dry fruits. Dropwort is sometimes grown in gardens.

Family	Rosaceae	
Synonym	*F. hexapetala*	
Status	Locally common	
Distribution	Mainly in England	
Height	30—60 cm	

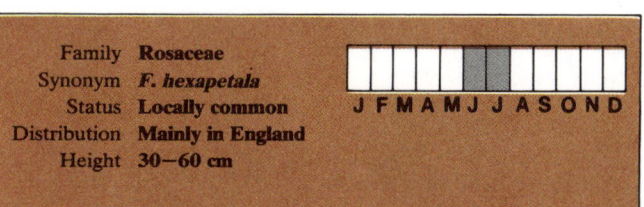

Sickle Medick
Medicago falcata

This yellow-flowered species derives both its common and Latin specific names from its sickle-shaped black seed pods. It has a densely branched root system from which grow prostrate and ascending stems. The alternately arranged leaves have three lance-shaped leaflets, with pointed tips, in which the central leaflet has a longer leaf-stalk than the two lateral ones. The flowers are borne in long-stalked racemes which grow in the axils of the leaves. When not in flower, this plant is sometimes mistaken for the cultivated Lucerne (*M. sativa*). The latter, however, has a more robust stem, pale violet flowers and spirally twisted pods. The warmth-loving Sickle Medick was locally cultivated for fodder at one time, growing throughout Europe and Asia especially in lime-rich soils.

Family	**Leguminosae**
Status	**Local**
Distribution	**Mainly in East Anglia**
Height	**20—25 cm**

J F M A M J J A S O N D

Black Medick
Medicago lupulina

A common Eurasian species found in dry grassland and fields in neutral and lime-rich soils. If compared with the related Sickle Medick, it has more slender stems and smaller leaves. The leaflets are finely toothed with rounded tips. From the axils of the stipulate leaves grow long-stalked compact clusters of very small (5 mm long) yellow flowers. The individual *Medicago* species are best told apart by their fruits: *M. sativa* produces spirally twisted pods, those of *M. falcata* are sickle-shaped and *M. lupulina* has one-seeded, kidney-shaped, markedly ribbed pods. Unlike the other two, *M. lupulina* is an annual species.

Family	**Leguminosae**
Other names	**Nonsuch**
Status	**Common**
Distribution	**Throughout much of Britain**
Height	**15—50 cm**

J F M A M J J A S O N D

White Clover

Trifolium repens

This perennial plant is common throughout the whole Northern Hemisphere. Its creeping stems root at the nodes and turn upwards at the tips, and bear long-stalked compound leaves with crescent-shaped spots across the leaflets. The leaves have three leaflets as a rule, but 'four-leaved clovers' can sometimes be found and are proverbially lucky. The leaflets are stalkless, finely toothed on the margins. Flowering stems, longer than the leaves, are terminated by spherical heads consisting of densely packed, white or pinkish flowers. They open from the bottom of the head upwards, drooping and turning brown after flowering. An important cultivated fodder plant, Clover also helps to improve the quality of the soil by the action of symbiotic bacteria living on its roots, which bind nitrogen from the atmosphere.

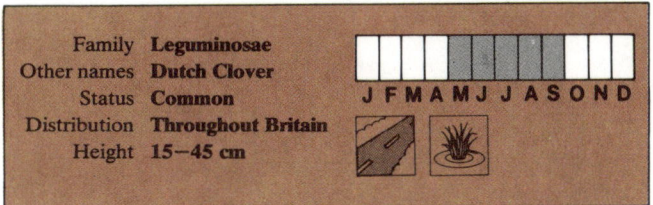

Family	**Leguminosae**
Other names	**Dutch Clover**
Status	**Common**
Distribution	**Throughout Britain**
Height	**15—45 cm**

J F M A M J J A S O N D

Lesser Yellow Trefoil

Trifolium dubium

This is one of the smallest trefoils, an annual plant with slender low-growing branched stems which are sparsely covered with alternate short-stalked leaves. Each leaf has three wedge-like leaflets and the central leaflet has a longer stalk than the two lateral ones. Sparse spherical flower-heads, the size of a pea, grow from the leaf axils and bear 10—25 very small pale yellow flowers which turn brownish when flowering has ended. This inconspicuous drought-loving trefoil is widely distributed in grasslands on acid clay soils in both lowland and mountain areas in Europe where, like all the other trefoils, it contributes to soil fertility by the action of its nitrogen-fixing root bacteria.

Family	**Leguminosae**
Synonym	***T. minus***
Other names	**Suckling Clover**
Status	**Common**
Distribution	**Throughout Britain**
Height	**10—30 cm**

J F M A M J J A S O N D

Milkvetch
Astragalus glycyphyllos

This relative of the vetches is a perennial robust plant with smooth stems, up to one metre long. The compound leaves have 4−7 pairs of oval leaflets and grow alternately along the stem in such a way as to make the stem look as if it were a zig-zag. Short-stalked racemes of 11−13 yellowish-white pea-like flowers are followed by smooth, somewhat sickle-shaped, many-seeded pods which are divided longitudinally into two cells. The plant grows in dry grassy places and open woodland in lowlands and hills of Europe and western Siberia where it is often inconspicuous for its greenish flowers merge into the background. It is supposed to increase the milk yield of goats (hence the common name) but cattle avoid it, presumably because of its bitter after-taste.

Family	Leguminosae
Status	Local
Distribution	Mainly in England and Scotland
Height	50−150 cm

J F M A M J J A S O N D

Kidney Vetch
Anthyllis vulneraria

This highly variable aggregate species splits into a number of small species which differ in morphology and in their ecological requirements. The true Kidney Vetch grows in dry grassy places throughout Europe, usually on shallow lime-rich soils like those found on the downs and limestone uplands. The erect stem bears two types of leaves: undivided basal leaves, and compound stem leaves with 3−5 pairs of ellipsoid leaflets and one large terminal leaflet. The stem is finely hairy and the yellow flowers are clustered into a large terminal head, made conspicuous by the 8−11 mm long tubular yellow-green sepals which are very hairy. This is a medicinal and a cultivated fodder plant. It was used at one time in herbal medicine for healing wounds (hence *vulneraria*) and for treating kidney stones, hence the common name.

Family	Leguminosae
Other names	Ladies' Fingers
Status	Locally common
Distribution	Scattered in Britain
Height	15−30 cm

J F M A M J J A S O N D

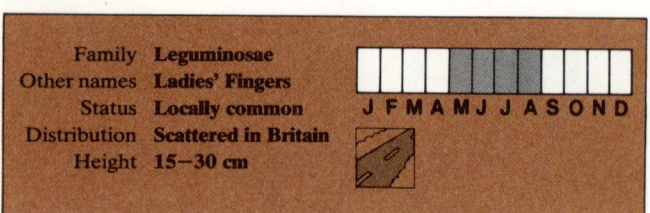

Crown Vetch

Coronilla varia

A conspicuous plant with whitish-pink flowers borne in umbels, followed by long pods which break up into one-seeded sections. The long compound leaves have 25 smooth narrow leaflets which fold along their axis for the night to prevent loss of heat. Crown Vetch is an important medicinal plant known since the Middle Ages and used in folk medicine in the treatment of heart weakness, for it stimulates the action of the heart. Its action is similar to that of Foxglove (digitalis) and like that plant it is poisonous in any but controlled small doses. Crown Vetch grows in grassy places, in fields and hills throughout much of Europe and has been introduced to Britain.

Family	**Leguminosae**												
Status	**Introduced**	J	F	M	A	M	J	J	A	S	O	N	D
Distribution	**Naturalized in scattered places**												
Height	**30–60 cm**												

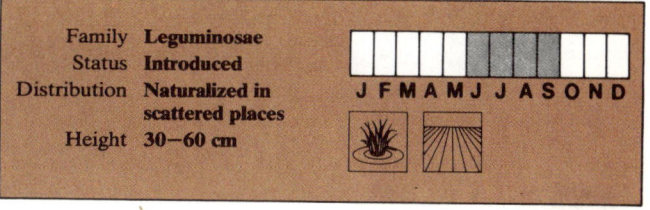

Sainfoin

Onobrychis viciifolia

This lime-loving plant of dry sunny slopes is often found in the wild from lowlands to the Alpine belt of Europe, especially in limestone uplands and chalk downs. It is cultivated as an excellent protein-rich fodder plant and its common name, Sainfoin, comes from the French word meaning 'wholesome hay'. The specific name reflects the similarity of its leaves to those of vetches; they are compound with 6–12 pairs of long leaflets and one terminal leaflet. Pink red-striped flowers are arranged in long-stalked racemes growing from the axils of the leaves and they are followed by rounded hairy crinkled pods, each containing one seed. The plant was used in herb medicine for poulticing boils and was supposed to increase the milk supply in nursing mothers.

Family	**Leguminosae**												
Synonym	*O. sativa*												
Other names	**Cock's Head**	J	F	M	A	M	J	J	A	S	O	N	D
Status	**Local**												
Distribution	**Mainly in southeast England**												
Height	**30–60 cm**												

Common Whitlow Grass
Erophila verna

This highly variable European and west Asian species is an inconspicuous short-lived plant. It can only be found in the winter and spring months, when it germinates, produces stems, leaves and flowers, bears fruits and dies. It grows in sandy soils both in lowland and mountain areas on rocks, screes, sea-cliffs and old walls. It has also been introduced as a weed to fields and waste land. From small basal leaf rosettes of broadly lance-shaped leaves grow erect stems bearing a few four-petalled white flowers which are soon followed by short erect fruits on long stalks.

Family	Cruciferae
Synonym	*Draba verna*
Status	Common
Distribution	Throughout Britain
Height	3—15 cm

J F M A M J J A S O N D

Common Rockrose
Helianthemum nummularium

This is a low-growing, densely branched semi-shrubby plant with a woody base and oval, opposite leaves bearing linear stipules below. Both the ascending stems and the entire leaves are finely hairy. Single yellow flowers are borne on long stalks and last only for a day, turning towards the sun as it travels across the sky. In old botanical books such plants were referred to as 'sun flowers', hence the Latin name *Helianthemum*. This variable European species grows locally in sunny places from lowlands to mountain areas, often in the shallow lime-rich soils of the limestone uplands and the chalk downs.

Family	Cistaceae
Synonym	*H. chamaecistus*
Status	Locally common
Distribution	Much of England, Scotland and Wales
Height	10—35 cm

J F M A M J J A S O N D

Hairy Violet
Viola hirta

Warmer parts of Europe and western Asia from lowlands to hills form the home of this perennial plant, in lime-rich soils of pastures and open woods. Like many violets it flowers in spring but it can be easily distinguished from the others by the dense spreading hairs which cover the leaves. Growing directly from an underground stem, the long-stalked heart-shaped leaves form a basal rosette — there are no running stems as there are in many other violets. The leaves have entire or finely toothed stipules on the underside. Violet or occasionally white, spurred and scentless flowers occur among the leaves in spring. The fruit, a spherical capsule, contains tiny seeds with an orange-coloured fleshy outgrowth which attracts ants who then disperse the seeds.

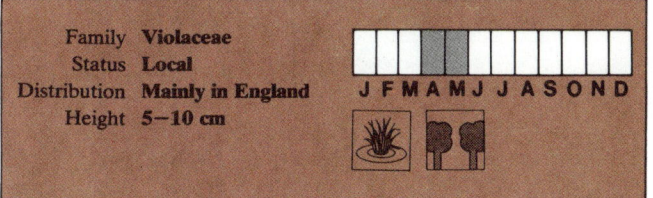

Family	Violaceae
Status	Local
Distribution	Mainly in England
Height	5—10 cm

J F M A M J J A S O N D

Heath Violet
Viola canina

This perennial violet produces from its rootstock many spreading stems to form a loose clump. Only stem leaves are present, there is no basal leaf rosette. Small stipules on the undersides of the rather triangular leaves are lance-shaped and fringed. The flowers, which grow on long stalks in the leaf axils, have pale bluish-violet petals protruding into a slightly curved paler spur. This is one of several violets which, besides the conspicuously coloured but sterile flowers, also forms closed green flowers later in the summer which are self-pollinated and bear fruit. Heath Violet is a variable species growing on poor soils on heaths and dry grassland inland and on sand dunes near the sea.

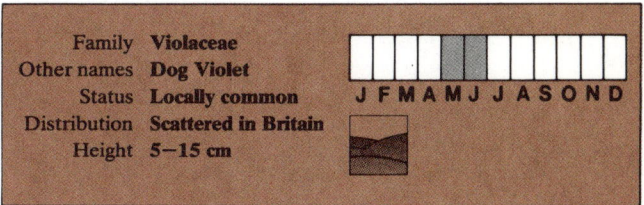

Family	Violaceae
Other names	Dog Violet
Status	Locally common
Distribution	Scattered in Britain
Height	5—15 cm

J F M A M J J A S O N D

Small-flowered Cranesbill

Geranium pusillum

This annual or biennial weed of fields, pastures and waste ground grows in a dry environment in all types of soil. It has densely branched stems spreading into a low, wide, rather sparse clump with long-stalked, rounded, deeply lobed, 7—9 partite leaves. The whole plant is covered with many short, fine hairs. The flowers are arranged in sparse two-flowered clusters on straggling flower stalks, each flower on a drooping stalk which becomes erect when the fruits have formed. The beaked fruit splits into five one-seeded portions, each with a sickle-shaped beak by which it becomes attached to the fur of animals and so dispersed. This adaptable species is distributed in Europe, western and central Asia and northern Africa.

Family	Geraniaceae
Status	Quite common
Distribution	Mostly in England and Wales
Height	15—30 cm

J F M A M J J A S O N D

Musk Mallow

Malva moschata

This tall perennial plant has erect branched stems with musk-scented flowers, coloured a pale pink with darker veining, growing from the upper leaf axils. Long-stalked basal leaves are palmately lobed while the stem leaves have 5—7 deeply divided lobes. The flowers have spreading sepals and five free, very separate petals. Numerous stamens surround the ovary which is later transformed into a disk-shaped hairy fruit of many segments surrounding a short column in the middle. The plant grows in all kinds of grassy places and hedgebanks throughout Europe. The leaves are sometimes used in treating coughs and colds but those of the related Marsh Mallow (*Althaea officinalis*) are much more effective.

Family	Malvaceae
Status	Locally common
Distribution	Rarer in north and west
Height	20—80 cm

J F M A M J J A S O N D

Common Milkwort
Polygala vulgaris

This blue-flowered perennial plant has weak branched stems growing in a sparse clump. It belongs to a complex aggregate species which is often divided into many subspecies or independent species. The most important distinguishing features are the wings at the sides of the compressed flowers. These are, in fact, two enlarged petal-like sepals which protect the three true petals; these are fused at the bottom into a tube and comb-like at the tips. The type species has rounded, rather oval wings slightly longer than the fruit, a capsule, and it is common in damp meadows. Another variant has pointed, lance-shaped wings which are never longer than the capsule and is found in the subatlantic region of Europe in heathland and open woodland.

Family	Polygalaceae		J F M A M J J A S O N D
Synonym	*P. oxyptera*		
Status	Relatively common		
Distribution	Throughout Britain		
Height	5–20 cm		

Purging Flax
Linum catharticum

An inconspicuous annual species, widely distributed in lowland meadows, among high-mountain grasses, on rocks and in sand dunes wherever the soil is damp in winter and dry in summer. It is a poisonous plant used as a laxative in folk medicine, hence its Latin and common names. This flax is much smaller than the other species of *Linum,* with slender erect branched stems bearing sparse clusters of small flowers on drooping flower-stalks. The petals are white with yellow blotches at their bases. After flowering the persistent sepals cover half of the five-celled globular capsules which contain many tiny seeds.

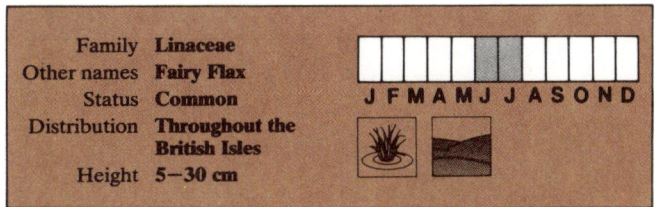

Family	Linaceae		J F M A M J J A S O N D
Other names	Fairy Flax		
Status	Common		
Distribution	Throughout the British Isles		
Height	5–30 cm		

Burnet Saxifrage
Pimpinella saxifraga

Burnet Saxifrage is a perennial plant found in the drier regions of northern Europe and Asia, especially on grassy downs and semi-steppes on calcareous soils. The slender erect stem is rounded, finely grooved and bears variously shaped compound leaves. It is terminated by several umbels of small white flowers which later develop into smooth rounded-ovoid one-seeded fruits. Together with the related Great Burnet Saxifrage (*P. major*), it has been used as a medicinal plant since the time of the Roman Empire to treat stomach troubles and to alleviate throat infections. The Mediterranean species, *P. anisum* (Anise or Aniseed) is even more effective as a throat and stomach medicine and is used in the manufacture of throat lozenges and cough syrups, as well as being the active ingredient of Gripe Water.

Family	**Umbelliferae**	
Status	**Relatively common**	
Distribution	**Throughout much of Britain**	
Height	**30—60 cm**	

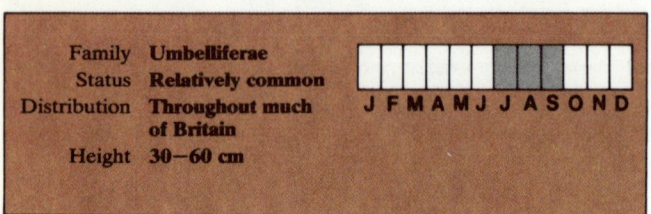

J F M A M J J A S O N D

Field Eryngo
Eryngium campestre

This spiny plant is superficially much more similar to a thistle than to an umbellifer, but the white flowers in umbels betray its real relationships. It is a tough perennial plant, a native of the Mediterranean region, which dies back to the ground each autumn. But the dried stems with ripened seeds are carried by the wind across slopes, field borders and pastures and the single-seeded fruits are dispersed on the way. In spring, the young greyish-green leaves emerge from the original perennial clump. The first leaves are simple, toothed and prickly but soon a basal rosette of prickly divided leaves is formed. The erect flower-bearing stems have smaller clasping leaves and small flowers, arranged in umbellate heads and supported by tough prickly bracts.

Family	**Umbelliferae**	
Status	**Rare. Probably introduced**	
Distribution	**Scattered in southern England**	
Height	**15—60 cm**	

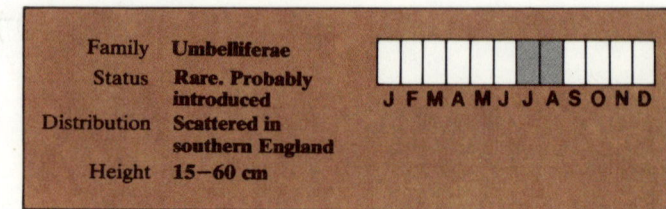

J F M A M J J A S O N D

Wild Carrot
Daucus carota

Usually biennial in its lifestyle, this plant forms a rosette of long-stalked dark green divided leaves in its first year and an erect bristly and leafy stem in the second year. This bears flat umbels of white flowers, usually with one sterile red or purple flower in the centre. The whole inflorescence, as well as the umbel of hooked one-seeded fruits, bears bristly hairs. The slender white root resembles that of the cultivated carrot (which is a subspecies of *D. carota*) in its scent, but not in its thickness. The whole plant is used in herb medicine to treat kidney complaints and gastric ailments, and of course the cultivated variety is well-known as a vegetable. Wild Carrot flowers until autumn in grassy and stony places throughout Europe, southwestern Asia and North America, particularly on calcareous soils and near the sea.

Family	Umbelliferae	
Status	Locally common	
Distribution	Mainly in south and west, and near the sea	J F M A M J J A S O N D
Height	30—100 cm	

Cypress Spurge
Euphorbia cyparissias

This plant is extremely invasive with long creeping underground stems from which grow many delicately fern-like leaves, soon covering large areas of ground. Like all spurges, the stems, leaves and flower-stalks are filled with an acrid milky juice which stains the skin and may cause blisters. The flowers are tiny, a central female flower consisting of a three-celled ovary surrounded by several male flowers each consisting of one stamen only. The flower cluster is surrounded by five enlarged bracts which look like petals, they are yellowish at first later turning red. Flowers and bracts are gathered into large umbel-like heads. Cypress Spurge grows in calcareous grassland throughout Europe but is only occasionally found in the British Isles where it may escape from gardens to grow in wasteland or hedgebanks.

Family	Euphorbiaceae	
Status	Usually a garden escape	
Distribution	Scattered, mainly in England	J F M A M J J A S O N D
Height	15—30 cm	

Bastard Toadflax

Thesium humifusum

This small warmth-loving perennial plant grows locally in European lowlands in grassland communities, especially in chalk and limestone areas. The slender branched stems bear alternate lance-shaped leaves and dense inflorescences of small white flowers. The pointed petal-like sepals are fused into a bell-shaped tube, greenish outside and white inside; there are no petals. The fruit is a nutlet cupped in the persistent sepals. Under each flower there are three bracts, one the same length as the fruit and two smaller bracteoles. This plant is a semi-parasite which, although capable of photosynthesis, also draws water and nutrients through special sucking roots which are attached to the roots of other plants.

		J F M A M J J A S O N D
Family	**Santalaceae**	
Synonym	***T. linophyllon***	
Status	**Local**	
Distribution	**Southern and central England**	
Height	**10—30 cm**	

Leafy Spurge

Euphorbia esula

The tough branched rootstock of this species produces many small branched stems, most of which are sterile, densely covered with more or less linear leaves and which exude a milky white sap when cut, like the rootstock and the flower stems. The relatively fewer flower stems bear broader leaves and rich terminal inflorescences with yellowish-green bracts. Leafy Spurge is similar to another more common spurge, *E. uralensis,* for which it may be mistaken, although *E. uralensis* is much larger, up to 80 cm tall, and has about equal numbers of sterile and flowering stems. The fruit of Leafy Spurge is a smooth green capsule with three seeds in separate compartments. It is a perennial plant widely distributed in Europe, particularly in lowland areas, but a rare introduction in Britain.

		J F M A M J J A S O N D
Family	**Euphorbiaceae**	
Status	**A rare introduction**	
Distribution	**Scotland and southern England**	
Height	**30—60 cm**	

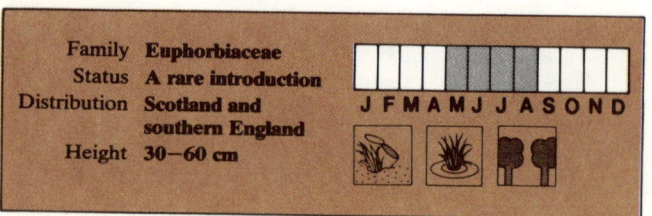

Nottingham Catchfly
Silene nutans

This plant has a basal rosette of spoon-shaped leaves, from which grow erect flowering stems with opposite stalkless leaves; these are covered with downy hairs on the lower surfaces and are sticky on the upper surfaces. In the leaf axils of the upper leaves grow drooping long-stalked flowers arranged in one-sided clusters. Each flower is composed of five deeply two-lobed petals enclosed in a narrow tube formed of five sepals. The fragrant flowers open at night and they are pollinated by moths; they are followed by many-seeded capsules which open by six teeth. The plant grows on dry stony slopes or cliffs, on rocks and walls and in open woods and on shingle foreshores, in the warmer areas of Europe and western Siberia.

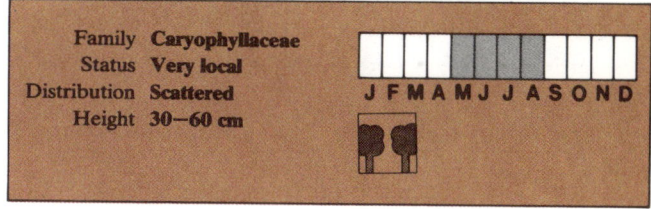

Family	Caryophyllaceae		
Status	Very local		
Distribution	Scattered		
Height	30—60 cm		

J F M A M J J A S O N D

Sticky Catchfly
Lychnis viscaria

This plant forms a perennial clump of long pointed, rather grass-like, dark green leaves. The clump actually consists of several non-flowering tufts which remain green throughout the year and erect flowering tufts in early summer. The common name comes from the stickiness of the stems around the nodes. The flowers are borne in terminal clusters, each has five purplish pink petals with five little erect scales at the centre of the flower. The flowers are followed by five-celled capsules. Sticky Catchfly grows in open places with dry, slightly acid soils, most commonly on cliffs, rocks, stony screes and grassy slopes. It is sometimes grown in large rock gardens and open flower borders.

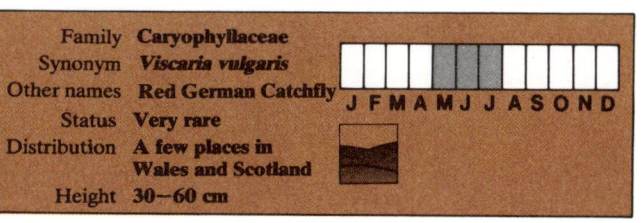

Family	Caryophyllaceae		
Synonym	*Viscaria vulgaris*		
Other names	Red German Catchfly		
Status	Very rare		
Distribution	A few places in Wales and Scotland		
Height	30—60 cm		

J F M A M J J A S O N D

Moss Campion
Silene acaulis

Moss Campions can be found in rock fissures of weathered rocks, on stony slopes and screes in both mountain regions inland and on rocks and cliffs near the sea, throughout much of the Northern Hemisphere. It is a favourite plant for rock gardens and forms a dense clump of linear leaves, fresh green from above with withered brown leaves beneath. It is ideally adapted for life in a crevice with its leafy cushions and its long questing roots. The solitary pink or occasionally white flowers are borne on short stalks growing on very short stems and are followed by many-seeded capsules.

Family	Caryophyllaceae
Status	Local
Distribution	Mainly in Scotland
Height	1—3 cm

J F M A M J J A S O N D

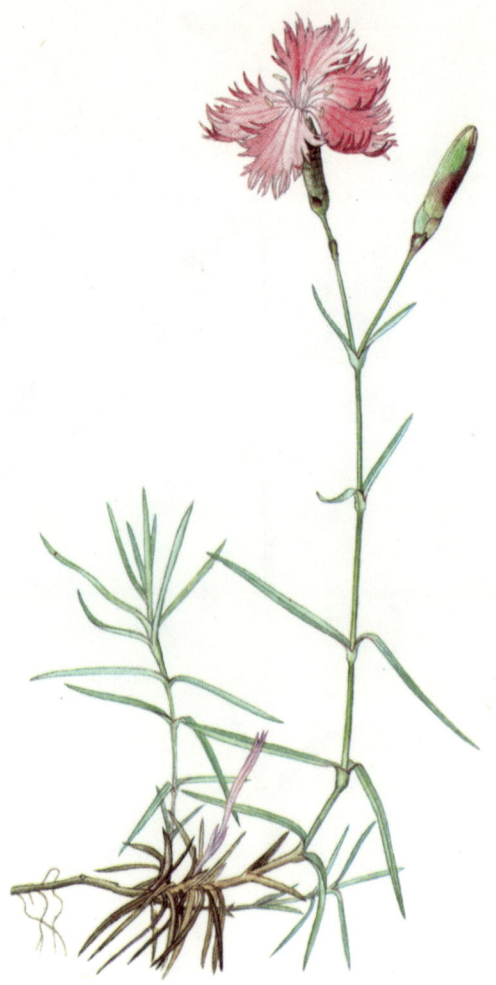

Cheddar Pink
Dianthus gratianopolitanus

This plant is found in a few scattered localities in western and central Europe; the only place where it grows in Britain is on the sides and the top of the gorge at Cheddar. It is included in the list of European endangered plant species and is protected by law in many European countries including Great Britain, West Germany and Czechoslovakia. The cushion-like clumps are formed of linear bluish-green leaves and may be covered by pinkish-red fragrant flowers in early summer, each with five finely toothed petals. The large attractive flowers are borne singly or in pairs on stalks growing from axils of the leaves. Several cultivated varieties are grown in rock gardens.

Family	Caryophyllaceae
Synonyms	*D. caesius,* *D. caespitosus*
Status	Very rare
Distribution	Cheddar cliffs
Height	10—25 cm

J F M A M J J A S O N D

Maiden Pink

Dianthus deltoides

This is an undemanding perennial plant which grows in dry grassy places and sunny banks in lowland areas throughout Europe and parts of western Siberia. It forms loose tufts of opposite, shortly linear leaves and the uppermost ones are transformed into scale-like bracts below the flowers. The five reddish sepals are fused into a tube partly enclosing the five finely toothed, typically carmine-red petals. There are white spots at the mouth of the flower. This species is one of the most attractive meadow plants and may be quite common in certain localities. It is protected in some European countries, Belgium for instance.

Family	Caryophyllaceae
Status	Local
Distribution	Scattered, except in Ireland
Height	15—40 cm

J F M A M J J A S O N D

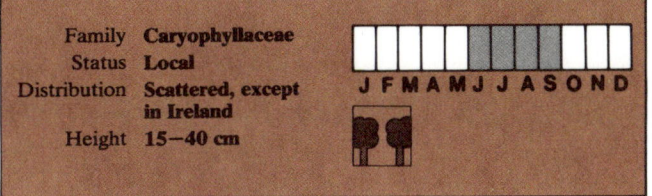

Deptford Pink

Dianthus armeria

Unlike many other pinks, the Deptford Pink is an annual plant with rather unattractive flowers. They are small, reddish and short-stalked, arranged in spherical clusters and hidden in tufts of green bracts which are as long as or longer than the petals. The plant consists of several erect, rather stiff stems, sparsely branched and bearing narrowly lance-shaped leaves which are borne in opposite pairs, fused together across the stem. The bottom leaves have blunt tips, the upper ones are pointed. The whole plant is sparsely covered with spreading hairs. It is scattered throughout much of Europe from lowlands to mountain elevations on poor sandy soils, in grassy places, roadside verges and hedgerows but is nowhere very common.

Family	Caryophyllaceae
Status	Rare
Distribution	Mainly in south and southeast
Height	30—60 cm

J F M A M J J A S O N D

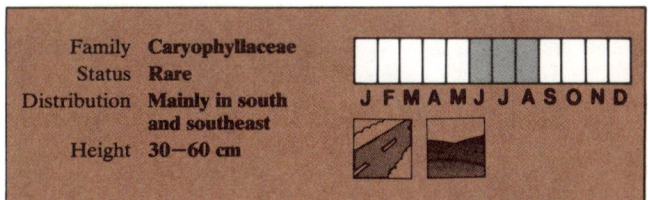

Lesser Stitchwort

Stellaria graminea

This perennial plant has relatively long but feeble ascending and always more or less curved stems. It resembles the similar Great Stitchwort (*S. holostea*) but its flowers are smaller and the stem and leaves are hairless. The grass-green narrowly lance-shaped leaves are stalkless and in the upper leaf axils grow wide open starlike flowers composed of alternating forked petals and narrow green sepals, both of equal length. The flowers are borne on long, often drooping stalks. The plant also produces small closed, so-called cleistogamous, flowers which are self-pollinated. This Eurasian species of lowlands and submontane regions grows in grassland and woodland communities especially on sandy soils.

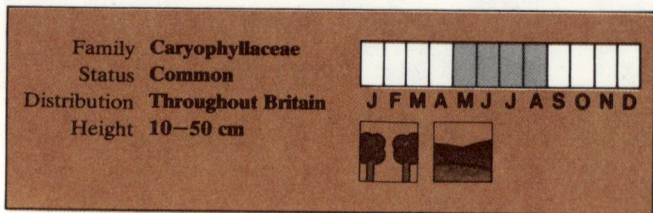

Family	Caryophyllaceae
Status	Common
Distribution	Throughout Britain
Height	10—50 cm

Field Mouse-ear Chickweed

Cerastium arvense

The grey-green clumps of this plant are common throughout the Northern Hemisphere, particularly in Europe. It is found from lowlands to hills, in dry grassy places especially on sandy soils. It has two types of stems: the sterile ones are weak, low-growing and rooting while the flowering stems are taller, branching above to form forked clusters of long-stalked flowers. The flowering shoots grow from the axils of the leaves which are fused at their bases; the lower leaf axils bear only sterile side shoots instead of flowering shoots. White bell-shaped flowers have the petals cleft to one third of their length. The fruit, a cylindrical capsule, opens by ten teeth at the top, and is borne on a drooping stalk which straightens up when the capsule ripens.

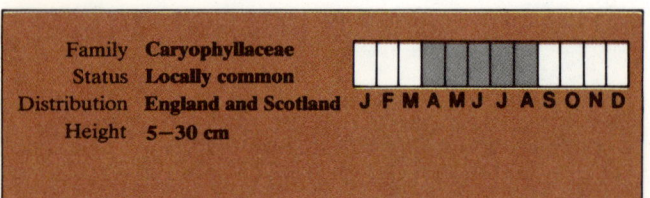

Family	Caryophyllaceae
Status	Locally common
Distribution	England and Scotland
Height	5—30 cm

Thrift

Armeria maritima

This plant grows in mountain grasslands and in crevices in mountain rocks and sea-cliffs throughout many of the maritime areas of the Northern Hemisphere. A subspecies is also found in the upper zones of salt marshes. When not in flower it could easily be mistaken for a grass, with its ground rosette of linear leaves. From this rosette emerge smooth rounded stems in summer, terminated by heads of densely packed red flowers. This hemispherical head is supported by dry membranous bracts which persist after the flowers have withered to enclose the dry papery fruits — the whole forms a light chaffy head which can be dispersed by the wind or water.

		J F M A M J J A S O N D
Family	**Plumbaginaceae**	
Other names	**Sea Pink**	
Status	**Local**	
Distribution	**Coastal and mountain areas**	
Height	**5—50 cm**	

Cowslip

Primula veris

This spring-flowering plant grows in grassy places, often on sloping hillsides and motorway verges, sometimes in large numbers. The large wrinkled leaves form a ground rosette, from the centre of which emerge several leafless flowering stems each bearing an umbel of yellow flowers. The petals are fused to form a tube with orange spots at its throat; this is partly enclosed by the sepals, also fused into a tube. The similar Oxlip (*P. elatior*) has larger paler petals and grows in woods on heavy soils. Individual flowers of the Cowslip differ in the relative lengths of their styles and stamens, a floral adaptation to ensure cross-pollination, short-styled plants being pollinated by pollen from short-filamented plants and vice versa. The flowers are used in herb medicine as a sedative and to make cowslip wine.

		J F M A M J J A S O N D
Family	**Primulaceae**	
Other names	**Paigle**	
Status	**Locally common**	
Distribution	**Throughout Britain but rare in Scotland**	
Height	**10—30 cm**	

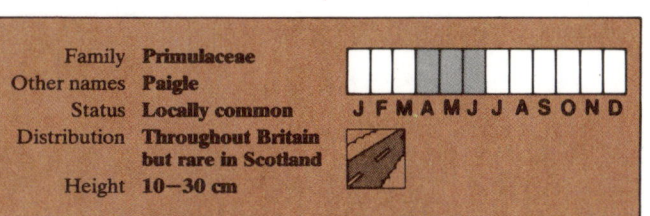

Spring Gentian
Gentiana verna

The beautiful solitary flowers of this plant grow on leafy stems from dense rosettes of pale green, oval or lance-shaped leaves. There may be many rosettes forming a large cushion. The sepals of the flower are fused to form a winged tube, up to 4 cm long, and the five spreading petal-lobes measure some 1.5 cm across. Spring Gentians grow on screes, limestone rocks and stony meadows at high-mountain elevations, but occur locally also in damp meadows in the submontane belt, throughout the temperate zone of Europe and western Asia. However, its existence is threatened by the recent changes in the techniques used in the cultivation of grassland.

Family	Gentianaceae
Status	Very local
Distribution	Mountain areas, especially in Wales
Height	5–15 cm

J F M A M J J A S O N D

Viper's Bugloss
Echium vulgare

This warmth-loving plant grows in sunny places in Europe and western Asia, most commonly in dry grassy or stony areas on sandy soils inland and on coastal dunes and sea-cliffs. It is a coarse biennial plant with several erect stems covered in conspicuous, tough spreading bristles, the stems growing from a basal clump of many lance-shaped leaves. The upright flowering stalk bears many small side clusters of blue flowers growing from the axils of stalkless lance-shaped leaves, which become smaller towards the top of the plant. The funnel-shaped flowers are purplish-red at first, later turning blue. The common name comes from the old use of this plant in herb medicine, for it was supposed to cure snakebite, particularly that of a viper. It is still used to alleviate fever and headaches.

Family	Boraginaceae
Status	Locally common
Distribution	More common in eastern areas
Height	25–100 cm

J F M A M J J A S O N D

Hound's Tongue

Cynoglossum officinale

This biennial or perennial plant grows in dry grassy places and in woodland edges, on stony slopes and waste places inland, but is more often found near the sea. The erect branched, densely leafy stems bear many one-sided clusters of bluish-red flowers. Four sharply spiny nutlets, which ripen after flowering, are enclosed by the persistent sepals. They are dispersed in the fur of various mammals. The common name, Hound's Tongue, comes from the shape and texture of the leaves which are supposed to resemble the tongues of dogs; they are lance-shaped and softly hairy and clasp the stem. This plant was used in herb medicine to treat burns and cuts.

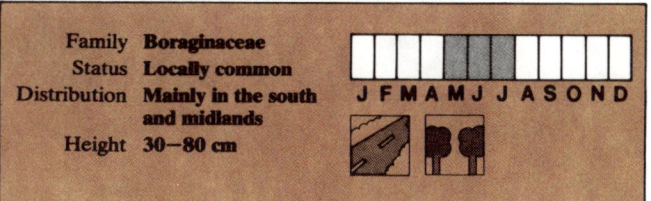

Family	**Boraginaceae**
Status	**Locally common**
Distribution	**Mainly in the south and midlands**
Height	**30—80 cm**

J F M A M J J A S O N D

Self-heal

Prunella vulgaris

A common grassland species of sun and shade, most often found on basic and neutral soils, which grows throughout Europe, Asia and north Africa from lowlands to mountain elevations. It has been introduced to North America and Australia. Its low-growing, sparsely hairy stems branch immediately above the roots to form small spreading clumps. Square ascending stems bear flowers packed tightly into terminal spikes which grow in the axils of the uppermost pair of leaves. The blue-violet, pink or white flowers are two-lipped with a helmet-shaped upper lip and a toothed lower lip. This plant was widely used in herb medicine to treat wounds and to stop bleeding. It is still in use as a gargle for sore throats and mouth ulcers.

Family	**Labiatae**
Status	**Common**
Distribution	**Throughout Britain**
Height	**5—30 cm**

J F M A M J J A S O N D

Basil-thyme

Acinos arvensis

An annual herb with ascending quadrangular stems covered with long soft hairs and bearing opposite pointed-oval leaves. Mauve two-lipped flowers grow in whorls in the leaf axils. This plant grows on dry open grassland, amongst rocks or in fields especially on calcareous soils. It can be used as a culinary herb either in mixed herbs or instead of thyme, although its flavour is rather milder than that herb. It was used in mediaeval herb medicine as a treatment for bruising and snakebites and is said to be a favourite food of sheep, imparting a fine flavour to the meat.

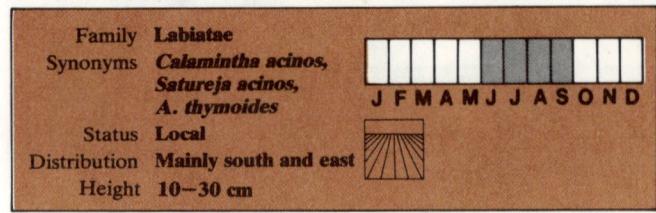

Family	Labiatae	
Synonyms	*Calamintha acinos,*	
	Satureja acinos,	
	A. thymoides	J F M A M J J A S O N D
Status	Local	
Distribution	Mainly south and east	
Height	10—30 cm	

Wild Thyme

Thymus praecox

This aromatic creeping plant forms cushion-like clumps of rooting stems which become woody at the base. It bears many small rounded aromatic leaves which grow flat to the ground and little heads of mauve flowers in summer. It grows in warm places on sun-warmed rocks and slopes on calcareous downs and acid heaths, in lowland hills and mountain areas and on sea-cliffs and sand dunes in coastal areas, throughout the warmer parts of Europe. It is one of several species of thyme which are difficult to distinguish from one another. Many *Thymus* species are used in medicine and as culinary herbs but Wild Thyme contains fewer active ingredients than the French Thyme (*T. vulgaris*), and is therefore less valuable as a herb. Thyme is used in many cough medicines as a treatment for bronchitis.

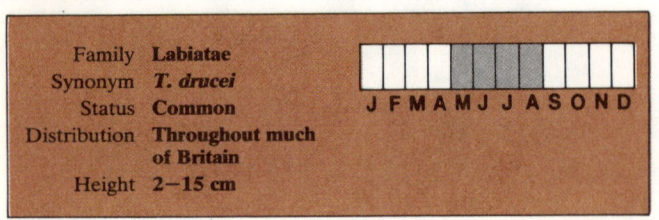

Family	Labiatae	
Synonym	*T. drucei*	
Status	Common	
Distribution	Throughout much	J F M A M J J A S O N D
	of Britain	
Height	2—15 cm	

Meadow Clary
Salvia pratensis

This pleasantly aromatic plant can be found growing in warm localities on calcareous soils, particularly on downs and limestone hills. It is a spreading plant with a few large roughly heart-shaped basal leaves and upright showy inflorescences. These latter consist of a series of whorls of dark blue flowers. The lipped flowers are adapted for cross-pollination by long-tongued bumblebees. The anthers and style are versatile, that is they can move in any direction; when the insect alights on the flower's lower lip, to suck the nectar deep down at the bottom of the long flower tube, it sets into action a lever mechanism which bends the anther down. The pollen, sprinkled on the insect's back, is transported to the stigma of the bent style of an older flower which has already lost its pollen.

Family	Labiatae												
Other names	Meadow Sage												
Status	Very local												
Distribution	Southern and central England												
Height	30—60 cm	J	F	M	A	M	J	J	A	S	O	N	D

Wild Marjoram
Origanum vulgare

This wild relative of the cultivated Marjoram, used in cooking, has tough quadrangular stems with short-stalked opposite oval leaves. The reddish stem branches into a compound inflorescence composed of many spherical clusters of dark pink or purplish fragrant flowers. The tiny individual flowers are borne in the axils of reddish bracts. Wild Marjoram grows in warm dry grassland and on hedgebanks especially on calcareous soils. It is said to originate from Asia and was probably introduced to Europe from Palestine in the 16th century. It was used by the ancient Greeks as an antidote for poisons. Today it is used to make marjoram tea which is a mild tonic and also as a pot herb for flavouring stews and casseroles especially with beef.

Family	Labiatae												
Status	Locally common												
Distribution	Rarer in northern areas	J	F	M	A	M	J	J	A	S	O	N	D
Height	30—80 cm												

Spiked Speedwell
Veronica spicata

A perennial plant of sunny slopes and stony grassy places, scattered through the lowlands and occasionally in the uplands of Europe. In Britain there are two subspecies, one found in the Brecklands of East Anglia, the other on limestone rocks in the Avon Gorge, in Wales and the Pennines but it is rare in all these localities. It is nowhere very common in the whole of Europe and in some countries it is on the list of protected species. In comparison with the other *Veronica* species, Spiked Speedwell is a relatively tall erect plant, with several unbranched stems growing from a creeping underground stem. The stems are glandular-hairy, particularly near the tops, and they bear opposite leaves with rounded teeth on their margins. Tiny blue-violet flowers form a dense terminal raceme on each stem.

Family	Scrophulariaceae
Status	Very rare
Distribution	Scattered
Height	20—55 cm

J F M A M J J A S O N D

Thyme-leaved Speedwell
Veronica serpyllifolia

This low-growing perennial plant has creeping rooting stems with undivided hairless leaves. The basal leaves are rounded, those on the stems are long-oval in shape with rounded teeth. From these creeping stems grow erect inflorescences with a few solitary, loosely arranged flowers; the tiny flowers have four whitish blue-veined petals, broadly spreading and fused at the base. They soon fall off, together with the two anthers, the whole forming a single structure. This leaves the fruiting capsule enclosed in the fused tubular sepals. The plant grows in all sorts of open grassy places throughout Europe, often growing in rather damp spots as well as dry ground.

Family	Scrophulariaceae
Status	Common
Distribution	Throughout Britain
Height	5—20 cm

J F M A M J J A S O N D

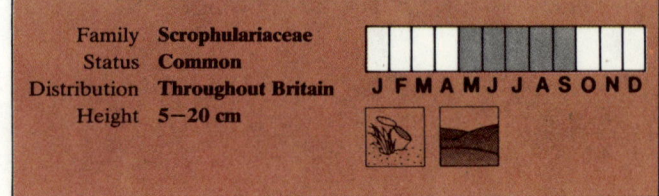

Aaron's Rod

Verbascum thapsus

A biennial plant with a rosette of large thick white-felted leaves in the first year and a tall unbranched flower spike in the second year. The lower part of the spike is clothed with white-felted clasping leaves whose bases run for some distance down the stem; and it bears many funnel-shaped yellow flowers, only a few of which are open at any one time. Aaron's Rod grows on warm sunny banks and hillsides, on roadsides and downland meadows, on dry soils throughout much of Europe and Asia except in the far north. The arrangement of the leaves on the flowering spike channels rain water down the stem to the taproot, an advantage to a plant growing on dry soil.

Family	**Scrophulariaceae**
Other names	**Great Mullein**
Status	**Relatively common**
Distribution	**Rarer in the north**
Height	**40—200 cm**

J F M A M J J A S O N D

Orange Mullein

Verbascum phlomoides

A similar plant to Aaron's Rod, this biennial species grows in stony grassland and cultivated ground in much of Europe except in the northern areas. It is only found as a rare casual in Britain. It has a rosette of stalked basal leaves and a flowering spike, all covered with dense white or yellowish woolly felt, which protects the plant from water loss. The stem leaves differ from those of Aaron's Rod — their bases do not clasp the stem to the same extent. The flowering spike bears widely spaced clusters of yellow flowers and there may be side branches at the base of the stem.

Family	**Scrophulariaceae**
Status	**A rare casual**
Distribution	**Occasional**
Height	**30—150 cm**

J F M A M J J A S O N D

151

Ribwort
Plantago lanceolata

Tall square flowering stems grow from a ground rosette of linear or lance-shaped leaves. These leaves have marked longitudinal veins (giving the plant its name), are pointed at the tips and gradually narrow into a basal stalk. The leafless flowering stem is terminated by a dense spike of tiny flowers. Markedly long pale filaments bearing yellow anthers protrude from the densely-packed insignificant brownish flowers; there are many narrow pointed bracts in the flower spike and the flowers are followed by glossy pale brown capsules each with 1−2 seeds. This plant is sometimes used in herb medicine, instead of its relative the Great Plantain (*P. major*), but it does not have the medicinal action of the latter plant.

Family	Plantaginaceae		J F M A M J J A S O N D
Other names	Narrow-leaved Plantain		
Status	Very common		
Distribution	Throughout Britain		
Height	5−50 cm		

Red Broomrape
Orobanche alba

Broomrapes lack the green pigment, chlorophyll, and are consequently unable to synthesise their food. Instead they are parasitic on various other plants. Red Broomrape is parasitic on members of the Labiatae, like Basil-thyme and Wild Basil, but more particularly on *Thymus* species, growing with these plants on sun-warmed rocky or stony slopes in the warmer parts of Europe and western Asia. It is confined to western rocky coasts in Britain, especially in Scotland. The plant attaches itself by the base of the stem to the host's roots. The waxy-looking stem appears in summer and is covered in tiny scales instead of leaves. It bears a raceme of yellow-pink tubular flowers in Europe although red flowers are more common in Britain (this variant is sometimes called *O. rubra*). The flowers are followed by capsules containing numerous seeds which are dispersed by water.

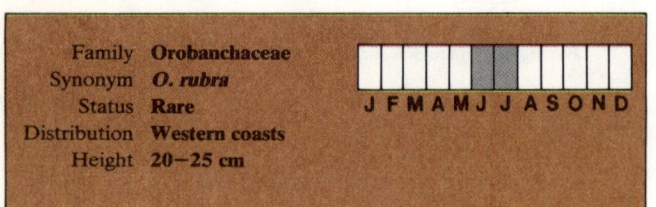

Family	Orobanchaceae		J F M A M J J A S O N D
Synonym	*O. rubra*		
Status	Rare		
Distribution	Western coasts		
Height	20−25 cm		

Lady's Bedstraw
Galium verum

This perennial plant attracts one's eye in a meadow by its mats of creeping stems with whorled leaves and dense terminal clusters of lemon-yellow, honey-scented flowers. The small funnel-shaped flowers have four-lobed petals and are followed by tiny spherical, finely warty double fruits which stick to the fur of animals and the plant is thus dispersed. The plant is characteristic of dry grassland on downs and limestone hills, in hedgebanks and on stable fixed dunes near the sea. It is still used in some areas for curdling milk for cheese making, as it has been for hundreds of years, and is sometimes called Cheese Rennet.

Family	Rubiaceae
Other names	Yellow Bedstraw
Status	Common
Distribution	Throughout much of Britain
Height	50—80 cm

J F M A M J J A S O N D

Hoary Plantain
Plantago media

This plantain has a ground rosette of leaves but they differ from those of Ribwort. They are large and oval with distinctive veins and they are divided into hairy blades and short stalks. The main root dies after germination of the seed and its function is taken over by many adventitious roots. The rootstock also dies back gradually until its lower end looks as if it had been bitten off. The pinkish-violet finely scented flowers are arranged in spikes, slender before the flowers open, but becoming much larger when the pink filaments, bearing anthers, protrude from the flowers. Hoary Plantain is widely distributed in Europe, western Asia and Siberia. The leaves are supposed to effect a cure for blight on fruit trees if rubbed on the affected part.

Family	Plantaginaceae
Status	Common
Distribution	Mainly in central and southern England
Height	15—45 cm

J F M A M J J A S O N D

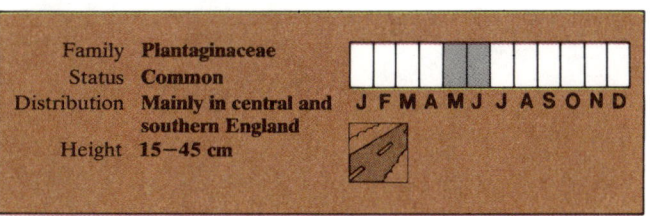

Squinancy Wort
Asperula cynanchica

This native of southern and southeastern Europe has spread to other warm European regions, growing at lower elevations on sun-warmed slopes and dry grassland inland and on stable fixed dunes on the coasts. Although a British native plant it is not a common species in this country. *Asperula* species bear long-tubed white flowers while the similar *Galium* species, often also white-flowered, have funnel-shaped short-tubed flowers. Squinancy Wort is a clump-forming plant with numerous slender branches and narrow one-veined greyish leaves in whorls of four. At one time it was used in herb medicine to treat quinsy, hence its other common name.

Family	**Rubiaceae**
Other names	**Quinsy-wort**
Status	**Locally common**
Distribution	**Southern and western areas**
Height	**5–30 cm**

J F M A M J J A S O N D

Field Scabious
Knautia arvensis

This is a common grassland plant of drier locations, distributed from lowlands to subalpine elevations throughout Europe and western Asia, particularly in chalk downs and limestone areas. From a perennial branching taproot grows a ground rosette of undivided long-stalked leaves and several erect stems. The stem leaves are deeply lobed with several pairs of lobes, grey-green and opposite. Individual small flowers are gathered together into long-stalked terminal heads, the outermost flowers of the head being larger than the central ones. The tiny sepals are bristle-like and there are four petals in each flower. Scabious was used in herb medicine to treat scabs and skin ulcers, hence the common name.

Family	**Dipsacaceae**
Synonym	***Scabiosa arvensis***
Status	**Common**
Distribution	**England, Wales and Eire**
Height	**30–80 cm**

J F M A M J J A S O N D

Harebell

Campanula rotundifolia

This bellflower has a basal clump of stalked, rounded, kidney-shaped leaves and several slender, more or less erect stems with pointed leaves. The erect stems bear solitary blue-violet, broadly bell-shaped flowers, each with little spreading sepals. The flowers are followed by fruiting capsules with many tiny seeds. Harebells grow throughout the Northern Hemisphere from lowlands to mountain elevations in dry grasslands, especially on poor soils both acid and calcareous. They also grow in stable fixed dunes in coastal areas. This little flower has a rich history of folklore, not as a medicinal plant but as belonging to the fairies and goblins or even to the Devil, together with the hare for which it is named.

Family	Campanulaceae
Other names	Scottish Bluebell, Fairy Thimbles
Status	Locally common
Distribution	Rare in southwest and Ireland
Height	15—30 cm

J F M A M J J A S O N D

Clustered Bellflower

Campanula glomerata

This is a decorative perennial species of dry grassy slopes or scrub, in the warmer regions of Europe especially on the calcareous soils of the downs and on sea-cliffs. The blue-violet or occasionally white bell-shaped flowers are borne at the top of many stout erect unbranched stems, growing from creeping underground stems. The stalkless flowers are either clustered into a single terminal head or form several smaller whorls in the axils of the upper leaves. The basal leaves are long-stalked and form ground hugging mats, the stem leaves are stalkless. There are several cultivated varieties of this plant which are grown in the flower border.

Family	Campanulaceae
Status	Local
Distribution	Mainly in southern and central England
Height	30—60 cm

J F M A M J J A S O N D

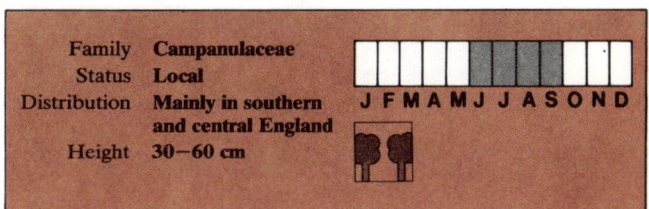

Rough Hawksbeard
Crepis biennis

This biennial plant is one of many similar composite plants, known as hawksbeards, hawkbits and hawkweeds. Hawksbeards can be identified by their single-seeded fruits which have many rows of soft white unbranched hairs and by their involucral bracts beneath the flower-heads which are all the same length and in one row. The plant forms a spindle-shaped root and a rosette of lobed, long-stalked basal leaves during its first year, in the second year producing a branched stem with several yellow flower-heads, all with identical ray florets and no disk florets. The stems are full of milky latex. Rough Hawksbeard is a common and adaptable species of dry grassland and damp meadows throughout many parts of Europe, especially on calcareous soils.

Family	Compositae	
Status	Locally common	
Distribution	Mainly southern and central England	J F M A M J J A S O N D
Height	50—120 cm	

Sheep's-bit
Jasione montana

Although related to bellflowers this biennial or perennial plant is not much like them at first glance. It forms a spreading clump of slender hairy stems, covered with stalkless linear leaves with wavy margins. The stems bear dense terminal heads of blue flowers, each flower with five deeply cleft linear petals and an extremely long style protruding from the centre. Sheep's-bit is locally common in lowland and mountain regions, growing in dry grassy places, sand dunes and open woods on lime-free soils. It is an indicator of very poor, sandy or stony soils both inland and near the sea. Often only the blue flower-heads can be seen growing in a rough pasture with coarse grasses, where it may be cropped by sheep.

Family	Campanulaceae	
Status	Locally common	
Distribution	Scattered throughout Britain	J F M A M J J A S O N D
Height	20—45 cm	

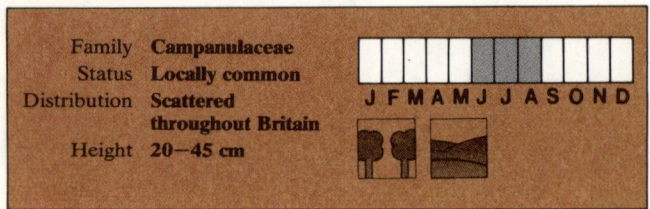

Autumnal Hawkbit

Leontodon autumnalis

Hawkbits can be distinguished from the other hawksbeards and hawkweeds by the two rows of pappus hairs on the single-seeded fruit, in which the innermost row of hairs is feathery and the outermost simple. Autumnal Hawkbit consists of a perennial ground rosette of hairless, entire or lobed leaves from which grow leafless flower-stalks bearing two or more dandelion-like flower-heads. The heads are formed of many golden-yellow ray florets which are streaked with red beneath. The plant grows in grassland from lowlands to mountain elevations throughout Europe and Asia; it may be found on stony slopes and screes in mountain areas, waste places and roadside verges in lowlands.

Family	**Compositae**	
Status	**Common**	
Distribution	**Throughout Britain**	J F M A M J J A S O N D
Height	**10—50 cm**	

Mouse-ear Hawkweed

Hieracium pilosella

The hawkweeds are a large genus of similar plants, most of which are extremely difficult to tell apart. However, Mouse-ear Hawkweed is rather different to all the others (belonging to a subgenus of its own) and is the only one with running stems. These root into the soil at intervals and form new rosettes of leaves (like strawberries do) so that large colonies of plants may result. The rosette leaves are linear in shape and from the centre of the rosette grows an erect flowering stem which bears a solitary flower-head with lemon-yellow ray florets, streaked with red beneath. The flower-heads of the other hawkweeds are a harsh yellow in colour and are borne in clusters. Mouse-ear Hawkweed grows in grassland on damp and dry soils, and on heathland and moors throughout Europe.

Family	**Compositae**	
Status	**Common**	
Distribution	**Throughout Britain**	J F M A M J J A S O N D
Height	**5—30 cm**	

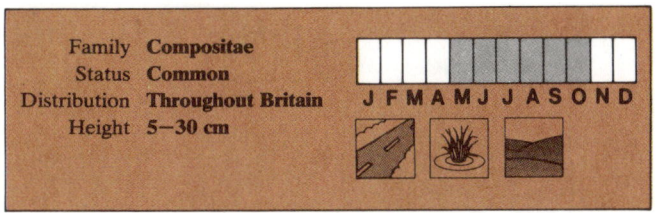

Alpine Coltsfoot
Homogyne alpina

This low-growing perennial plant grows in high-mountain meadows and mountain forests, particularly in subalpine spruce and dwarf pine woods and poor pastures. It is usually found in acid soils rich in minerals and organic matter and saturated with water from long-lying snow. It grows only in two localities in Britain, one in Scotland and the other in the Outer Hebrides. In spring, the creeping underground stems produce rosettes of rounded kidney-shaped, rather leathery leaves with prominent white-felted veins. From the rosette grow several, almost leafless, woolly reddish stems each terminating in a solitary flower-head. The tiny, densely packed florets are reddish or whitish, the inner ones being tubular and the outer ray florets. The single-seeded fruits have a snow-white pappus of hairs.

Family	**Compositae**	
Synonym	*Tussilago alpina*	
Other names	**Purple Coltsfoot**	J F M A M J J A S O N D
Status	**Very rare**	
Distribution	**Two localities only**	
Height	**15—30 cm**	

Goldilocks
Aster linosyris

This relative of the asters differs from those plants in its flowers, since it has no ray florets, only tubular disk florets making up the flower-heads. It is a perennial plant with many erect slender stems bearing a dense cover of linear alternate leaves. These are hairless, one-veined and rough on the margins. The flower-heads are borne in large leafy clusters terminating the stems. This plant grows on sunny stony slopes and rocks and in sandy places in the warmest parts of Europe, often near the sea and on calcareous soils. It is rare in Britain, growing only in a few places on limestone cliffs on the western coastline.

Family	**Compositae**	
Synonyms	*Chrysocoma linosyris,*	
	Linosyris vulgaris,	
	Crinitaria linosyris	J F M A M J J A S O N D
Status	**Very rare**	
Distribution	**Scattered on**	
	western sea-cliffs	
Height	**20—50 cm**	

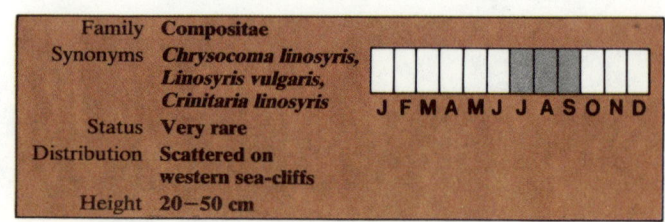

Blue Fleabane

Erigeron acer

This roughly hairy annual or biennial plant has a basal rosette of entire, rather spoon-shaped leaves and an erect tough stem which branches to form the inflorescence. The stem leaves are stalkless and lance-shaped. The small flower-heads appear blue from a distance but in reality they have pale violet ray florets and yellowish tubular disk florets. The cylindrical involucre beneath the flower-heads is formed by linear hairy bracts and the single-seeded fruits have white, red-tinged hairs. Common Fleabane grows in dry grassland, on walls and sunny banks especially on disturbed ground, on chalk downs and other calcareous soils throughout the Northern Hemisphere. It also grows on sand dunes in coastal areas.

Family	Compositae	
Status	Locally common	
Distribution	England, Wales and Ireland	
Height	10—30 cm	

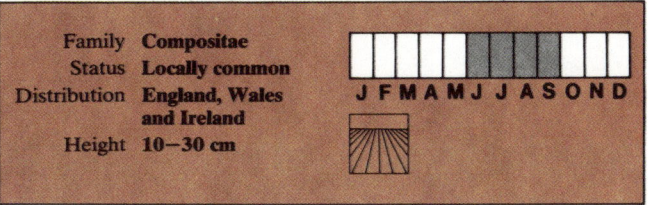

J F M A M J J A S O N D

Brown Knapweed

Centaurea jacea

A common lowland European species similar to the familiar Hardheads (*C. nigra*) of the downs and other grassland areas. Several tough erect, more or less cottony stems are clothed with hairy stalkless leaves and bear solitary flower-heads each 3—4 cm across. The flower-heads of knapweeds are distinctive with a large dark, more or less globular involucre beneath the head and enclosing the buds, and with large sterile fringing ray florets around the outside of the head. The involucral bracts of Brown Knapweed are pale brown beneath and membranous; the ray florets are reddish-purple in colour. This species grows in grassland and waste places.

Family	Compositae	
Status	Rare	
Distribution	Southeast England	
Height	30—80 cm	

J F M A M J J A S O N D

Carline Thistle

Carlina vulgaris

Carline Thistle is a stiff erect, usually biennial plant with lobed prickly-margined leaves, the lowermost often withered in dry weather. It grows in dry or extremely dry calcareous grasslands and its tough prickly surface protects it from both drought and grazing sheep and rabbits. The stem bears several small clusters of flower-heads, each measuring 2–3 cm across and consisting entirely of yellow tubular disk florets. Around the rim of the involucre is a ring of large yellow bracts which look like petals. They spread out in dry weather and close up when the air is damp. The flowers used to be hung up outside cottage doors at one time, and were used to forecast the weather. Dead flower-heads may persist on the plants through the winter.

Family	**Compositae**	
Status	**Locally common**	
Distribution	**Rarer in the north**	
Height	**15–50 cm**	J F M A M J J A S O N D

Stemless Thistle

Cirsium acaule

This prickly plant has a conspicuously short, more or less underground stem with a rosette of large lobed, very prickly leaves in the centre of which grow a few stalkless reddish-purple flower-heads. The heads are composed of tubular florets only and grow from a large greenish-purple, rather spiny involucre. The fruiting heads which follow are composed of many single-seeded fruits bearing long feathery hairs, a feature which distinguishes thistles of the genus, *Cirsium,* from the thistles of the genus, *Carduus,* which have simple hairs. Stemless Thistle grows in the warmer parts of Europe, especially on chalk downs and limestone hills in short grassland where constant grazing keeps the vegetation short.

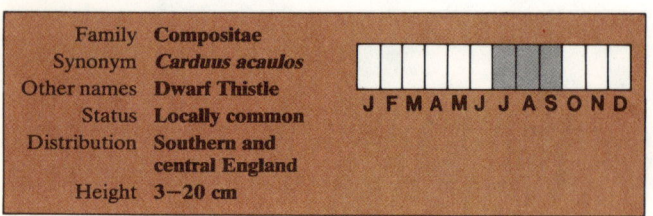

Family	**Compositae**	
Synonym	***Carduus acaulos***	
Other names	**Dwarf Thistle**	
Status	**Locally common**	J F M A M J J A S O N D
Distribution	**Southern and central England**	
Height	**3–20 cm**	

Sand Leek
Allium scorodoprasum

This plant grows from an underground bulb which produces numerous bulbils so that soon a small clump of plants is formed. From each bulb grows an erect tough stem sheathed with narrow leaves and terminated by a spherical umbel of bell-shaped reddish-purple flowers. The whole plant, and especially the bulb, smells strongly of garlic. The small sparse umbel bears not only flowers but also a number of purplish bulbils. The inflorescence is at first enclosed in a membranous two-valved sheath, which opens to expose the flowers and persists beneath the umbel during flowering. This warmth-loving plant grows locally in vineyards in many parts of Europe and also on poor dry grassland and stony ground.

		J F M A M J J A S O N D
Family	**Liliaceae**	
Status	**Very local**	
Distribution	**Northeast England and Scotland**	
Height	**60–100 cm**	

Star of Bethlehem
Ornithogalum umbellatum

This monocotyledonous plant grows in large clumps, from bulbs that produce many bulbils each year so that soon there is a large cluster of bulbs where at first there was only one. The bulbs have a distinctive onion-like smell, as does the foliage to a lesser extent. Six to nine long-linear, rather soft leaves with a wide white stripe down the middle emerge from each bulb in late winter, to be followed in spring by a leafless flowering stalk bearing a terminal cluster of flowers. The glistening white star-like flowers are composed of six petals, each with a green band on the back; they open only in bright sunlight. This plant is more common in the Mediterranean region than in more northerly areas of Europe where it is probably introduced. It is grown in gardens in Britain, from whence it often escapes to grow in grassy places.

		J F M A M J J A S O N D
Family	**Liliaceae**	
Status	**Locally naturalized**	
Distribution	**Scattered, mainly in England and Wales**	
Height	**10–30 cm**	

Tassel Hyacinth

Muscari comosum

This robust bulbous plant produces three or four fleshy, broadly linear grooved stems and a flowering stem which is terminated by a striking inflorescence with two types of flowers. The lower flowers are fertile, green-brown in colour and spread outwards on short stalks, while the upper blue-violet bell-shaped flowers are sterile and grow on long upright stalks. Both flower-types have six petals. This very decorative plant flowers at the end of spring and beginning of summer in warm places and sunny slopes. It grows rarely in northern European lowland and hill regions but is much more common in the Mediterranean. It may sometimes be found as a weed in dry sandy fields.

Family	**Liliaceae**	
Synonym	*Hyacinthus comosus*	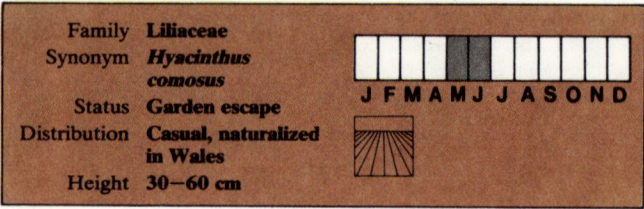
Status	**Garden escape**	
Distribution	**Casual, naturalized in Wales**	
Height	**30—60 cm**	

Green-winged Orchid

Orchis morio

This orchid was once common throughout much of Europe except the most northern parts, but it is now scattered or rare and has disappeared from many of its original habitats, in spite of its being protected by law in some European countries. This is due mostly to the introduction of modern farming techniques and chemicals into meadowland and to the extensive ploughing-up of the downs to grow wheat. From a clump of lance-shaped unspotted dark green leaves grows an erect flower-stalk sheathed in leaves and terminated by a few flowers. The purple flower has green-veined petals, the uppermost forming a helmet, the lowermost forming a dark-spotted lip broader than it is long, and the side petals forming rounded lateral lobes. The spur is straight and as long as or shorter than the ovary.

Family	**Orchidaceae**	
Status	**Locally common**	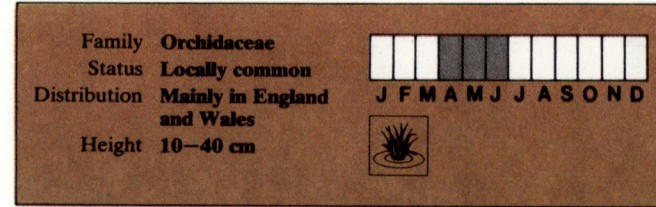
Distribution	**Mainly in England and Wales**	
Height	**10—40 cm**	

Species featured
in this section

Species featured
in another section

Pheasant's Eye

Adonis aestivalis

This is a small annual weed found on calcareous soils especially in corn fields in the warmer areas of Europe and southwestern Asia. It has an erect branched stem with many finely divided leaves. Each leaf is basically three-lobed, the lobes deeply divided into many linear segments. The solitary terminal flowers are bright red in colour with a darker spot at the base of each petal. The plant is poisonous, with a poison rather like that of foxglove but stronger; like that plant, Pheasant's Eye is used in the treatment of heart weakness, especially when the digitalis from foxgloves does not work. But the risks involved in its use are much higher.

Family	Ranunculaceae		J F M A M J J A S O N D
Status	Introduced		
Distribution	Occasionally naturalized in the south		
Height	20—60 cm		

Corn Buttercup

Ranunculus arvensis

Buttercups grow in many habitats — meadows, woodland, water, waste ground, mountains and fields. This species, Corn Buttercup, is found in corn fields, especially on calcareous soils in the warmer areas of Europe. It is an undesirable element in green fodder as it is poisonous like the entire family, and the rough prickly single-seeded fruits hurt the cattle's mouths. This pale green annual plant has a ground rosette composed of simple long-stalked leaves, from which grows an erect stem with lower leaves divided into three wedge-shaped segments and narrow unstalked upper leaves. The small pale yellow flowers grow in clusters terminating the erect stems.

Family	Ranunculaceae		J F M A M J J A S O N D
Other names	Corn Crowfoot		
Status	Locally common		
Distribution	Mainly in the south and southeast		
Height	20—60 cm		

Forking Larkspur
Delphinium consolida

This annual field weed has leaves deeply divided into linear segments and blue-purple flowers growing in sparse racemes in the leaf axils. The flowers have five petal-like sepals, one of which is elongated into a spur. The four true petals are modified into nectaries, one of them forming a spur inside the sepal spur. The flowers are followed by smooth pods, each containing ten seeds which look like small cones covered with horizontal rows of scales. Forking Larkspur was introduced into Europe from western Asia together with field crops, mainly cereals. It is a somewhat poisonous plant which has the effect of lowering the blood pressure and slowing the pulse.

Family	**Ranunculaceae**	
Status	**Rare casual**	
Distribution	**Mostly found near ports**	
Height	**20—40 cm**	J F M A M J J A S O N D

Parsley Piert
Aphanes arvensis

This small grey-green relative of the Lady's Mantles is an annual plant with a branched stem forming a sparse, rather sprawling clump. The dense leaves are short-stalked and deeply cleft into 3—5 wedge-shaped segments. Tiny yellow-green flowers grow in sparse clusters in the leaf axils; each has four green sepals and no petals and is followed by one-seeded fruits. Parsley Piert grows throughout the Northern Hemisphere as a field and garden weed and in grassy places such as pastures, fallow land and on waste ground in many different kinds of soil.

Family	**Rosaceae**	
Synonym	***Alchemilla arvensis***	
Status	**Common**	J F M A M J J A S O N D
Distribution	**Throughout Britain**	
Height	**5—20 cm**	

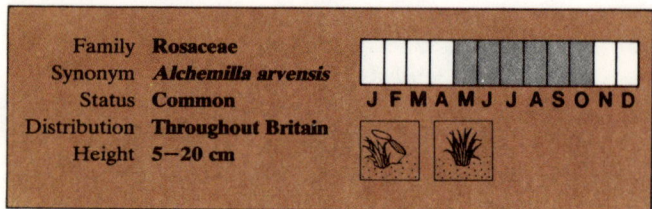

Tuberous Pea

Lathyrus tuberosus

This climbing or prostrate perennial plant has a scrambling stem and compound leaves. Each leaf has a single pair of leaflets and is terminated by branched tendrils; there is an arrow-shaped stipule at the bottom of the leaf-stalk. The small fragrant racemes of crimson pea-like flowers may equal the beauty of the garden sweet peas and the individual blossoms have markedly large standard petals. Tuberous Pea used to be grown in western Europe as a vegetable rich in starch — the name refers to the small black underground tubers which form on the roots. They are edible, sugary, slightly bitter with a delicate nut-like flavour. The plant grows in the warmer regions of Europe and western Asia on heavy clay soils, especially in corn fields and hedgerows from lowlands to the hills.

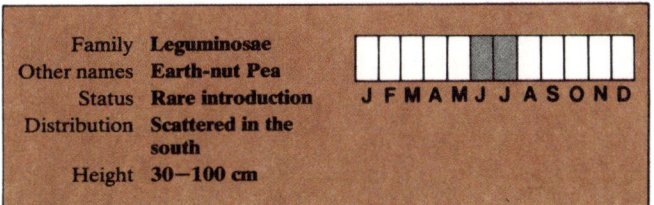

Family	**Leguminosae**													
Other names	**Earth-nut Pea**													
Status	**Rare introduction**													
Distribution	**Scattered in the south**													
Height	**30—100 cm**													

J F M A M J J A S O N D

Hairy Tare

Vicia hirsuta

This slender tare has trailing stems which may grow over 50 cm in length. It has compound leaves, each with up to ten pairs of alternately arranged leaflets and a terminal branched tendril by which the tare clings to other plants. Long-stalked racemes of 3—6 whitish, pea-like flowers grow in the leaf axils and are followed by softly-hairy two-seeded pods. Hairy Tare is often mistaken for its relative, Smooth Tare (*V. tetrasperma*), which has fewer leaflets to each leaf (up to six) and smooth seed-pods with four seeds in each. Hairy Tare grows in cornfields and grassy places often in poor soils; it improves the fertility of these soils with the nitrogenous bacteria living in the nodules on the fine lateral roots of the taproot.

Family	**Leguminosae**													
Status	**Common**													
Distribution	**Throughout Britain**													
Height	**15—60 cm**													

J F M A M J J A S O N D

Red Clover
Trifolium pratense

This is a common perennial meadow plant and an important component of green cattle fodder, enriching it with proteins and minerals. The cultivated variety is grown mainly in subalpine regions and the wild form grows in all kinds of grassy places, roadside verges and gardens throughout Europe and much of western Asia. It has an erect stem and many leaves, each with three leaflets. The leaves are quite distinctive for each long-oval leaflet has a white crescent-shaped spot near the base. The small reddish-purple flowers grow in dense heads terminating the stems; they are rich in nectar and very attractive to bees which pollinate the flowers. This clover is an important source of nectar for hive bees and clover honey is one of the best kinds.

Family	Leguminosae
Status	Common
Distribution	Throughout Britain
Height	15—40 cm

J F M A M J J A S O N D

Lucerne
Medicago sativa

Lucerne is a cultivated plant of Asiatic origin, often grown as a valuable fodder plant in many parts of Europe. It sometimes escapes and becomes naturalized in waste ground. It has erect stems with compound leaflets and dense racemes of violet pea-like flowers growing in the leaf axils. The seed pods are spirally coiled and contain many seeds. Cultivated plants are often hybrids between Lucerne with pale violet flowers and Sickle Medick (*M. falcata*) which has yellow flowers. The hybrid is called *M. varia* and has a great variety of forms with flowers in all colours from yellow-green to purple-brown, growing in short racemes. The pods of the hybrid are a cross between the sickle-shaped fruits of Sickle Medick and the double or triple spirals of Lucerne.

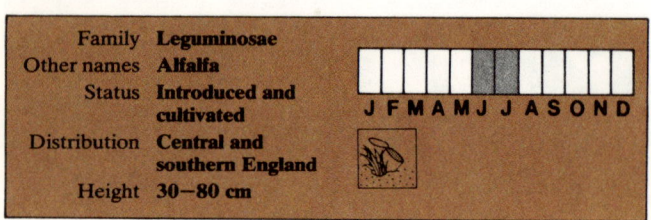

Family	Leguminosae
Other names	Alfalfa
Status	Introduced and cultivated
Distribution	Central and southern England
Height	30—80 cm

J F M A M J J A S O N D

Long Prickly-headed Poppy

Papaver argemone

This small annual weed grows in fields and waste places in the warmer areas of Europe and central Asia, on many different kinds of soil. It has a long taproot and a basal rosette of long-stalked divided leaves. An erect stem grows from the basal rosette, also bearing divided leaves although the stem leaves are stalkless. The whole plant is covered with stiff bristly hairs. The terminal flowers each have four red petals with a black spot at the base of the petal. They are followed by long narrow, strongly grooved, rather bristly capsules. Poppy capsules are very distinctive, rather like pepper-shakers with a ridged top and many holes in a ring around the top through which the seeds are shaken out.

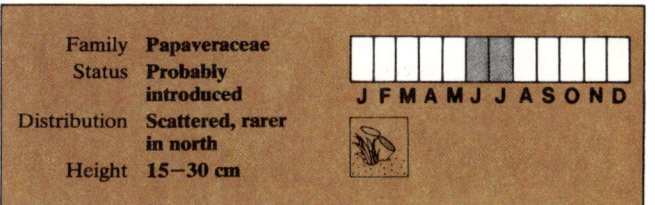

Family	Papaveraceae		
Status	Probably introduced		J F M A M J J A S O N D
Distribution	Scattered, rarer in north		
Height	15–30 cm		

Hare's-foot Clover

Trifolium arvense

This species is rather different from the other clovers. It is an annual plant with low-growing branched stems which bear terminal long-stalked flower-heads of an unusual grey-pink colour; both sepals and petals are the same colour. The oval hairy heads are reminiscent of the soft fur of a hare's foot, hence the common name. The long-haired sepals are fused into a tube with five long hairy teeth and they conceal the small pea-like flowers for the sepals are twice as long as the petals. The fruit is an indehiscent pod enclosed in the persistent sepals, which turn brownish in colour. The hairy stem bears alternate long-stalked leaves, each with three narrow wedge-shaped leaflets having soft silky hairs on both sides. Hare's-foot Clover is often common in dry light sandy soils in fields, grassy places and sand dunes throughout much of Europe.

Family	Leguminosae		
Status	Locally common		J F M A M J J A S O N D
Distribution	Throughout Britain		
Height	8–30 cm		

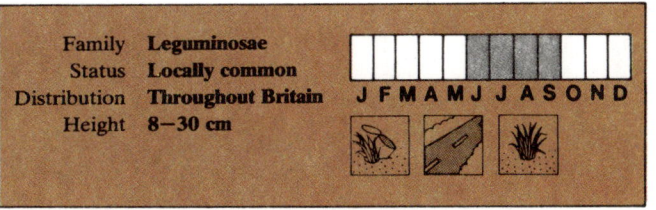

Field Poppy
Papaver rhoeas

This annual plant was common at one time in cornfields and arable land, but is now much more rarely seen in such fields due to modern agricultural techniques. It still grows in waste places and on roadsides, especially near the fields where it was once so common. It has a basal rosette of divided or lobed leaves, from which grows an erect stem with stalkless lobed leaves. The whole plant is covered with many bristly hairs. Each bright red-petalled flower has a black centre, made up of many black anthers, and it remains open only for a day, after which the petals fall and the seed capsule forms. The capsules are smooth and ridged without bristles, but with the distinctive pepperpot action. Field Poppy is used in herb medicine as a mild soothing remedy for coughs and throat infections.

Family	**Papaveraceae**
Status	**Locally common**
Distribution	**Rarer in north and west**
Height	**30—90 cm**

J F M A M J J A S O N D

Common Fumitory
Fumaria officinalis

This variable plant has a branched acrid root from which grow several sprawling stems and deeply divided leaves. The whole plant is smooth and hairless and bluish-green in colour, somewhat smoky as its name suggests and the smell of the roots brings tears to the eyes as smoke does. The flowers are borne in long erect racemes with up to 40 flowers, and are strangely shaped with long pinkish petals and a keel at the back. In Britain the petals are black-tipped but European forms may have no black tips to the petals. The flowers are followed by rounded nutlets, each with one seed. Fumitory grows on cultivated land and disturbed ground, especially on lighter soils. It is used in herb medicine to treat constipation and to prevent water retention by stimulating the kidneys.

Family	**Papaveraceae**
Status	**Locally common**
Distribution	**Throughout Britain**
Height	**15—30 cm**

J F M A M J J A S O N D

Charlock

Sinapis arvensis

This common and invasive field weed grows in lowlands, especially on basic fertile soils in arable land, on roadsides and on waste ground throughout Europe and much of the rest of the world. It is an annual plant usually with an unbranched stem and sparse hairs. The lowermost leaves are long-stalked and lyre-shaped, the upper stalkless, undivided, often coarsely toothed. The shining yellow flowers appear during the early summer months, opening from the bottom of the racemes upwards. They have spreading sepals, half the length of the petals, and are followed by erect cylindrical seed pods, each with a long beak. The young leaves can be used to add flavour to a salad or omelette and the seeds to make mustard, like the cultivated mustards.

Family	Cruciferae	
Synonym	*Brassica arvensis*	
Other names	Wild Mustard	J F M A M J J A S O N D
Status	Common	
Distribution	Throughout Britain	
Height	30—60 cm	

Small Alison

Alyssum alyssoides

Small Alison is a small annual plant with several stems growing directly from a single root without forming a basal leaf rosette; many small lance-shaped leaves cover the stems and the whole plant is covered with a dense down of grey hairs. The racemes of stalked flowers, borne at the ends of the stems, are composed of many smallish pale yellow or whitish flowers, opening from the bottom of the inflorescence upwards. The whole raceme lengthens as it gets older and produces many circular fruits, each with one or two winged seeds. The flowers are inconspicuous when compared to those of some of the other alisons, which have bright yellow flowers. This low-growing spring-flowering plant grows mainly on sandy soils in dry sunny parts of Europe.

Family	Cruciferae	
Synonym	*A. calycinum*	
Status	Rare introduction	J F M A M J J A S O N D
Distribution	Scattered in eastern areas	
Height	10—30 cm	

Hoary Cress

Cardaria draba

This is a perennial weed which was introduced into Britain at the beginning of the 19th century. Its deeply penetrating creeping roots make it a difficult weed to eradicate and, if left unchecked, it soon colonises large areas choking the other plants present. The erect stems are covered with shallowly toothed ovoid leaves clasping the stem with their arrow-shaped bases. The upper part of the stem branches into several many-flowered racemes with white flowers growing on long stalks. These mature into unwinged heart-shaped fruits tipped by long styles; they do not break open but break up into one-seeded portions which are then dispersed. Hoary Cress is a native of central Asia but it has become widely naturalized in many parts of Europe. At one time its seeds were ground up and used as pepper.

		J F M A M J J A S O N D
Family	**Cruciferae**	
Synonym	*Lepidium draba*	
Other names	**Thanet Cress**	
Status	**Becoming locally common**	
Distribution	**Mainly in south and east**	
Height	**20—50 cm**	

Field Penny-cress

Thlaspi arvense

Penny-cresses are usually spring-flowering plants, some annual and others perennial. Their compressed round fruits are said to resemble pennies, giving them their common name. Field Penny-cress is a pale green annual plant which has no leaf rosette, unlike many of the annual crucifers. The stems are erect and unbranched with alternate arrow-shaped leaves which clasp the stems with their bases. The white four-petalled flowers are borne in a terminal raceme, short and dense at first, becoming elongated and sparse as the fruits ripen. The fruit is heart-shaped, broadly winged and deeply notched with a tiny remnant of the style in the notch. Field Penny-cress grows in arable land and waste places throughout Europe and much of Asia.

		J F M A M J J A S O N D
Family	**Cruciferae**	
Status	**Locally common**	
Distribution	**Mainly south and east**	
Height	**10—50 cm**	

Wild Radish

Raphanus raphanistrum

This plant is one of the most widespread field weeds. Because of its yellow flowers and generally similar appearance, it is often mistaken for Charlock, but it can be reliably identified by its sepals which are pressed against the petals while in Charlock the sepals are open and spreading. Wild Radish is a large annual plant with an erect stem and lyre-shaped divided lower leaves, toothed or lobed upper leaves. The whole plant is covered in bristly hairs. The flowers vary in colour from white or pale lilac to yellow, they are borne in loose racemes and are followed by distinctive fruits. These are beaked and cylindrical in shape with 3−8 seeds and they do not split open but break into single-seeded sections along the lines of the deep constrictions.

Family	**Cruciferae**	
Other names	**White Charlock**	
Status	**Common**	J F M A M J J A S O N D
Distribution	**Throughout Britain**	
Height	**30−60 cm**	

Yellow Ball Mustard

Neslia paniculata

This is an annual plant, tall and slender with a coarsely hairy greyish-green stem and an inflorescence of yellow flowers at the top. The lowermost leaves are oblong with narrow stalks, but further up the stem the leaves become lance-shaped with arrow-shaped bases clasping the stem. Terminal racemes of golden-yellow flowers open from the bottom upwards, elongating in fruit with distinctive hard ball-like fruits growing on long stalks. Each fruit has one seed, a short pointed tip and is covered with a network of fine wrinkles. This Eurasian species grows on fertile clay soils in cornfields and amongst root and tuber crops, also in wastelands particularly in lowland areas.

Family	**Cruciferae**	
Synonym	***Myagrium paniculatum***	
Status	**Casual**	J F M A M J J A S O N D
Distribution	**Occasional**	
Height	**15−80 cm**	

Wild Mignonette

Reseda lutea

Wild Mignonette is an annual or biennial plant with a rosette of basal leaves from which grows a relatively erect short branched stem, rough in texture and with longitudinal ridges. The basal leaves soon wither but there are many stem leaves; these are divided with blunt lobes growing almost at right angles to the central blade. The stems are terminated by loose racemes of greenish-yellow flowers, each with six sepals, six petals split into many linear segments and many yellow stamens. The capsules which follow the flowers are oblong in shape, covered with tubercles and open at the top to release the many seeds. Wild Mignonette grows on roadside verges, railway embankments, waste ground and arable land, more rarely in vineyards, especially on calcareous soils in central and southern Europe.

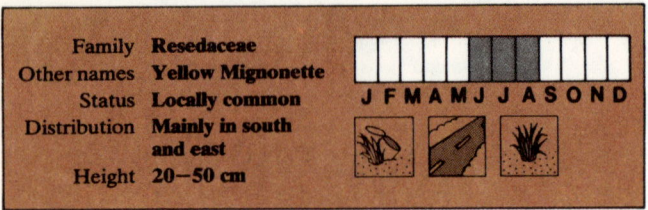

Family	Resedaceae	
Other names	Yellow Mignonette	
Status	Locally common	J F M A M J J A S O N D
Distribution	Mainly in south and east	
Height	20—50 cm	

Wild Pansy

Viola tricolor

This species is often mistaken for the Field Violet (*V. arvensis*), both are common field weeds growing in waste ground and on cultivated land, but *V. tricolor* grows mostly in acid soils while *V. arvensis* prefers basic soils. There is also a subspecies of *V. tricolor* that grows on sand dunes and in grassy places near the sea. Wild Pansy is an annual or perennial plant with several branched stems forming a sprawling clump. The long-stalked leaves are simple, variable in shape and there are large lobed stipules where the leaf-stalk joins the stem. The pansy flowers are blue-violet in colour with a long spur at the back; sometimes they are partly white or yellow but they are never entirely yellow or yellow-white like the flowers of *V. arvensis*. The stems and leaves are occasionally used in ointments to treat skin rashes like eczema.

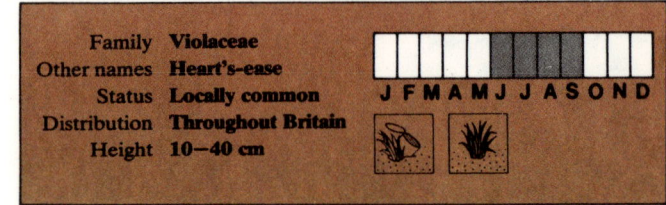

Family	Violaceae	
Other names	Heart's-ease	
Status	Locally common	J F M A M J J A S O N D
Distribution	Throughout Britain	
Height	10—40 cm	

Upright Yellow Sorrel

Oxalis europaea

Originally a North American species, this oxalis has spread as a weed throughout Europe and Asia. It is increasingly common in central and western Europe in gardens, arable land and wasteland in towns and villages, spreading by means of seeds and creeping underground stems. It has a solitary erect stem with whorls of three-lobed leaves and small clusters of yellow five-petalled flowers growing in the axils of the leaves. The flowers are followed by large cylindrical capsules with many seeds.

Family	Oxalidaceae	
Status	Locally common	
Distribution	South and central England	
Height	10—40 cm	

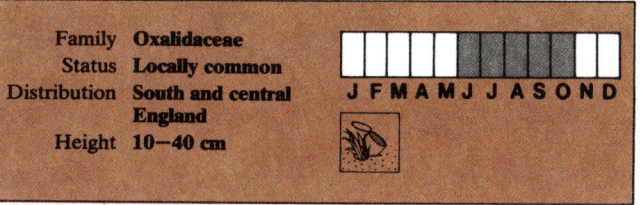

J F M A M J J A S O N D

Common Stork's-bill

Erodium cicutarium

This undemanding plant is common in Europe and Asia from lowlands to mountain foothills in dry grassland and arable fields, especially on sandy soils and near the sea; it also grows on sand dunes on the coast. It forms a small clump of finely divided leaves and straggling flower branches with clusters of four pink flowers. These are followed by long-beaked dehiscent fruits. The fruit does not release individual seeds but splits into five sections, each terminated by a long spirally coiled awn which looks like a corkscrew. In dry weather the awn shortens and forms a close coil but it straightens with increasing humidity; the effect is to drill the seed into the ground. This hygroscopic property can be used to predict the weather.

Family	Geraniaceae	
Status	Locally common	
Distribution	Mainly in south and east	
Height	10—60 cm	

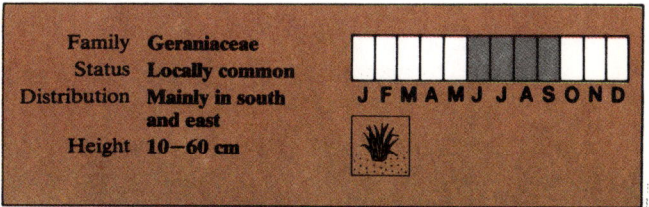

J F M A M J J A S O N D

175

Fool's Parsley
Aethusa cynapium

This is usually a tall annual plant with a smooth waxy hollow stem and compound leaves with many toothed triangular leaflets. Sometimes it only grows up to 30 cm tall, in which case it can be mistaken for parsley, a serious error for this plant contains the same poison as Hemlock, hence the name Fool's Parsley. The poison causes a burning sensation in the throat and dizziness. Terminal umbels of white flowers are borne on the stems and long drooping bracts can be seen beneath the umbels. The flowers are followed by egg-shaped deeply grooved fruits. Fool's Parsley grows in cultivated ground throughout much of Europe.

Family	Umbelliferae
Other names	False Parsley
Status	Common
Distribution	Rare in the north
Height	10—120 cm

J F M A M J J A S O N D

Cultivated Flax
Linum usitatissimum

One of the oldest medicinal and utility plants, Cultivated Flax was probably developed from the biennial or perennial species *L. bienne,* and has been cultivated since the Neolithic period. It was probably native to Mesopotamia and Egypt. It is grown for its linseed oil which is used in the paint industry and also for protecting wood (especially cricket bats); for its linseed cake which is formed of the remains of the seeds after the oil has been pressed out and is used as cattle food; and for its fibres which form the basis of linen. It is a tall erect annual plant, with a solitary stem covered with numerous linear leaves and an inflorescence of bright blue flowers. The fruits are rounded five-celled capsules, nondehiscent in the cultivated flax. It is usually grown in good fertile soils with a high percentage of organic material.

Family	Linaceae
Status	Rare. Sometimes cultivated
Distribution	Occasional
Height	30—60 cm

J F M A M J J A S O N D

Sun Spurge

Euphorbia helioscopia

An annual plant, a common weed of cultivated ground throughout Europe. It has a hairless erect stem with alternate oval leaves and a terminal head of flowers, all filled with the milky juice found in all spurges. This is said to be useful for burning off warts although care is needed to ensure that the surrounding skin is not damaged. The minute flowers consist of a ring of male flowers, each with a single stamen, surrounding a single female flower consisting of a single stalked ovary. These tiny flower clusters are cupped in green bracts and many are gathered together to form the flat terminal flower-heads. The flowers are followed by three-celled capsules which split open with an explosive crack, expelling the seeds. These have fleshy outgrowths which attract ants who carry them away.

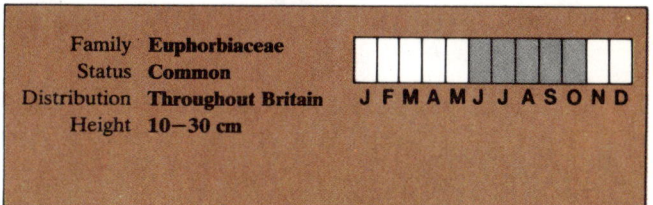

Family	**Euphorbiaceae**	
Status	**Common**	
Distribution	**Throughout Britain**	J F M A M J J A S O N D
Height	**10—30 cm**	

Small Nettle

Urtica urens

Like the Common Stinging Nettle (*U. dioica*), this plant has erect angular stems and opposite toothed leaves, all covered with stinging hairs. However, it differs in several significant ways from that plant. It is annual and it is monoecious (that is, it bears both male and female flowers on the same plant, unlike the Stinging Nettle which has separate male and female plants). The small unisexual flowers are crowded into numerous clusters in the axils of the leaves. The female flowers are more numerous than the males; both have sepals which are pale green, bristly and stinging, there are no petals. The single-seeded fruits are enclosed in the persistent sepals and are covered with glandular hairs. Small Nettle grows in wasteland and cultivated land, especially in light sandy soils throughout the Northern Hemisphere.

Family	**Urticaceae**	
Other names	**Annual Nettle**	
Status	**Locally common**	J F M A M J J A S O N D
Distribution	**Much of Britain**	
Height	**15—45 cm**	

Dwarf Spurge
Euphorbia exigua

This small pale green annual is one of the smallest species of its genus and grows as an arable field and garden weed in the warmer regions of Europe as well as in northern Africa and Asia Minor. It grows often in calcareous clay soils with root and tuber crops, vegetables and corn. It has an erect, sometimes branched stem, smooth and hairless and blue-green in colour, with alternate linear leaves and loose terminal clusters of flowers. The flowers are similar to those of the Sun Spurge. The capsules are three-celled and smooth, and contain pale grey seeds which are attractive to ants by way of their fleshy appendages.

Family	Euphorbiaceae
Status	Common
Distribution	England, Wales and Scotland
Height	5—30 cm

J F M A M J J A S O N D

Buckwheat
Fagopyrum esculentum

An erect annual plant, smooth with purple-tinged stems and alternate heart-shaped leaves. The pink or white pink-tinged flowers grow in spikes in branched inflorescences, opposite to the leaves. The flowers are bell-shaped with petal-like sepals and no petals. They are followed by large brown nuts. This plant was widely cultivated in the Middle Ages as a cereal and fodder plant, but was later replaced by other grains. It is now being grown again and the nuts are ground into flour and used to make pancakes, porridge and bread. It is also used in herb medicine to treat eczema and liver complaints and is rich in minerals. It grows best in damp ground and, in the wild, is found in waste places and cultivated land.

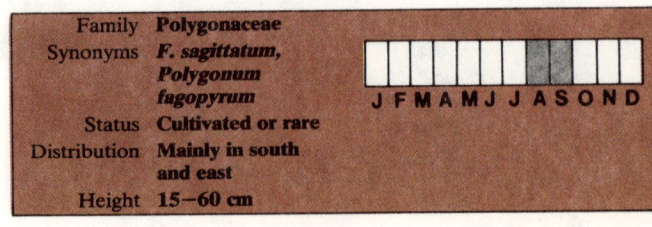

Family	Polygonaceae
Synonyms	*F. sagittatum, Polygonum fagopyrum*
Status	Cultivated or rare
Distribution	Mainly in south and east
Height	15—60 cm

J F M A M J J A S O N D

Broad-leaved Dock

Rumex obtusifolius

This tough perennial plant grows in cultivated ground, waste places, gardens and hedgerows, usually in disturbed soil. It grows best in good soil which makes it a troublesome weed. It is firmly anchored in the ground by its long taproot, from which grows a basal clump of long-stalked leaves each with a large, broadly elliptical blade, smooth entire margin and a blunt end. From this clump grows an erect branched stem with lance-shaped leaves on the lower part and many whorls of small green flowers, followed by whorls of distinctive three-sided fruits. Each fruit is green with one large red tubercle in the centre.

Family	**Polygonaceae**												
Status	**Common**												
Distribution	**Throughout Britain**	J	F	M	A	M	J	J	A	S	O	N	D
Height	**50—120 cm**												

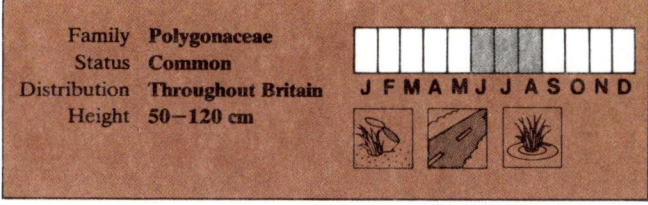

Curled Dock

Rumex crispus

Another perennial European species that often grows in the company of Broad-leaved Dock in fields and meadows, wasteland and gardens, roadsides and hedgerows throughout the Northern Hemisphere from lowlands to mountain areas. It also grows on shingle foreshores and on stable sand dunes in coastal areas. It can be distinguished from the previous species by the curly edges of its long lance-shaped pointed leaves which form the ground rosette. It has a stout taproot from which grow several erect stems with many whorls of green flowers followed by heart-shaped three-sided fruits. Each fruit has three red tubercles in the centre, one larger than the other two. The roots are used in herb medicine as a laxative and to treat irritations of the skin and throat.

Family	**Polygonaceae**												
Status	**Common**												
Distribution	**Throughout Britain**	J	F	M	A	M	J	J	A	S	O	N	D
Height	**30—100 cm**												

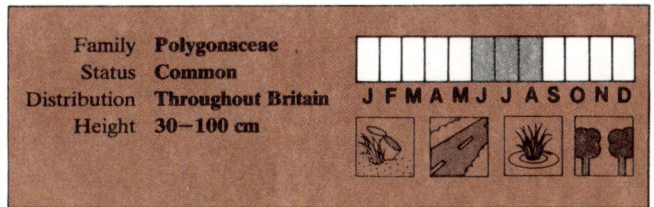

Night-flowering Campion

Silene noctiflora

This leafy annual plant grows in lowland areas, in arable land especially on light sandy soils. It has an erect stem with large simple leaves, all covered with glandular very sticky hairs. The flowers are borne in pairs in small clusters terminating the stems. Unlike the majority of flowering plants, this one opens its flowers in the evening. They remain rolled up in the day, showing only their dull yellow undersides, but open as the day cools until their pink upper surfaces and their fragrance attracts the moths which act as pollinators. The flowers are followed by brown egg-shaped capsules which open by six teeth at the top to release the seeds.

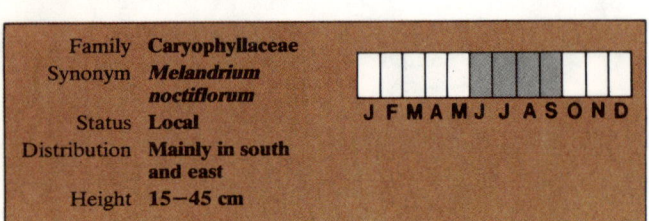

Family	Caryophyllaceae		
Synonym	*Melandrium noctiflorum*		
Status	Local		
Distribution	Mainly in south and east		
Height	15—45 cm		

J F M A M J J A S O N D

Corn Cockle

Agrostemma githago

Once a common and undesirable annual weed of cornfields, this plant has now been virtually eliminated by modern farming techniques, so that there is a certain anxiety about its survival. It was native to the Mediterranean and spread from there with the cereals with which it grew. In the past, the black-brown poisonous seeds were often mixed in flour during milling, turning it grey and bitter. An admixture of five per cent was dangerous for man and cattle. The seeds contain a toxic saponin which has a laxative effect at first, later penetrating the blood system and damaging the red blood cells. Corn Cockle has tall stems and opposite linear leaves, all covered with silky white hairs. The solitary reddish-purple flowers have woolly sepals, each elongated into a long linear tooth. The warty black seeds are borne in egg-shaped capsules.

Family	Caryophyllaceae		
Synonyms	*Lychnis githago, Githago segetum*		
Status	Rare		
Distribution	Mainly in south and east		
Height	50—100 cm		

J F M A M J J A S O N D

Thyme-leaved Sandwort
Arenaria serpyllifolia

This tiny annual or biennial plant is often overlooked. It is a small field weed, found mostly on poor light soils among root and tuber crops and winter cereals; also on bare ground in wasteland and chalk downs, on walls and sea cliffs. It cannot compete with taller growing plants and is therefore most likely to be found on bare ground. This sandwort forms a small clump of trailing stems covered with small oval roughly hairy, opposite leaves in the axils of which grow the flowers. These are tiny, solitary with five white petals alternating with five green sepals. They are followed by flask-shaped capsules partly enclosed by the persistent sepals.

Family	Caryophyllaceae
Status	Common
Distribution	Throughout Britain
Height	5–20 cm

J F M A M J J A S O N D

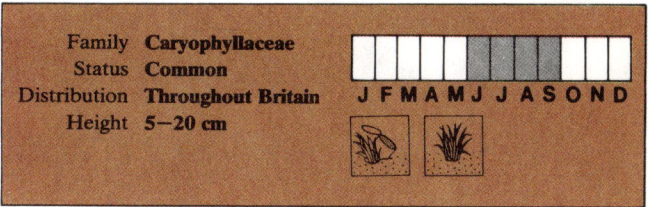

Corn Spurrey
Spergula arvensis

Corn Spurrey is an annual plant with weak grass-green stems, hairless below and glandular above. The linear leaves grow in whorled clusters, and from the axils of the leaves grow branched inflorescences of white flowers on long stalks. Corn Spurrey was used as a food plant up to the Middle Ages, the seeds were ground up and used to make porridge; it is still used as a cattle fodder plant in some parts of Europe, when it is said to improve the quality of the milk. When growing in cornfields it is an undesirable weed for it reduces the yield of wheat and other cereals. It usually grows in sandy acid soils and is found throughout much of the world.

Family	Caryophyllaceae
Status	Locally common
Distribution	Throughout Britain
Height	10–40 cm

J F M A M J J A S O N D

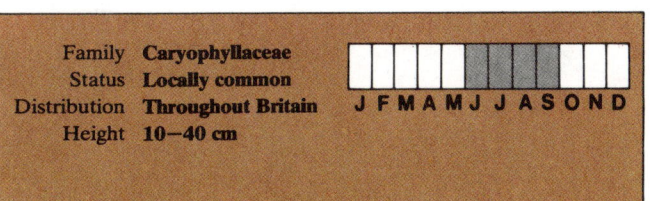

Sand Spurrey
Spergularia rubra

Sand Spurrey grows in barren sandy lime-free, rather acid soils in fields and waste ground throughout the whole of the Northern Hemisphere. This small annual plant has thin trailing stems forming spreading clumps, and narrow linear pointed flat leaves growing in pairs on the stems. At the base of the leaves are silvery-brown rather membranous stipules. The flowers have reddish-pink petals alternating with green sepals and are borne in small terminal clusters. They are followed by small brown capsules opening by three valves to release the ovoid warty seeds.

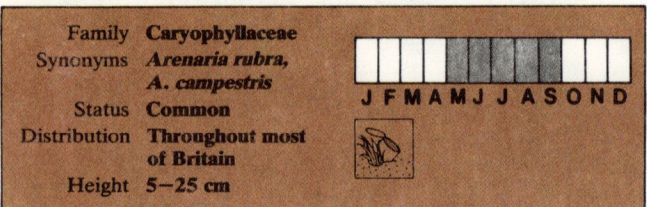

Family	**Caryophyllaceae**	
Synonyms	***Arenaria rubra, A. campestris***	
Status	**Common**	
Distribution	**Throughout most of Britain**	
Height	**5—25 cm**	

Annual Knawel
Scleranthus annuus

This plant was not always included in the family Caryophyllaceae. At one time it was classified, together with its relatives in the genera *Herniaria, Corrigiola* and *Illecebrum,* into the family Illecebraceae. They all have dry one-seeded fruits which do not split open, very different to the many-seeded capsules of the rest of the Caryophyllaceae. Annual Knawel is an annual or biennial plant with branched trailing stems and opposite narrow awl-shaped leaves joined together across the stems by their membranous margins. The tiny green flowers grow in dense clusters in leaf axils; they have five green sepals and no petals and are probably self-pollinated. The plant grows in dry cultivated ground and waste places on lime-free sandy soils throughout much of the Northern Hemisphere.

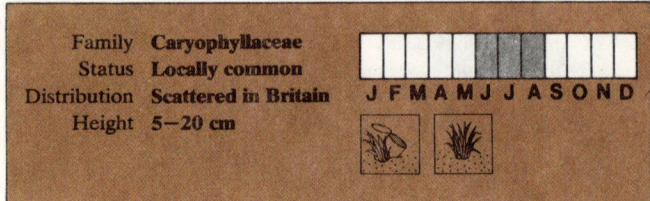

Family	**Caryophyllaceae**	
Status	**Locally common**	
Distribution	**Scattered in Britain**	
Height	**5—20 cm**	

All-seed

Chenopodium polyspermum

This European and western Siberian species is a tall annual plant with a rather weak erect branched stem, often with a reddish tinge. This colour is often also seen on the long stalks of the oval hairless leaves and on the leaves themselves. The flowers grow in small clusters, which are in turn grouped into long loose inflorescences growing in the leaf axils. The flowers are rather star-like, each with five rounded green sepals and no petals; they are followed by thin membranous fruits with characteristic black pitted seeds. All-seed grows in waste places and cultivated ground in fields and gardens, especially in wet places.

Family	Chenopodiaceae
Status	Locally common
Distribution	South and central England
Height	15—60 cm

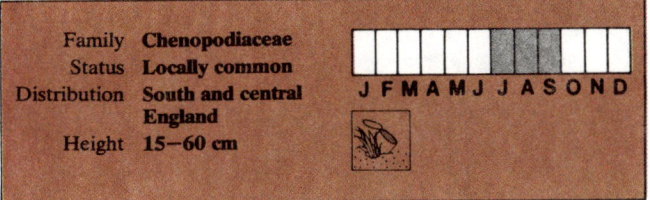

J F M A M J J A S O N D

Scarlet Pimpernel

Anagallis arvensis

Scarlet Pimpernel is an annual or perennial plant with weak trailing branched stems and stalkless oval opposite leaves. From the axils of these leaves grow the solitary funnel-shaped brick-red flowers on long stalks. Flowering occurs from spring to autumn with only a few flowers open at any one time. The flowers open only in the morning and early afternoon in sunshine and remain closed in cloudy or wet weather — this feature gives the plant its name of Shepherd's Weather Glass. The fruits are glossy spherical capsules enclosed in the sepals and opening by a lid at the top to release the small seeds. This plant grows throughout many of the temperate parts of the world, on cultivated land, on roadsides and on stable sand dunes.

Family	Primulaceae
Other names	Shepherd's Weather Glass
Status	Common
Distribution	England, Wales and Ireland
Height	5—30 cm

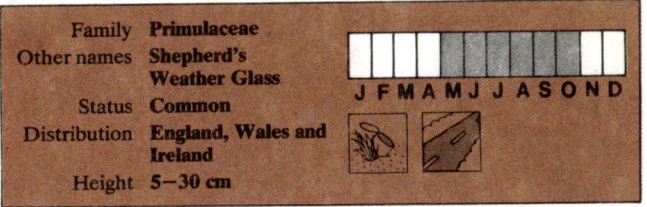

J F M A M J J A S O N D

Bugloss
Anchusa arvensis

This coarse annual or biennial plant is covered with rough spreading bristly hairs. It has an erect stem with stalkless long lance-shaped leaves with wavy margins. The funnel-shaped flowers are borne in terminal one-sided branched clusters; they are pink in bud, turning blue as they open and they each have a white throat. The flowers are followed by four warty elongated nutlets enclosed in the persistent sepals. Bugloss grows in light sandy soils or on chalk downs in cultivated land and heathland especially near the sea.

Family	Boraginaceae		J F M A M J J A S O N D
Synonym	*Lycopsis arvensis*		
Status	Locally common		
Distribution	England, Wales and Scotland		
Height	20—40 cm		

Lesser Bindweed
Convolvulus arvensis

This is a common weed in many different habitats throughout the temperate regions of the world. It grows in wasteland and gardens, arable land and hedgerows, roadsides and railway embankments inland, and is a common plant of shingle foreshores and waste land near the sea, especially on basic soils. It is difficult to eradicate because of the massive root and underground stem system, penetrating to a depth of 3—5 metres. The long slender stems with long-stalked leaves and flowers are prostrate or twine left-handedly about other plants and wire fences. The pink or white broadly funnel-shaped flowers grow in the axils of the arrow-shaped leaves and are open in the morning, closed after midday. The fruits are 2—4 seeded capsules. This bindweed can be used in herb medicine as a laxative and to alleviate fevers.

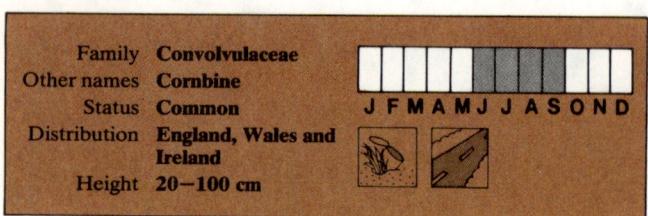

Family	Convolvulaceae		J F M A M J J A S O N D
Other names	Cornbine		
Status	Common		
Distribution	England, Wales and Ireland		
Height	20—100 cm		

Corn Gromwell

Lithospermum arvense

Like many of the annual weeds of cornfields and arable land, this plant is much less common than it used to be, due to modern agricultural techniques and selective weedkillers. It grows in dry soils in cultivated ground and wasteland throughout Europe and much of Asia. It has an erect stem growing from a long taproot and lance-shaped alternate leaves. The lower leaves usually wither before the flowering period. The funnel-shaped flowers are small, yellowish white or occasionally bluish, and grow in short terminal clusters which elongate during flowering. The five hairy sepals are fused to form a tubular calyx which persists after flowering to enclose the four pointed warty nutlets. A single specimen may produce up to 200 fruits.

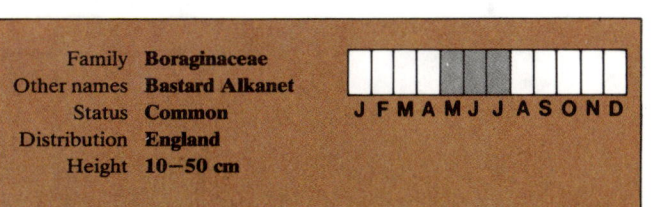

Family	**Boraginaceae**	
Other names	**Bastard Alkanet**	
Status	**Common**	
Distribution	**England**	
Height	**10—50 cm**	

J F M A M J J A S O N D

Common Forget-me-not

Myosotis arvensis

This is an erect or rather sprawling annual plant with a basal rosette of rounded-oval leaves from which grow several erect leafy inflorescences, all covered with short hairs. At the beginning of the summer the blue flowers are borne in tightly curled one-sided clusters, but these elongate and straighten as the summer goes on. Each funnel-shaped flower has a yellow ring at its centre. The flowers are followed by dark brown shiny nutlets enclosed in the persistent sepals. This forget-me-not grows throughout Europe and western Asia in cultivated ground, in gardens and arable land, in woodland and on stable sand dunes near the sea.

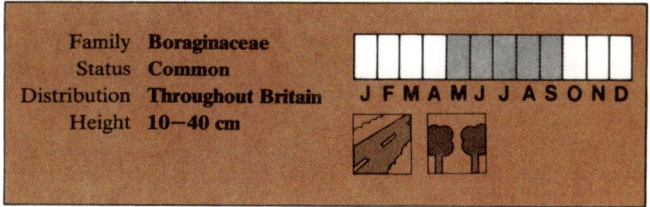

Family	**Boraginaceae**	
Status	**Common**	
Distribution	**Throughout Britain**	
Height	**10—40 cm**	

J F M A M J J A S O N D

Red Deadnettle
Lamium purpureum

This is an annual plant which germinates from seed in winter and soon forms leafy clumps, low and spreading in open waste ground and cultivated land, taller and looser in habit in woodland. The four-angled stems are erect, bearing many coarsely toothed hairy opposite leaves and purplish-red flowers growing in whorls in the axils of the upper leaves, which often become purple like the flowers. Each flower is two-lipped with a hooded upper lip concealing the anthers and a three-lobed lower lip forming a landing platform for pollinating bees. The four nutlets which form the fruit are concealed at the bottom of the sepal tube.

Family	Labiatae
Status	Very common
Distribution	Throughout Britain
Height	10—35 cm

J F M A M J J A S O N D

Henbit
Lamium amplexicaule

An annual plant with erect stems bearing rounded lobed leaves, the lowermost with long stalks, the upper ones with shorter stalks. The pinkish-purple flowers grow in a few sparse whorls in the axils of the upper leaves; each has five sepals fused into a tube which is covered in long white hairs. The flowers are two-lipped, rather like those of Red Deadnettle, but slimmer and protruding further from the sepals than in that plant. Henbit also produces small closed flowers in unfavourable weather and these are self-pollinated. The flowers are followed by four triangular nutlets enclosed by the persistent sepals. This plant grows in dry cultivated ground throughout much of Europe except the far north.

Family	Labiatae
Status	Relatively common
Distribution	Mainly in eastern areas
Height	10—25 cm

J F M A M J J A S O N D

Common Hempnettle

Galeopsis tetrahit

This annual plant has erect stems which are swollen just beneath the places where the leaves join the stem (the nodes). The stems are covered with glandular red-tipped hairs, particularly in the swollen areas. The opposite leaves are oval or lance-shaped, toothed and hairy, with whorls of flowers in the axils of the uppermost ones. Each flower has four hairy sepals fused to form a tubular calyx with five long pointed teeth. The flower is two-lipped, the upper lip hooded, the lower lip with three teeth and with darker markings in the centre. Flower colour varies considerably from pink or purple to white. Common Hempnettle grows in arable land, heathland or woods often in wetter ground, throughout Europe.

Family	**Labiatae**	
Status	**Common**	
Distribution	**Throughout Britain**	J F M A M J J A S O N D
Height	**10—40 cm**	

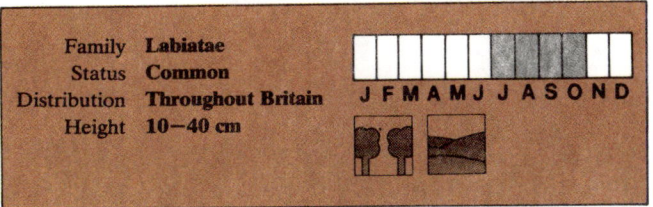

Large-flowered Hempnettle

Galeopsis speciosa

This species can be distinguished from the Common Hempnettle (*G. tetrahit*) by its less swollen stems and yellow-tipped, not red-tipped, glandular hairs which cover all the stems. It is a robust plant with erect stems, opposite toothed leaves and several whorls of flowers. The flowers are two-lipped, like those of the Common Hempnettle, but pale yellow in colour with a violet three-lobed lower lip and they protrude far out of the tubular sepals. This Large-flowered Hempnettle grows in cultivated ground throughout Europe and Asia, especially in moist peaty soil, from lowlands to the lower mountain elevations.

Family	**Labiatae**	
Status	**Local**	
Distribution	**Scattered over Britain**	J F M A M J J A S O N D
Height	**50—100 cm**	

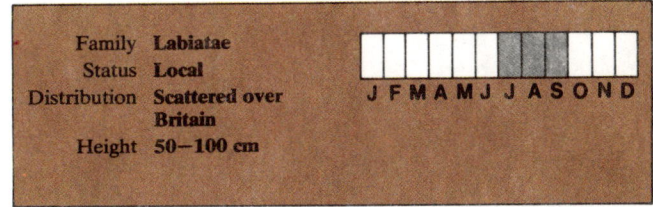

Black Nightshade

Solanum nigrum

The poisonous Black Nightshade belongs to the same family as the Tomato (*S. lycopersicum*) and the Potato (*S. tuberosum*). It is an annual herb with erect stems and simple broadly oval, slightly lobed leaves, forming a rather bushy upright plant. It bears small clusters of white flowers in the leaf axils. The flowers are characteristic of the family; they are broad and funnel-shaped with five petals and a central yellow cone formed by the stamens. The flower-clusters are followed by clusters of berries, definitely poisonous in the green stage but becoming less so when ripe and black. This plant is related to the Woody Nightshade (*S. dulcamara*), a climbing plant with purple flowers and red berries. Black Nightshade grows in cultivated ground in gardens and arable land and on wasteland throughout much of the world.

Family	Solanaceae	
Status	Common	
Distribution	Mainly in England	J F M A M J J A S O N D
Height	10—80 cm	

Corn Mint

Mentha arvensis

A very variable perennial plant with more or less erect branched stems and oval toothed leaves growing in opposite pairs. This mint smells quite unlike the others and, if growing in a field of peppermint, can spoil the scent and flavour of the other plants. It has dense whorls of small lilac funnel-shaped flowers growing spaced out along the stems and not in dense whorled spikes like those found in the other common mint, *M. aquatica*. Corn Mint grows in arable fields, meadows and open woodland, especially in damper spots, throughout much of Europe. A variety of Corn Mint, *M. arvensis* var. *piperascens,* is grown in Japan for the high content of menthol in the peppermint oil extracted from it.

Family	Labiatae	
Status	Common	
Distribution	Throughout Britain	J F M A M J J A S O N D
Height	15—50 cm	

188

Ivy-leaved Speedwell

Veronica hederifolia

This is a low-growing plant with many branched ascending hairy stems. The lower leaves are opposite, the upper ones alternate, sparsely hairy and stalked. They are pale green and thick, rounded or oval in shape with 2 or 3 small lobes near the base. From the axils of the leaves grow the small flowers, measuring 2–2.5 mm across, with pale blue or whitish petals, shorter than the green sepals. The flowers are followed by hairless ovoid capsules which are enclosed in the persistent sepals. There are two cells in the capsule, each containing two seeds. Ivy-leaved Speedwell is an annual plant which sometimes germinates in the autumn. It flowers in the spring. It grows in cultivated ground throughout Europe and much of Asia.

Family	Scrophulariaceae	
Status	Common	
Distribution	Throughout Britain	J F M A M J J A S O N D
Height	5–30 cm	

Fingered Speedwell

Veronica triphyllos

This short-lived annual plant flowers in spring. It is a low-growing spreading plant with little-branched stems and sparsely hairy opposite rounded leaves. The leaves are deeply palmately lobed with 3–5 large oblong lobes, the lowermost leaves are stalked, the uppermost stalkless. In the axils of the leaves grow flowers on long hairy glandular flower-stalks, in sparse terminal racemes. The deep blue funnel-shaped flowers are followed by rounded glandular-hairy capsules containing egg-shaped seeds. This speedwell was originally a European steppe species which has spread to fields and wasteland communities in many lowland areas of Europe. It is rare in Britain, growing in sandy fields in a few localities in Norfolk and Suffolk.

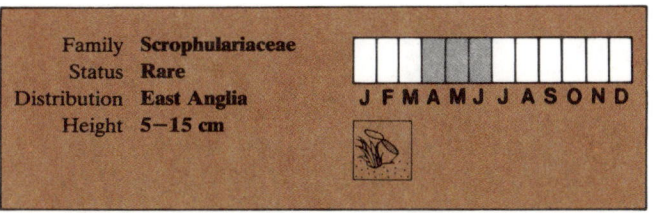

Family	Scrophulariaceae	
Status	Rare	
Distribution	East Anglia	J F M A M J J A S O N D
Height	5–15 cm	

Buxbaum's Speedwell

Veronica persica

The scientific name of this speedwell reflects the probable place of its origin in Persia. It was introduced to Europe in the 19th century when it escaped from a botanical garden in Germany, and it has spread widely in fields and gardens since then. It is a remarkably resistant plant, growing and even flowering in a mild winter. It is an annual plant with many branched stems forming a sprawling clump. The bright blue flowers are funnel-shaped with four petals; the lowermost petal is often paler than the others, sometimes even whitish. The flowers grow in the axils of the rounded lobed hairy leaves; they do not last long, the petals soon fall off as a single unit together with the stamens, leaving the two-lobed capsule enclosed by the persistent sepals.

Family	**Scrophulariaceae**	
Synonyms	***V. buxbaumii,***	
	V. tournefortii	
Status	**Common**	
Distribution	**Throughout Britain**	
Height	**15—40 cm**	

J F M A M J J A S O N D

Small Toadflax

Chaenorhinum minus

This small annual plant has an erect much-branched stem, covered in glandular hairs. The dark green leaves are lance-shaped, opposite at the base and alternate higher up the stem. The tiny solitary flowers grow on long stalks from the upper leaf axils; they are highly distinctive, rather like small snapdragons, purple in colour with a gaping mouth and a small spur at the back. The fused sepals are much shorter than the petals and have five linear teeth. The flowers are followed by ovoid capsules partly concealed by the persistent sepals. This light-loving species grows in all kinds of soils in arable land, vineyards and waste ground in central and southern Europe. In Britain it is also likely to be found in railway sidings, on walls and chalk cliffs.

Family	**Scrophulariaceae**	
Synonym	***Linaria minor***	
Status	**Common**	
Distribution	**England, Ireland**	
	and Wales	
Height	**5—20 cm**	

J F M A M J J A S O N D

Greater Yellow Rattle

Rhinanthus angustifolius

This is one of the semi-parasitic species of the family Scrophulariaceae. Its roots become attached to the grasses on which it is parasitic, obtaining water and nutrients from the host. But it is not wholly dependent on the host, it has green leaves and can photosynthesise food with its leaves. Greater Yellow Rattle is an annual plant with an erect little-branched sparsely hairy stem. The stem is quadrangular, black-lined and bears lance-shaped deeply toothed opposite leaves. At the top of the stem is the terminal inflorescence of hooded yellow stalkless flowers, each with violet teeth. The flowers are partly concealed by the sepals which are fused to form a swollen bladder-like calyx which persists after flowering to enclose the capsule. The plant grows in cornfields, damp meadows or dunes throughout Europe, but is rare in Britain.

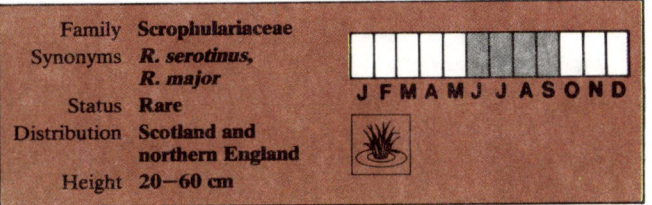

Family	Scrophulariaceae
Synonyms	*R. serotinus, R. major*
Status	Rare
Distribution	Scotland and northern England
Height	20—60 cm

J F M A M J J A S O N D

Red Bartsia

Odontites verna

This is a common plant of fields and fallow ground, wasteland and roadsides from lowlands to submontane elevations in Europe and Asia. At one time it was used in herb medicine to alleviate toothache, hence its Latin name. It is an erect annual plant with a branched stem and opposite lance-shaped leaves. The flowers are borne in long slender terminal racemes; they are a dull red in colour, two-lipped with a hooded upper lip and a three-lobed lower lip with rounded teeth. The four sepals are fused into a bell-shaped calyx, which persists after flowering to enclose the fruiting capsule. Red Bartsia is like the eyebrights in that it is semi-parasitic in its way of life; its roots obtain water and nutrients from the roots of grasses.

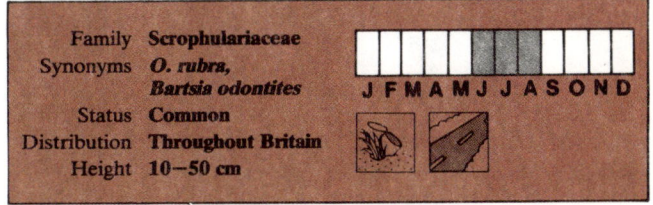

Family	Scrophulariaceae
Synonyms	*O. rubra, Bartsia odontites*
Status	Common
Distribution	Throughout Britain
Height	10—50 cm

J F M A M J J A S O N D

Great Plantain

Plantago major

This is a low-growing perennial herb with a basal rosette of large rounded stalked leaves, each with 5—9 veins. From the leaf rosette grow several leafless flower stalks terminated by elongated cylindrical spikes of green flowers. The spike is as long as or longer than the stalk. Each tiny flower has four greenish sepals and four membranous yellowish-white petals. The most noticeable feature of the flowering spike is the stamens, which have white filaments and lilac or yellow anthers projecting out at right angles to the flowering spike. Since the flowers open from the bottom of the spike upwards, there appears to be a ring of stamens which travels upwards as the flowers open. Great Plantain is a common weed of wasteland and cultivated ground throughout Europe and Asia. It is used in herb medicine to treat diarrhoea and piles.

Family	Plantaginaceae	J F M A M J J A S O N D
Status	Common	
Distribution	Throughout Britain	
Height	5—30 cm	

Field Cow-wheat

Melampyrum arvense

This is an attractive plant with a solid erect branched stem and opposite stalkless lance-shaped leaves, entire at the base of the plant but with long teeth higher up the stem. The flowers are borne in rather loose terminal spikes in the axils of pinkish bracts; they are pink with pink lips and a yellow throat. They are tubular in shape and partly enclosed by the green sepals which are also fused into a tube. The sepals persist after flowering to enclose the two-seeded capsules. This rather hairy annual plant is a semi-parasite growing in grassy places and in arable fields from lowlands to hillsides throughout Europe. It is rare in Britain, however, growing only in a few cornfields in southern England and East Anglia.

Family	Scrophulariaceae	J F M A M J J A S O N D
Status	Rare	
Distribution	South England and East Anglia	
Height	15—50 cm	

Lamb's Lettuce

Valerianella dentata

This annual field herb has a basal rosette of rounded-oval leaves and slender stems with a few opposite simple lance-shaped leaves. These have one or two pairs of teeth at the base. The tiny bluish-white flowers are crowded into heads, borne in rather loose terminal inflorescences, similar to those of a common relative, *V. locusta,* Corn Salad; *V. dentata* also has solitary flowers in the axils of the branches. The ovary of this plant is three-celled but only one fertile seed is produced, in a cell that is much larger than the other two. Lamb's Lettuce grows in cultivated ground, especially in cornfields, mainly in lowland areas but also in mountain regions throughout central and southern Europe.

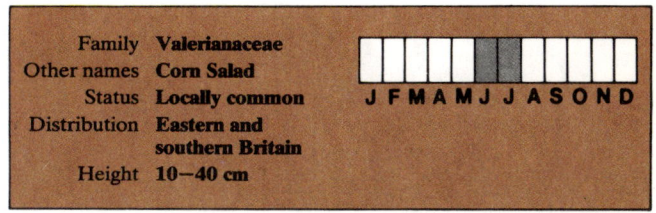

Family	Valerianaceae
Other names	Corn Salad
Status	Locally common
Distribution	Eastern and southern Britain
Height	10—40 cm

J F M A M J J A S O N D

Field Madder

Sherardia arvensis

This roughly hairy plant is an annual weed of arable fields and waste places. It probably originated in the warm regions around the Mediterranean Sea, but now it grows throughout Europe and many other temperate areas of the world. It has numerous prostrate or ascending square stems, forming a low clump. The stalkless pointed, one-veined leaves grow in whorls of four in the lower parts of the stems, and in whorls of five or six in the upper parts. The pink or violet flowers are borne in dense clusters at the tips of the stems, cupped by several green bracts so that the flower clusters look like posies. Each flower is funnel-shaped with a long tube projecting from the short sepal-tube. This persists to enclose the single-seeded fruits which are prickly and covered with white hairs; they are dispersed by animals when they become caught in their hair.

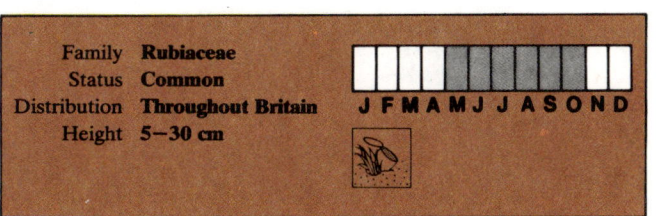

Family	Rubiaceae
Status	Common
Distribution	Throughout Britain
Height	5—30 cm

J F M A M J J A S O N D

Prickly Sowthistle

Sonchus asper

There are two related annual sowthistles which are common weeds of cultivated ground and waste places throughout Europe and northern Asia. Both produce basal rosettes of leaves from seeds which often germinate in the autumn and overwinter, and tall erect flower stalks, filled with milky juice, in the summer. The stem leaves of Prickly Sowthistle have ear-like projections which clasp the stem while the stem leaves of *S. oleraceus* (Smooth Sowthistle), although they too clasp the stem, do not have the ear-like projections. The flowers are yellow, like those of a dandelion, with many strap-shaped ray florets and are borne in clusters terminating the stem. The single-seeded fruits are crowned with two whorls of simple white hairs.

Family	**Compositae**
Other names	**Prickly Milkthistle**
Status	**Common**
Distribution	**Throughout Britain**
Height	**30—80 cm**

J F M A M J J A S O N D

Corn Chamomile

Anthemis arvensis

This aromatic annual or overwintering plant has a woolly branched stem with divided leaves, often woolly beneath especially when they are young. The solitary flower-heads are borne on long stalks; they have broad white ray florets around the outside and a central dome of yellow tubular disk florets. The single-seeded fruits which follow, are whitish in colour, smooth and hairless in texture with ribs running along their length. Corn Chamomile is a common plant in arable fields and fallow land and in wasteland, on calcareous soils throughout much of the British Isles except the far north, and in Europe.

Family	**Compositae**
Status	**Locally common**
Distribution	**Throughout Britain**
Height	**15—50 cm**

J F M A M J J A S O N D

Wild Chamomile

Matricaria recutita

This annual aromatically scented plant forms a clump with several erect smooth stems, finely divided hairless leaves and solitary daisy-like flower-heads. Each head has a ring of outer white ray florets, which turn downwards soon after the flower-head opens, and inner yellow tubular disk florets growing on a hollow receptacle. The flowers are followed by pale grey hairless single-seeded fruits. Wild Chamomile grows in cultivated ground, wasteland and waysides throughout much of the world. It is used in herb medicine to a lesser extent than the true Chamomile (*Chamaemelum nobile*), but is still effective in the treatment of gastric upset, spasm and wind, especially in children, and as a nerve tonic.

Family	**Compositae**
Synonyms	***M. chamomilla,*** ***Chamomilla recutita***
Other names	**German Chamomile**
Status	**Locally common**
Distribution	**Southern and central England**
Height	**15—60 cm**

J F M A M J J A S O N D

Cornflower

Centaurea cyanus

Once a common sight in cornfields, this attractive plant is another casualty of modern farming techniques, in particular the more efficient cleaning of grain. It can still be found occasionally in waste ground and on roadsides throughout Europe, but even in these places it is rare. It is an annual plant, with a branched wiry erect stem, lower lyre-shaped leaves and upper lance-shaped leaves, all greyish in colour and covered with cottony hairs. The solitary flower-heads are borne on long cottony stalks; they have cottony involucres and ray florets only, the outermost bright blue in colour and the innermost reddish-purple. The single-seeded fruits which follow, are silver-grey with a crown of short reddish hairs.

Family	**Compositae**
Other names	**Bluebottle**
Status	**Rare**
Distribution	**Scattered**
Height	**30—80 cm**

J F M A M J J A S O N D

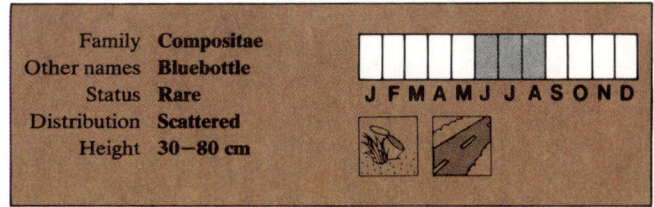

Scotch Thistle

Onoropordon acanthium

This is a biennial plant which forms a rosette of oblong lobed prickly-edged leaves in the first year. In the second year an erect winged prickly stem grows up to 1.5 metres tall; it has stalkless toothed prickly leaves. The red-violet flower-heads are borne on long stalks in the axils of the leaves. They have spherical involucres with spreading spines below and many tubular florets forming a dense head. The flowers are followed by greyish-brown single-seeded fruits, each with a ring of long, pale red toothed hairs. The stem of this plant is covered with cottony hairs which were used to stuff mattresses and pillows. It has played an important role in British history as the national emblem of Scotland.

Family	Compositae			
Other names	Cotton Thistle			
Status	Local	J F M A M J J A S O N D		
Distribution	Mainly in the south			
Height	30—150 cm			

Creeping Thistle

Cirsium arvense

A very common weed of roadsides, waste places and cultivated land throughout Europe, with creeping underground roots which make it almost impossible to eradicate. It forms wide spreading colonies of many erect flowering shoots, with divided lance-shaped prickly-edged leaves, larger at the base and becoming smaller towards the top of the plant. The flower-heads are often quite small, reddish-purple in colour with many ray florets. They are followed by many dark brown single-seeded fruits with long brownish hairs, transforming the plants with many balls of fluffy brownish hairs as each flowering head bursts open to release the fruits.

Family	Compositae			
Synonyms	*Serratula arvense,*			
	Carduus arvensis	J F M A M J J A S O N D		
Status	Very common			
Distribution	Throughout Britain			
Height	30—150 cm			

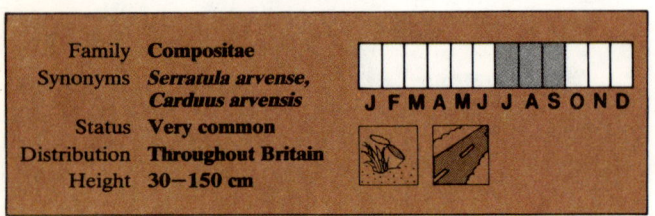

Species featured in this section

Species featured in another section

Great Spearwort
Ranunculus lingua

This is a much less common plant than the Lesser Spearwort, growing in scattered marshes and fens throughout Europe and Asia. It is much taller, with creeping stems rooting into the mud in which it grows and turning upwards to form erect flowering stalks, up to 150 cm tall. The stem leaves are linear, rather grass-like with bases clasping the stem and from the axils of the upper leaves grow several few-flowered inflorescences. The flowers are yellow, typically buttercup-like in their form and followed by typical buttercup fruits. Like the other members of the genus *Ranunculus,* this plant is poisonous with acrid sap and is avoided by cattle.

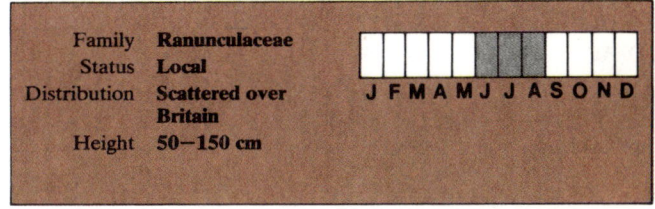

Family	Ranunculaceae		
Status	Local		
Distribution	Scattered over Britain		
Height	50—150 cm		

J F M A M J J A S O N D

Lesser Spearwort
Ranunculus flammula

Lesser Spearwort grows throughout much of Europe and Asia in marshes, wet meadows and shallow bodies of water, often on the grassy banks of ponds and in the water where it floats upon the surface. It is a perennial species with a short rootstock and sinuous prostrate stems up to 50 cm long, branched and often rooting at the lower nodes. The whole plant is smooth and hairless, coloured yellow-green, with many simple linear to lance-shaped leaves, those at the base of the stem with stalks while those higher up the stem are stalkless. Long grooved flower-stalks bear small yellow flowers, up to 1.5 cm across, followed by clusters of ovoid single-seeded fruits, each with a short beak. Lesser Spearwort is poisonous to cattle and to man, with blistering acrid sap.

Family	Ranunculaceae		
Status	Common		
Distribution	Throughout Britain		
Height	10—50 cm		

J F M A M J J A S O N D

Celery-leaved Buttercup
Ranunculus sceleratus

The most poisonous species of all the buttercups and crowfoots, the acrid sap of this species produces blisters if it comes into contact with the skin. It grows scattered throughout the Northern Hemisphere in marshy meadows, ditches and on the banks of ponds, sometimes growing even in the water where it may float on the surface. The terrestrial form has stalked divided leaves; those on the lower part of the stem have three forked lobes and those on the upper part, three linear segments. All are slightly fleshy and both the stem and leaves are smooth and glossy. The stem branches into a multiflowered inflorescence of many small pale yellow flowers. The petals are only slightly larger than the sepals and soon fall off, to be followed by a large aggregate of up to 100 single-seeded fruits.

Family	**Ranunculaceae**	
Other names	**Celery-leaved Crowfoot**	
Status	**Common**	J F M A M J J A S O N D
Distribution	**Throughout much of Britain**	
Height	**20—60 cm**	

Common Water Crowfoot
Ranunculus aquatilis

Like many other water plants, Water Crowfoot is rooted into the mud of the bottom of the water in which it grows, and its erect stem has two types of leaves. The submerged leaves are short-stalked and divided into fine segments arranged in bunches, but where the stem emerges into the air the leaves are floating with long stalks and flat rounded, three- to five-lobed kidney-shaped blades. The flowers grow on long stalks above the water. Each one has five white petals with a bright yellow blotch at the base of each petal. They are followed by clusters of single-seeded fruits, often hairy in texture, at least while they are young. Water Crowfoot grows in ponds, canals, ditches and slow-moving rivers throughout Europe.

Family	**Ranunculaceae**	
Status	**Common**	
Distribution	**Throughout much of Britain**	J F M A M J J A S O N D
Height	**10—200 cm**	

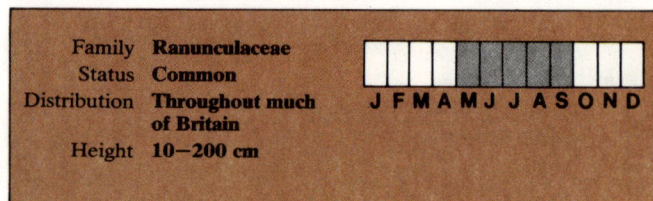

Riverine Water Crowfoot

Ranunculus fluitans

Unlike the other aquatic members of the genus *Ranunculus,* described here, this species grows in fast-flowing water in streams and rivers in both uplands and lowlands in southern and central Europe, but is absent from the more northerly areas. Its robust stems are firmly rooted to the bottom and may reach up to five metres in length, pulled downstream by the running water. Its submerged leaves are streamlined, with many long linear segments, up to 30 cm in length; it has no floating leaves. The plant has many small white flowers, borne on long stalks which project above the surface of the water. The flowers are unusual for they may have up to 10 overlapping petals which remain on the flower for some time.

Family	Ranunculaceae		
Status	Locally common		
Distribution	Mainly in England and Wales		
Height	50–500 cm		

J F M A M J J A S O N D

Common Meadow Rue

Thalictrum flavum

This quietly attractive plant grows in marshes, wet meadows and beside streams throughout Europe and northern Asia. It has creeping underground stems and many upright unbranched stems with compound leaves. Each leaf is divided and subdivided into numerous oblong leaflets. The yellowish flowers are borne in dense clusters at the tops of the stems, they are sweetly scented but petal-less and the colour comes from the conspicuous long yellow filaments and anthers. The flowers are followed by single-seeded dry brown fruits, each with six distinct ridges running along its length. Common Meadow Rue has been used in herb medicine as a laxative.

Family	Ranunculaceae		
Status	Locally common		
Distribution	England, Wales and Ireland		
Height	40–100 cm		

J F M A M J J A S O N D

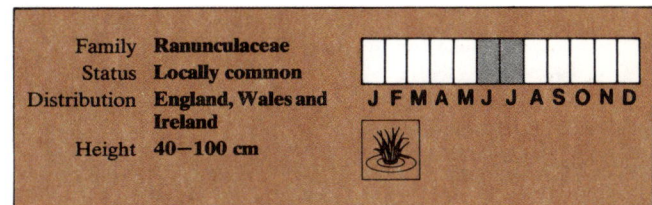

Monkshood

Aconitum napellus

A very poisonous plant, although it is highly decorative and often grown in gardens. It is a perennial, growing on the banks of upland streams, in damp screes and mountain meadows in the mountain and foothill regions in Europe and northwestern Asia. Its poisonous nature is due mostly to the presence of an alkaloid which is most highly concentrated in the root tubers. These are gathered and used in the preparation of potent pain-killers and sedatives, used only on the advice of a doctor. An old folk legend has it that the poison is in fact the saliva of the gatekeeper of the underworld, the many-headed dog Cerberus. Monkshood is a tall plant with a basal clump of divided leaves and tall branched stems bearing racemes of blue flowers. The flowers are distinctive, with large blue 'hoods' and they are followed by clusters of many-seeded pods.

Family	Ranunculaceae
Synonym	*A. anglicum*
Status	Local
Distribution	Southwestern England and Wales
Height	50—150 cm

J F M A M J J A S O N D

Marsh Marigold

Caltha palustris

This perennial plant grows in wet meadows, in marshes and on the damp banks of streams and ponds from lowland to mountain areas throughout the Northern Hemisphere. A very variable species, it has several subspecies in Europe and varies in form from large erect almost bushy plants to smaller creeping forms, with prostrate stems which root at the nodes where they touch the ground. It has large heart-shaped leaves, usually growing in a basal clump not on the stem, and an erect inflorescence of many bright yellow flowers in spring. The flowers are followed by clusters of many-seeded brown pods which split open at the top and along the sides to release the seeds. Marsh Marigold is poisonous like other members of this family.

Family	Ranunculaceae
Other names	Kingcup
Status	Common
Distribution	Throughout Britain
Height	15—50 cm

J F M A M J J A S O N D

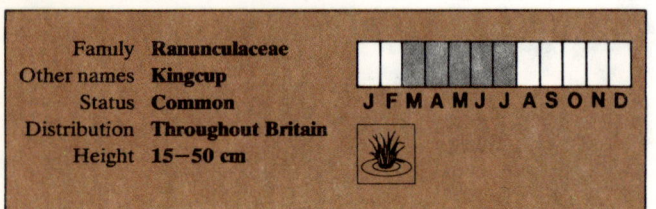

White Water-lily
Nymphaea alba

White Water-lily is a perennial plant, firmly rooted in the muddy bottom of the lakes and ponds in which it grows, by its thick fleshy creeping stem and numerous lateral roots. The rounded leathery leaves and white flowers are borne on long stalks, produced directly from the creeping stem and varying in length with the depth of the water. The flowers are conspicuous, up to 10 cm across and formed of many greenish-white sepals which pass gradually into 15—20 pure white petals which are replaced towards the centre by yellow-white petaloid stamens. The spongy fruiting capsule is drawn to the bottom of the pond after flowering, for its stalk coils up like a spring. It splits open to release the seeds which have special flotation devices and rise to the surface to be dispersed.

Family	Nymphaeaceae
Synonyms	*Castalia alba, C. speciosa*
Status	Local
Distribution	Throughout Britain

J F M A M J J A S O N D

Yellow Water-lily
Nuphar lutea

This plant grows in still and slow-moving waters in lowland areas of Europe and Siberia. The flowers and long-stalked leaves grow directly from a thick underground stem creeping in the mud. The leaves are entire, rounded in shape with a heart-shaped wedge at the base and the length of the leaf-stalk varies with the depth of the water. At the beginning of spring, small globose yellow flowers smelling of stale wine or brandy, open above the water surface. They are followed by the distinctive flask-shaped fruits — the 'brandy bottles' — which are buoyed up by air spaces in the tissues. The fruits float away from the parent plant until they finally disintegrate and the seeds sink to the mud and germinate.

Family	Nymphaeaceae
Other names	Brandy Bottle
Status	Local
Distribution	Throughout much of Britain

J F M A M J J A S O N D

Alternate-leaved Golden Saxifrage

Chrysosplenium alternifolium

In wet alder carr and shady fens, woodland springs and streams with rocky banks grows this tiny spring-flowering golden saxifrage. It often grows in large masses for it has many creeping leafless runners, from which grow rooted clumps of very long-stalked rounded kidney-shaped leaves and erect inflorescences. Each flowering stalk has one short-stalked rounded leaf and a terminal cluster of flowers with many yellow-green bracts. The individual flowers are small and petal-less, with four yellow-green sepals arranged in a cross and much nectar secreted by the receptacle. They are followed by brown capsules opening along the inner edges of the carpels to release the seeds.

Family	Saxifragaceae
Status	Local
Distribution	England, Wales and Scotland
Height	15—20 cm

J F M A M J J A S O N D

Water Avens

Geum rivale

A clump-forming perennial plant of wet meadows and marshes, streamsides and wet woodland in lowland and upland areas, usually on basic soils, throughout almost all of the Northern Hemisphere. The leaves are lyre-shaped with several smaller leaflets near the base of the leaf-stalk and one large terminal leaflet, mostly growing from the crown of the plant to form a dense clump. The few inflorescences are borne on taller drooping stems and consist of a few drooping reddish flowers, each with several overlapping petals. The fruits are distinctive, persistent reflexed sepals cupping spiny globular aggregates of single-seeded fruits, each with a long curved hairy appendage. This has a kink in the middle which breaks when touched and clings to animal fur or clothing.

Family	Rosaceae
Status	Common
Distribution	Northern areas of Britain
Height	30—60 cm

J F M A M J J A S O N D

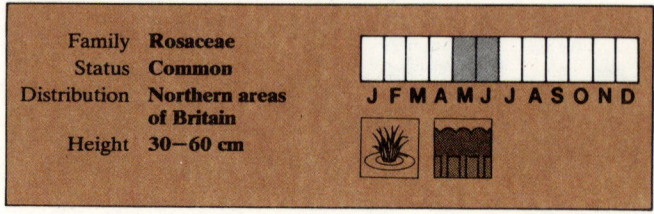

Meadowsweet

Filipendula ulmaria

This is a tall perennial plant which often forms dense 'thickets' on the banks of ponds and in ditches, in wet meadows and marshes in lowland and upland areas throughout much of Europe and Asia. It has many compound leaves in each of which large pairs of toothed leaflets alternate with smaller pairs. From each clump grow little branched, erect leafy stems with dense terminal clusters of tiny yellowish-white, sweetly scented flowers. The individual flowers have five creamy-white petals, many stamens and several ovaries. These later ripen into characteristic twisted many-seeded pods. The flowers yield a medicinal drug containing a salicylate, similar to aspirin, used to treat fevers.

Family	**Rosaceae**		
Synonym	***Spiraea ulmaria***		
Distribution	**Throughout Britain**		
Height	**50—150 cm**		

J F M A M J J A S O N D

Purple Loosestrife

Lythrum salicaria

The locally common Purple Loosestrife grows in fens and marshes, permanently wet woods and on the banks of lakes and ponds and ditches, from lowlands to the foothills of Europe and Asia. It often grows with Yellow Loosestrife (*Lysimachia vulgaris*), Yellow Flag (*Iris pseudacorus*) and in reed beds with the Common Reed, *Phragmites communis*. A clump consists of several tough erect quadrangular stems, with entire lance-shaped leaves arranged in whorls of three or in opposite pairs. The flowers grow in whorls in the axils of the upper leaves; each flower has six reddish-purple petals and twelve stamens. Three forms of flowers differing in the length of the style from short, medium to long can be found on different plants, with stamens to match, but a short-styled flower has only medium and long stamens; thus self-pollination is prevented.

Family	**Lythraceae**		
Status	**Locally common**		
Distribution	**England, Wales and southern Scotland**		
Height	**50—100 cm**		

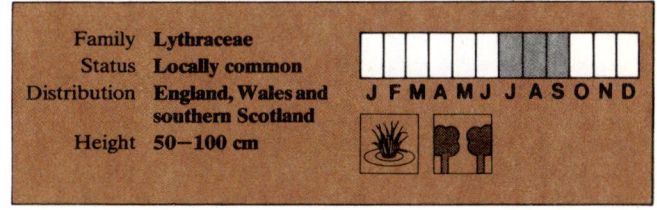

J F M A M J J A S O N D

Great Hairy Willowherb

Epilobium hirsutum

Most willowherbs are hard to distinguish from each other because of their similarity and tendency to cross-breeding. This species is a large-flowered robust perennial plant with an erect stem and can be recognised by the spreading, almost woolly hairs which cover the stem. It has many opposite oblong or lance-shaped toothed leaves and solitary purple flowers, growing in the axils of the upper leaves. The stigmas of these flowers are distinctive — four-lobed and star-like, creamy in colour and showing up clearly against the purple petals. The fruits that follow are long slender capsules which split open along their length to release hairy 'parachuted' seeds which are soon dispersed by the wind. Great Hairy Willowherb often forms large colonies on the banks of streams and in marshes and wet meadows throughout much of Europe and Asia.

Family	**Onagraceae**		
Other names	**Codlins and Cream**		
Status	**Common**	J F M A M J J A S O N D	
Distribution	**Throughout most of Britain**		
Height	**70—130 cm**		

Large Bittercress

Cardamine amara

This small perennial plant is found in wet shady places, in woodland springs and near shady streams, in fens and wet ground, often forming large colonies. It is particularly associated with wet alder carr and grows throughout Europe and Asia. It spreads by means of creeping underground stems with lateral roots and many side shoots. Its smooth erect stems bear compound leaves, each composed of 3—4 pairs of stalkless leaflets and one larger terminal leaflet, and a terminal raceme of white flowers. The flowers have four spreading petals and prominent violet anthers on the stamens. They are followed by long slender pods with one row of seeds in each.

Family	**Cruciferae**		
Status	**Locally common**	J F M A M J J A S O N D	
Distribution	**England and Scotland**		
Height	**10—60 cm**		

206

Great Yellow-cress

Rorippa amphibia

This is a perennial cress which grows on the margins of ponds, lakes and streams, in drainage canals and ditches throughout Europe, Siberia and northern Africa together with many other plants typical of this sort of habitat. It forms a rosette of variable broadly lance-shaped leaves, from which grow many short leafless side-shoots (stolons); each forms a new plant so that a spreading colony is formed. From the centre of the rosette grows an erect hollow stem with alternate variable leaves and a terminal raceme of golden-yellow conspicuous flowers. The four petals are almost twice the length of the sepals. The flowers are followed by small rounded fruits growing on long stalks.

Family	Cruciferae		
Other names	Great Watercress		J F M A M J J A S O N D
Status	Locally common		
Distribution	Central and southern England, Ireland		
Height	40—120 cm		

Marsh Yellow-cress

Rorippa islandica

Yellow- cresses are water-loving marsh or aquatic plants. *R. islandica* is an annual or biennial plant, often growing near rivers, streams and ditches but it is particularly characteristic of damp muddy low-lying ground where water stands only in winter and damp arable fields and meadows. It is found throughout Europe. It has an erect hollow stem, lobed basal leaves with 3—6 pairs of lobes and upper stalkless leaves which clasp the stem with their bases. From the axils of the upper leaves grow long-stalked dense racemes of small yellow flowers. Their pale yellow petals are the same length as the sepals and soon fall off. They are succeeded by oblong fruits shorter than their stalks, each with a short beak and many seeds in a row.

Family	Cruciferae		
Other names	Marsh Watercress		J F M A M J J A S O N D
Status	Quite common		
Distribution	Scattered over much of Britain		
Height	10—80 cm		

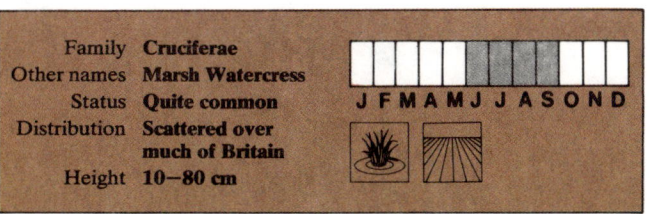

Creeping Yellow-cress
Rorippa sylvestris

This is another perennial cress that grows in similar places to the annual species, *R. islandica;* often the two plants are found together. It grows in muddy damp soil in low-lying ground where the water lies in winter, on the edges of ponds and lakes, also in damp fields and meadows. Sometimes this creeping plant can be a troublesome weed in damp areas in gardens. It forms a rosette of deeply lobed, lance-shaped leaves from which stolons radiate out to form new plants. One or more erect leafy stems bear terminal racemes of golden-yellow flowers; the flowers have four petals which soon fall off and leave a long oblong pod with many seeds.

Family	Cruciferae	J F M A M J J A S O N D
Status	Frequent	
Distribution	Mainly in England and Wales	
Height	20—60 cm	

Touch-me-not
Impatiens noli-tangere

Along woodland tracks where the ground is wet and beside woodland streams, this plant grows with its relative the Small Balsam (*I. parviflora*), although this latter plant usually grows in the drier spots. Touch-me-not is an annual plant with an erect hairless stem which has swollen nodes and alternate oval toothed leaves. Both the stem and the leaves are very juicy and wither after even a short dry spell. The flowers grow in small clusters, suspended on long stalks under the upper leaves. They are bright yellow, brown-spotted and helmet-shaped with a long curved spur at the back. They are followed by narrow capsules which are under great tension when ripe and burst on the slightest touch (hence the common name), ejecting the seeds several metres away from the parent plant.

Family	Balsaminaceae	J F M A M J J A S O N D
Status	Very local or rare	
Distribution	Mainly in the Lake District	
Height	30—100 cm	

Cowbane

Cicuta virosa

A very poisonous perennial plant, with a strong resemblance to Hemlock (*Conium maculatum*). It can be distinguished from that plant for Hemlock has purple spots on its stems where Cowbane has none. Cowbane grows in the shallow water of ponds, ditches and marshes throughout the Northern Hemisphere. The roots grow from a fleshy hollow oval underground stem which slightly resembles celery; it has a pleasant carrot-like smell and a sweetish taste but is deadly poisonous. The largest concentration of the poison, cicutoxine, occurs at the time of flowering. From this underground stem grows an erect hairless stem bearing compound leaves composed of many sharply-toothed leaflets and small flowers in bractless compound umbels.

Family	Umbelliferae
Other names	Water Hemlock
Status	Very local
Distribution	Scattered, mainly in Ireland
Height	60—120 cm

J F M A M J J A S O N D

Fine-leaved Water Dropwort

Oenanthe aquatica

This perennial plant grows in the shallow, often stagnant, water of ponds and drainage ditches, especially in marshes or fenlands throughout much of Europe except the far north. It contains a poisonous substance, oenanthotoxine; the popular usage of its seeds as an expectorant to alleviate bronchial infections is therefore somewhat risky and an overdose produces dizziness and intoxication. It spreads by means of short creeping stems and soon forms a clump of stout upright stems with finely divided leaves, sheathed at the base where they join the stem; submerged leaves have filamentous leaflets, in aerial leaves the leaflets are lance-shaped. Opposite to the leaf-stalks grow bractless compound umbels of small white four-petalled flowers, followed by single-seeded fruits.

Family	Umbelliferae
Other names	Water Fennel
Status	Locally common
Distribution	England, Wales and Ireland
Height	30—120 cm

J F M A M J J A S O N D

Amphibious Bistort

Polygonum amphibium

This species grows throughout Europe on land or in water — it has rather different growth forms for the two habitats. The aquatic form grows in ponds, canals and ditches and has long creeping stems, up to three metres long, which root at the nodes and which bear long-oval hairless leaves floating on the water surface. The terrestrial form grows on river banks and on pond edges and has erect or ascending stems, up to 75 cm tall, with roots growing only from the lowest nodes and with hairy lance-shaped leaves. In both forms the cup-shaped pink flowers grow in slender cylindrical spikes; each has five stamens and large club-shaped stigmas. The flowers are followed by glossy black triangular single-seeded fruits, enclosed in the persistent flowers which become dry and withered.

Family	Polygonaceae	
Status	Quite common	
Distribution	Throughout much of Britain	
Height	30—100 (300) cm	

J F M A M J J A S O N D

Starwort

Callitriche platycarpa

A small perennial plant growing in the still and slow-moving waters of ponds, ditches and lowland streams throughout all of the Northern Hemisphere. Its slender stems float in deeper water, or creep on the bottom in shallow water or in times of drought. The submerged simple opposite leaves are attached to the stems by their gradually narrowing bases, but the uppermost leaves form a terminal floating rosette reminiscent of a star; this rosette is found only in relatively deep water. The minute flowers grow in the axils of the rosette leaves and are monoecious; the male flowers have a single stamen, the female ones have one ovary with two styles. They are followed by four-lobed keeled fruits, separating into four winged seeds.

Family	Callitrichaceae	
Synonyms	C. polymorpha, C. verna	
Status	Locally common	
Distribution	Throughout lowland Britain	
Height	5—25 cm	

J F M A M J J A S O N D

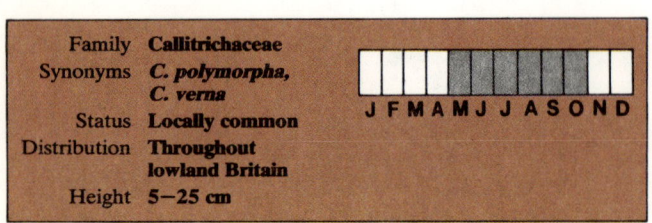

Small Water-pepper
Polygonum minus

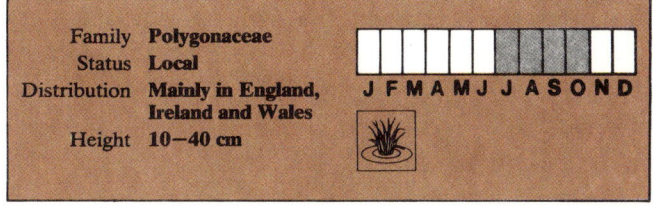

A similar species to *P. hydropiper,* with spreading branched ascending stems and narrow lance-shaped leaves. The leaves have conspicuous fringed ochraea at their bases where they join the stem. The flowers are borne in slender inflorescences growing in the axils of the leaves; they are rather different to those of the Water-pepper, pink or occasionally white in colour and without glandular spots. The fruits which follow are black and shiny. This annual plant grows in shallow water beside ponds, in ditches and marshes and also in damp meadows throughout much of Europe except the north. It is not acrid to the taste.

Family	Polygonaceae	J F M A M J J A S O N D
Status	Local	
Distribution	Mainly in England, Ireland and Wales	
Height	10—40 cm	

Water-pepper
Polygonum hydropiper

This annual plant is native to Europe, Asia and north Africa and has been introduced to North America, Australia and elsewhere. It grows in ponds and ditches or in damp low-lying ground in meadows and woodland, usually on acid soils. It has smooth erect stems with large lance-shaped leaves and slender nodding inflorescences growing in the axils of the upper leaves. The flowers are cup-shaped, greenish and covered with yellow glandular spots; they are followed by matt dark brown or black fruits. This plant is acrid and burning to the taste but is used in herb medicine to stop bleeding. Fresh bruised leaves are applied to cuts and grazes and an infusion is used for internal bleeding.

Family	Polygonaceae	J F M A M J J A S O N D
Other names	Smartweed, Biting Persicaria	
Status	Common	
Distribution	Throughout Britain, except for the north	
Height	25—60 cm	

Golden Dock
Rumex maritimus

This annual plant has a clump of oblong or lance-shaped leaves, from which grows an erect leafy stem with a dense inflorescence at the top. The stem leaves are similar in shape to the basal leaves, becoming narrower and linear towards the top of the stem. The flowers are borne in whorls, crowded together to form a dense spike. Each one is greenish with three green outer sepals and three yellow-brown finely toothed inner sepals. These persist to enclose the three-cornered fruits, becoming golden-yellow in colour and turning the whole plant golden-yellow from a distance — hence the common name. Golden Dock is found throughout Europe except in the north, growing in bare muddy ground beside reservoirs and ponds, especially where the water is brackish, or occasionally in damp grassland.

Family	**Polygonaceae**
Status	**Local**
Distribution	**Mainly in England**
Height	**30–100 cm**

J F M A M J J A S O N D

Water Chickweed
Myosoton aquaticum

This is a perennial plant reminiscent of the stitchworts, from which it can be distinguished by having five styles in the flower while *Stellaria* (stitchwort) species have three styles. It has brittle branched, prostrate or ascending, rooting stems with opposite, heart-shaped ovate leaves, those near the base of the stem with stalks, the upper ones without stalks. The white flowers are borne in leafy clusters at the top of the stem; each has five deeply forked petals, ten stamens and five styles. The flowers are followed by brown capsules which split open by five valves, almost to half their length, to release the many small seeds. Water Chickweed grows throughout much of lowland Europe in marshes, ditches and ponds, in damp woods and beside streams.

Family	**Caryophyllaceae**
Synonyms	***Cerastium aquaticum, Stellaria aquatica***
Status	**Common**
Distribution	**Mainly in England and Wales**
Height	**15–120 cm**

J F M A M J J A S O N D

Yellow Loosestrife

Lysimachià vulgaris

This is a decorative perennial plant of the water margins of lakes, rivers, fens and ditches. It is sometimes grown in gardens, together with the still more attractive *L. punctata*. It has creeping stems which spread rapidly in damp soil and soon a large colony is established with many stout erect stems. The lance-shaped leaves grow in opposite pairs or in whorls of three or four and in the axils of the uppermost leaves grow small clustered inflorescences of yellow flowers. These are funnel-shaped with five green orange-bordered sepals and five yellow petals. Yellow Loosestrife has a long history in herb lore and was strewn around cattle and horses to calm them − to 'loose strife'. It seems to drive away flies and other biting insects and is sometimes dried and burned on cottage fires to repel insects.

Family	**Primulaceae**	
Status	**Locally common**	
Distribution	**Scattered throughout much of Britain, except the north**	
Height	**50−150 cm**	

J F M A M J J A S O N D

Bogbean

Menyanthes trifoliata

This perennial plant has a scattered distribution in bogs and marshlands, at the edges of ponds and lakes in lowlands and mountain areas of the Northern Hemisphere. It is becoming increasingly rare in the wild as its distinctive three-lobed leaves have been overcollected for medicinal purposes, but the plant is now protected by law. The large trefoil-like leaves grow directly from a thick creeping underwater stem, as do the stout leafless racemes of five-petalled pinkish flowers, both leaves and inflorescences emerging above the surface of the water. The flowers are large and characteristically fringed with many white cottony hairs. Bogbean is used in herb medicine as a highly effective tonic and treatment for scurvy, skin disorders and rheumatism.

Family	**Menyanthaceae**	
Other names	**Buckbean, Marsh Trefoil**	
Status	**Locally common**	
Distribution	**Throughout Britain**	
Height	**15−30 cm**	

J F M A M J J A S O N D

Common Comfrey
Symphytum officinale

This waterside perennial plant was added to ointments in the Middle Ages and used to treat broken bones; it is still an important medicinal herb promoting the healing of damaged tissues and is used to treat wounds and bruises. Because of the high content of mucilage in its leaves, it is also an effective laxative and treatment for gastric ulcers. It forms a large clump of coarse hairy lance-shaped leaves and several leafy erect, roughly hairy flowering stems, with one-sided clusters of flowers growing in the axils of the upper leaves. The bases of the stem leaves run down the length of the stem for some distance, giving it the appearance of being winged. The flowers are tubular, pink in bud, becoming creamy-white as they open. Comfrey grows beside ponds, ditches and streams and in other damp places throughout Europe.

Family	Boraginaceae
Other names	Knitbone
Status	Common
Distribution	Throughout much of Britain
Height	30—100 cm

J F M A M J J A S O N D

Fringed Water-lily
Nymphoides peltata

This aquatic plant has floating rounded, heart-shaped, leathery leaves like those of the water-lily (*Nymphaea*), but very much smaller — only 3—10 cm across. The leaves grow on long stalks from creeping rhizomes anchored into the mud at the bottom of the water. Long-stalked flowers grow from the axils of the leaves. They are quite large and conspicuous, funnel-shaped and measuring up to 3 cm across, with five golden-yellow fringed petals. The flowers are followed by fruiting capsules. The floating leaves and flowers of this decorative plant can be seen on the surface of backwaters, slow-moving rivers and ponds, in the lowlands of Europe and Asia, where it is protected by law in many countries.

Family	Menyanthaceae
Status	Local
Distribution	Mainly in south-eastern England
Height	80—150 cm

J F M A M J J A S O N D

Water Mint

Mentha aquatica

This water-loving mint grows in wet marshes, fens and woodlands, on the edges of ponds and in ditches in the warmer regions of Europe and in Africa. It is a peppermint-scented perennial plant with more or less erect leafy angular reddish stems, rooting at the lower nodes and forming a spreading colony. The leaves are oval in shape, coarsely toothed and hairy and in the axils of the upper leaves grow the small flowers, crowded into whorled spherical heads. The individual flowers are tiny, bluish-purple in colour with four petals. This mint may be used in herb medicine in the preparation of peppermint tea and used to alleviate coughs, colds and flu.

Family	Labiatae
Status	Common
Distribution	Throughout Britain
Height	20—80 cm

J F M A M J J A S O N D

Marsh Woundwort

Stachys palustris

Another old medicinal plant which grows beside ponds, streams and ditches; also in marshland and sometimes as a weed in arable land and gardens in most of Europe. Its leaves have antiseptic properties and can be used to bind wounds and staunch bleeding as they have been for centuries. It is a robust plant with creeping underground stems from which grow many leafy erect quadrangular stems. The leaves are borne in opposite pairs, they are lance-shaped, coarsely toothed and hairy. The whole plant has an unpleasant smell when bruised. The two-lipped hooded purple flowers are borne in whorls in the axils of bracts at the tops of the stems; the whorls are closely packed together and form a dense spike.

Family	Labiatae
Status	Common
Distribution	Throughout Britain
Height	30—100 cm

J F M A M J J A S O N D

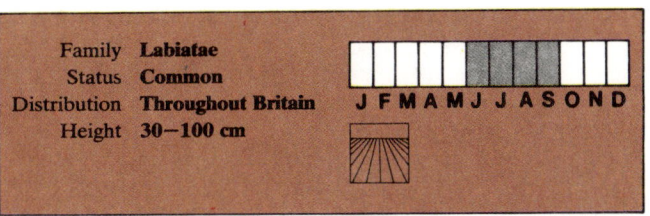

Gipsy-wort

Lycopus europaeus

Legend has it that gypsies used the black dye from this plant to dye their skin so that they could pass as Egyptians or African fortune tellers. Whether or not they did, it is certainly true that a good strong black dye can be obtained from the leaves. Gipsy-wort grows in marshes and in fens, beside ponds and rivers and ditches throughout Europe and much of Asia. It is a robust perennial plant with creeping underground stems from which grow many, more or less erect, leafy stems. The leaves are ovate or lance-shaped, coarsely toothed and grow in opposite pairs. The small white purple-spotted flowers grow in dense whorls in the axils of the leaves and are followed by dry flattened nutlets enclosed in sepals.

Family	**Labiatae**
Status	**Common**
Distribution	**Mainly in England, Wales and Ireland**
Height	**20–100 cm**

J F M A M J J A S O N D

Brooklime

Veronica beccabunga

Water margins or small streams and ditches with slow-moving water, marshes and wet meadows provide perfect habitats for the common Brooklime, where it grows with watercress, water forget-me-nots and Water Speedwell (*V. anagallis-aquatica*). Often at least part of the plant is submerged. From thick creeping rhizomes grow semi-succulent stems, creeping and rooting from the lower nodes while the tips turn upwards; the whole plant forms a tangled mat. The small opposite leaves are smooth, succulent and glossy and in their axils grow long-stalked racemes of blue funnel-shaped flowers, followed by rounded hairless capsules enclosed by persistent sepals.

Family	**Scrophulariaceae**
Status	**Common**
Distribution	**Throughout Britain**
Height	**20–60 cm**

J F M A M J J A S O N D

Water Speedwell

Veronica anagallis-aquatica

This speedwell often grows with Brooklime in slow-moving streams and ditches, but it is also found in wet muddy pond edges and in damp meadows. It resembles Brooklime with creeping thick hollow succulent stems, rooting at the nodes, and stalkless glossy ovate or lance-shaped, fleshy leaves. Stalked racemes of blue flowers, denser than in Brooklime, grow from the axils of opposite leaves, on the upward-turning parts of the stems. The petals are pale blue with darker veining, sometimes pink or white. This is a variable perennial plant, occurring in several subspecies, throughout many parts of the world, some subspecies growing in water, others in more terrestrial habitats.

Family	Scrophulariaceae													
Status	Relatively common	J	F	M	A	M	J	J	A	S	O	N	D
Distribution	Scattered over much of Britain												
Height	15—80 cm												

Northern Bedstraw

Galium boreale

This northern species grows beside mountain streams and in wet mountain flushes, on rocky screes and moraines; also on shingle beaches and in damp areas in stable sand dunes. It is found in lowlands and mountain areas throughout many parts of northern and central Europe. It forms a dense mat of erect slender quadrangular stems, with many whorls of four lance-shaped three-veined leaves. The stems bear dense terminal clusters of white funnel-shaped flowers, each with four petals. The flowers are followed by many brown bristly fruits growing in pairs, which are dispersed by animals.

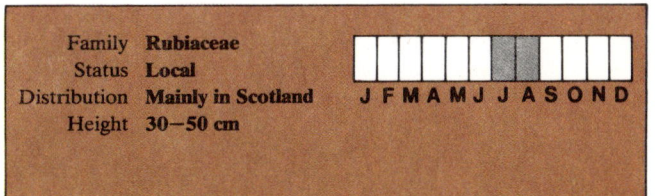

Family	Rubiaceae													
Status	Local	J	F	M	A	M	J	J	A	S	O	N	D
Distribution	Mainly in Scotland												
Height	30—50 cm												

217

Marsh Hawksbeard
Crepis paludosa

Fens, moist meadows, streamsides and wet woodland provide an ideal habitat for this perennial species, which grows in lowlands and foothills in the northerly areas of Europe. It forms a basal rosette of long-stalked, lobed lance-shaped leaves and an erect leafy stem. The stem leaves are stalkless, arrow-shaped and embrace the hollow ridged stem with their pointed ear-like bases. The stem bears several clusters of yellow flower-heads, formed only of strap-shaped ray florets and followed by single-seeded fruits with dingy-white simple hairs. The fruits are dispersed by the wind, helped by the parachutes of hairs.

Family	**Compositae**		
Synonyms	*Hieracium paludosum, Aracium paludosum*		J F M A M J J A S O N D
Status	**Locally common**		
Distribution	**Northern Britain**		
Height	**40—80 cm**		

Marsh Valerian
Valeriana dioica

A small bright green perennial plant with short creeping underground stems, a clump of basal leaves supported on long stalks, and a short erect leafy flowering stem. The stem leaves are stalkless and deeply lobed. The flowers are borne in a terminal head, male and female on separate plants; they are funnel-shaped with pinkish petals. Marsh Valerian, like all valerians, has a bitter taste and an odd smell, very attractive to cats. It grows in fens, marshes and wet meadows throughout much of Europe although it is much rarer in northern areas than in the south.

Family	**Valerianaceae**		
Status	**Locally common**		J F M A M J J A S O N D
Distribution	**Mainly in England and Wales**		
Height	**10—30 cm**		

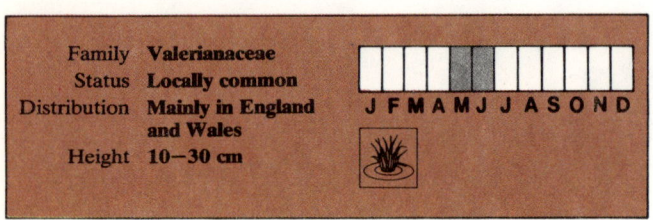

Nodding Bur Marigold

Bidens cernua

This plant grows throughout much of Europe and Asia, except in the north, in ponds, ditches and beside streams or in low-lying ground where water collects during the winter but not in summer. It is an annual which forms a large clump of erect leafy stems, with many opposite pairs of toothed stalkless pale green leaves. In the axils of these leaves are borne the distinctive nodding flower-heads, growing on long drooping stalks and each one cupped in an outer row of large green leaf-like bracts and an inner row of smaller darker, more petal-like bracts. All the florets are of the tubular disk form, dull yellow in colour and followed by single-seeded barbed fruits which catch in the fur of animals and so are dispersed.

Family	**Compositae**	
Status	**Locally common**	
Distribution	**Mainly England, Wales and Ireland**	
Height	**10—70 cm**	

J F M A M J J A S O N D

Field Milkthistle

Sonchus arvensis

This field thistle is common throughout Europe in damp low-lying fields, on the banks of streams and ponds inland, and on the driftlines of marshland and saltmarshes near the sea where it tolerates salt in the soil and water. Because of its long branched underground stem system which reaches a depth of 50—100 cm, it is one of the most difficult of weeds to eradicate. From buds on the upper roots, near the soil surface, grow many new shoots and so a wide colony is formed. The glossy, spiny-lobed leaves are attached by their heart-shaped bases to the upright hollow stem, clasping them with rounded ear-like bases. The yellow flowers are borne in flower-heads in large loose clusters, opening in sunny weather in the morning only. They are followed by single-seeded fruits, each with two rows of simple hairs.

Family	**Compositae**	
Other names	**Field Sowthistle**	
Status	**Common**	
Distribution	**Throughout Britain**	
Height	**50—150 cm**	

J F M A M J J A S O N D

Tripartite Bur Marigold
Bidens tripartita

This species grows in similar habitats to the previous one, but is less likely to be found in low-lying ground, preferring ditches, streamsides and the banks of ponds and lakes. It is a similar annual clump-forming plant with many erect leafy stems but its leaves are lobed, with three to five toothed lobes, not lance-shaped as in *B. cernua*. The flower-heads grow in the axils of the leaves, they have long, more or less erect stalks and similar bracts to the previous species. The florets are all tubular, dull yellow, and followed by barbed single-seeded fruits. This plant was used in herb medicine at one time, in the treatment of kidney stones and bladder problems and to alleviate fevers.

Family	**Compositae**	
Other names	**Water Agrimony**	
Status	**Locally common**	
Distribution	**Mainly England, Wales and Ireland**	
Height	**15—60 cm**	

J F M A M J J A S O N D

Marsh Cudweed
Gnaphalium uliginosum

An annual plant of wet or damp places in sandy fields, in puddles in the ruts of paths and tracks, in damp heathland throughout Europe and western Asia on acid soils. It forms a small branched clump of ascending stems, all covered with whitish woolly hairs. The leaves are alternately arranged, lance-shaped and woolly on both surfaces. The flowers are borne in terminal clusters of flowering heads; each head is cupped in two rows of pale brown bracts and is composed solely of yellowish tubular disk florets. They are followed by many single-seeded hairy fruits. An infusion of Marsh Cudweed leaves can be used in herb medicine as a gargle.

Family	**Compositae**	
Status	**Common**	
Distribution	**Throughout Britain**	
Height	**5—20 cm**	

J F M A M J J A S O N D

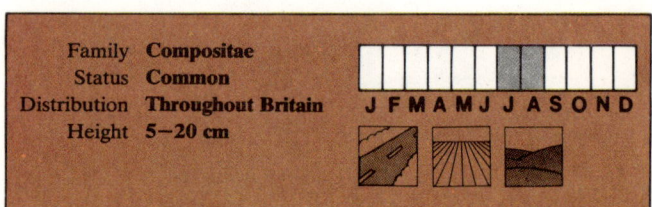

Butterbur

Petasites hybridus

This is a spring-flowering plant, growing in wet meadows, in wet woodland and especially beside upland streams where it may form large colonies, throughout much of Europe except the far north. First to emerge from the creeping underground stems in spring, are the stout hollow. unbranched reddish stems with terminal heads of pale purplish flowers, growing taller as flowering progresses. The male and female flowers are borne on separate plants; in Britain the male plants are much more common than the female ones, which are only found in a few northern English counties. The leaves appear after flowering and form a large clump; each leaf is long-stalked, heart-shaped and shallowly toothed on the margin, up to 90 cm across when fully mature. This is an old medicinal plant, its rootstock yielding a drug used to treat heart troubles, coughs and colds.

Family	**Compositae**	
Synonyms	***Tussilago petasites, P. vulgaris***	
Status	**Locally common**	
Distribution	**Throughout Britain**	
Height	**30—150 cm**	

J F M A M J J A S O N D

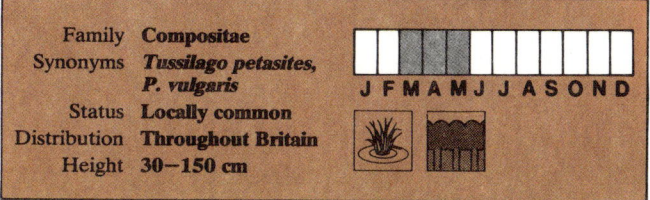

Hemp Agrimony

Eupatorium cannabinum

This is a stout perennial plant with a clump of stalked lance-shaped basal leaves and many erect reddish stems. These bear many lance-shaped toothed leaves, all growing in opposite pairs. The pinkish-purple flowers are borne in terminal clusters, growing in the axils of the uppermost leaves; each cluster is composed of many very small flower-heads having only 4—5 tubular florets in each head. The single-seeded fruits which follow have a single row of toothed hairs. Hemp Agrimony grows in fens and marshes, wet woodland, in ditches and beside streams from lowlands to mountains in the warmer areas of Europe; it may also be found growing at the bases of sea-cliffs in more northerly areas. It is an old medicinal plant which was used in the treatment of liver disorders at one time.

Family	**Compositae**	
Status	**Common**	
Distribution	**Throughout Britain except the north**	
Height	**50—150 cm**	

J F M A M J J A S O N D

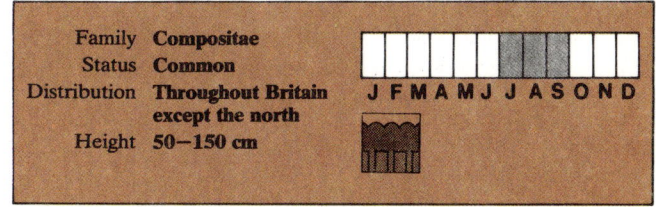

Common Water Plantain

Alisma plantago-aquatica

This robust perennial aquatic plant grows rooted in the muddy edges of slow-moving streams and rivers, beside ponds and in ditches and canals, throughout the temperate regions of the Northern Hemisphere. It has a short tuberous rhizome from which grows a rosette of long-stalked entire leaves which resemble those of the plantain, hence the common name. The tall graceful stem bears a loose pyramidal cluster of pale pink flowers arranged in whorls of three or more. Each flower has three sepals and petals and is followed by a distinctive fruit composed of many flattened seeds arranged in a horizontal whorl. In some countries the rhizome and leaves of this plant are collected and used, as they have been for centuries, as an effective treatment for kidney stones, gravel, cystitis and dysentery.

Family	**Alismataceae**
Status	**Locally common**
Distribution	**Throughout Britain, except the north**
Height	**30—100 cm**

J F M A M J J A S O N D

Welted Thistle

Carduus acanthoides

This biennial plant forms a ground rosette of sinuous lobed leaves in the first year, which withers in the second year when a leafy flowering stem with flowers and fruits is produced. The flowering stem is spinous-winged with tough spiny, deeply lobed leaves and large spiny, pale reddish-violet flower-heads, measuring about 3 cm across, growing in clusters on short spiny-winged stalks in the axils of the leaves. The flowering heads are formed of tubular disk florets only and are followed by many single-seeded fruits with white hairs. Welted Thistle grows in moist wasteland and roadside verges, beside streams and in damp meadows in lowland Europe.

Family	**Compositae**
Status	**Common**
Distribution	**Mainly in England and Wales**
Height	**30—100 cm**

J F M A M J J A S O N D

Flowering Rush

Butomus umbellatus

This spectacular plant grows in the shallow water of ponds and canals, beside slow-moving rivers, in ditches and reed beds together with Arrowhead, Water Plantain and Yellow Flag. It is found throughout the lowland areas of Europe and Asia. Its leaves are grass-like, growing in a clump from a rhizome beneath the mud, and they protrude well above the surface of the water. The clump also produces several rounded leafless flowering stems, terminated by rich umbel-like inflorescences composed of 15−30 long-stalked flowers. Each flower has six reddish-pink petals with darker veins, nine stamens and six ovaries which form many-seeded fruits after pollination.

Family	Butomaceae	
Status	Local	
Distribution	Mainly in central and southern England, Ireland	J F M A M J J A S O N D
Height	50−150 cm	

Arrowhead

Sagittaria sagittifolia

This is an erect plant growing on the edges of ponds and slow-moving rivers, in marshes and ditches in shallow water or in mud throughout Europe, Asia and North America. It has slender creeping stems which colonise the mud and two types of leaves. The leaves growing above the water are long-stalked and markedly arrow-shaped while the submerged ones are thin and linear in shape. The leafless flowering stems grow upright from the creeping stems to emerge above the water. They are triangular in cross-section and bear several whorls of flowers, three to five in each whorl. The flowers are either male or female, male flowers borne towards the top of the inflorescence while female flowers are borne near the bottom. The flowers have three broad whitish petals, each with a dark violet patch in the centre.

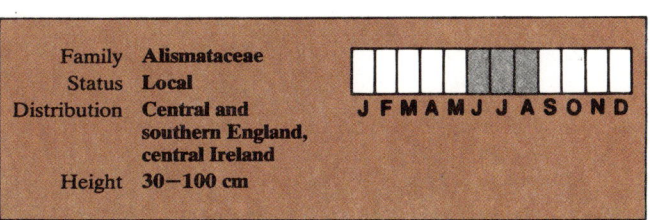

Family	Alismataceae	
Status	Local	
Distribution	Central and southern England, central Ireland	J F M A M J J A S O N D
Height	30−100 cm	

Canadian Pondweed

Elodea canadensis

This aquatic plant was introduced into Europe in 1836 from North America via the British Isles, and now grows in slow-moving water, ponds and canals throughout much of the Continent. It is an extremely invasive species, spreading rapidly by vegetative means for the European plants are almost entirely female, male plants are very rare and flowers are not pollinated. However, the submerged stems are very brittle and any portions which break off can form a new plant. In the winter, special buds are formed in the axils of the leaves and sink to the bottom when the rest of the plant dies back, to grow into new plants in the spring. The brittle stems may be short or very long with many dense whorls of translucent dark green oval leaves, growing in threes. They may be rooted at the bottom or floating near the surface.

Family	Hydrocharitaceae
Synonym	*Anacharis canadensis*
Status	Introduced. Common
Distribution	Throughout Britain except the north
Height	30—60 cm

J F M A M J J A S O N D

Common Frogbit

Hydrocharis morsus-ranae

This plant grows in still shallow water in lakes and backwaters, ponds, reservoirs and ditches, usually in areas where the water is rich in calcium, in Europe and Asia. It is not a common plant and is protected by law. Its small leaf rosettes float near the surface of the water so that the long-stalked rounded kidney-shaped leaf blades lie on the surface and the long roots dangle. The white male and female flowers protrude above the water surface on long stalks, two male flowers and one female flower growing together from a large membranous sheath. The fruits are semi-leathery capsules which burst irregularly when ripe. In the autumn Frogbit produces long thin stems with winter buds, which fall off to overwinter in the mud at the bottom of the water and grow into new plants in the spring.

Family	Hydrocharitaceae
Status	Local
Distribution	Southern and central England and Ireland
Height	15—30 cm

J F M A M J J A S O N D

Broad-leaved Pondweed

Potamogeton natans

A creeping plant with many underground stems which rapidly colonise the rich mud in which it grows. It prefers shallow water, no more than one metre or so deep, in ponds, lakes and canals, or slow-moving rivers and ditches and grows in such habitats throughout the Northern Hemisphere. From the creeping stems grow two types of leaves; thin linear submerged leaves and long-stalked floating leaves with oval blades which appear to be jointed just below the junction between blade and stalk. The flowers are small, greenish, growing in long-stalked dense spikes in the axils of the leaves and are followed by dense fruiting spikes.

Family	**Potamogetonaceae**
Synonym	*P. hibernicus*
Status	**Common**
Distribution	**Throughout Britain**
Height	**60—150 cm**

J F M A M J J A S O N D

Curled Pondweed

Potamogeton crispus

A creeping plant, like the previous species, with many creeping underground stems growing in the mud at the bottom of ponds and lakes, slow-moving rivers and canals throughout Europe and Asia. However, unlike *P. natans*, it has only one kind of leaves. They are very distinctive, submerged, translucent, long and lance-shaped with blunt ends, strongly undulating and giving the plant its name of Curled Pondweed. The leaves are arranged alternately on the simple little-branched stem. The short flowering spikes are borne on long slender stalks and have only a few flowers, followed by long-beaked fruits. The plant spreads by seeds and by winter buds which are detached in the autumn, overwinter in mud and produce new plants in spring.

Family	**Potamogetonaceae**
Synonym	*P. serratus*
Status	**Common**
Distribution	**Throughout Britain**
Height	**30—120 cm**

J F M A M J J A S O N D

Sweet Flag
Acorus calamus

Colonies of this plant grow from tangled sweet-scented rhizomes at the margins of ponds, canals and slow-moving rivers, among sedges, bulrushes and reeds. The narrow flat sword-like leaves usually have wavy margins and the yellowish flowers are borne in dense spikes growing on leafless flowering stalks. Until the beginning of the 16th century, only the candied rhizomes of the plant were known in Europe, sold as a rare Turkish delicacy. Once introduced into Europe, the scented leaves were used to strew the floors of houses, halls and churches and the rhizome was, and still is, used extensively in herb medicine as a stimulant and tonic. The medical tonic known as Stockton Bitters comes from the rhizome of Sweet Flag; the rhizome can be used to flavour beer and liquor, powdered as a spice like cinnamon or used in perfumery.

Family	Araceae	
Other names	Sweet Sedge	
Status	Introduced. Local	
Distribution	Mainly in central and southern England and Ireland	
Height	30—150 cm	

J F M A M J J A S O N D

Yellow Flag
Iris pseudacorus

This distinctive plant has large clumps of sword-shaped leaves growing from thick fleshy rhizomes, often forming large colonies on the banks of ponds and canals as well as in ditches, marshes, fens and wet woodland throughout Europe and Asia. The yellow flowers are borne in small clusters, each sheathed by a large green bract, terminating tall leafless flowering stalks. Each flower has three large outer petals bent downwards and three smaller ones, linear in shape and semi-erect. The yellow three-branched petal-like style is longer than the inner petals and has one stamen under each branch. The flowers are followed by long greenish capsules which turn brown as they dry and split open to release the seeds.

Family	Iridaceae	
Other names	Wild Iris	
Status	Common	
Distribution	Throughout Britain	
Height	60—120 cm	

J F M A M J J A S O N D

226

Great Reedmace
Typha latifolia

On the edges of ponds, lakes and canals, in marshes, fens and ditches, wherever the muddy bottom is rich in organic remains, a dense mesh of reed mace rhizomes and roots captures silt and detritus, slowly raising the muddy bottom in the same manner as mangroves do in the sea. From the mat of thick creeping stems, grow many long broadly linear leaves, taller than the flowering spikes. The flowers are borne in flowering spadices, terminating the leafless stems. The bottom female one is greenish-yellow at first while the male spadix is closely attached to its top and is brownish-orange in colour. After pollination by wind, the female spadix becomes a fruiting spike, dark velvety brown in colour. Dried reedmace leaves are used in basket-making and roasted rhizomes can be used as a coffee substitute.

Family	Typhaceae		
Other names	Bulrush, Cat's Tail		
Status	Common		
Distribution	Throughout Britain except the north		
Height	100—250 cm		

J F M A M J **J A S** O N D

Bog Arum
Calla palustris

This poisonous species grows throughout much of the Northern Hemisphere and is now protected as a rare and decorative plant in some countries. In spite of this it is becoming increasingly rare, like so many wetland plants, since it cannot survive the disappearance of its natural habitat of muddy marshes and swamps with shallow warm water, wet alder woods and waterside communities. The creeping jointed rhizomes, hidden in the mud of woodland ponds and moorland pools, produce long-stalked heart-shaped entire leaves, often forming dense masses. The funnel-shaped spathes, white inside and green outside, grow in early summer together with the spikes of tiny greenish flowers. They are pollinated by slugs and insects and followed by spikes of red berries with violet seeds.

Family	Araceae		
Status	A rare garden escape		
Distribution	Occasional		
Height	15—30 cm		

J F M A M **J J A** S O N D

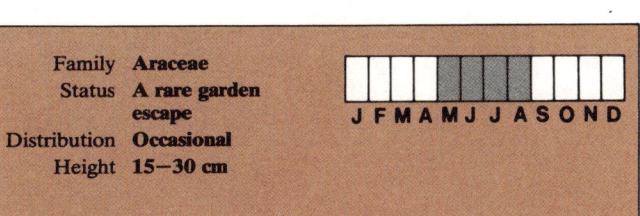

Lesser Reedmace
Typha angustifolia

This plant has a similar distribution throughout the Northern Hemisphere to Great Reedmace, but is much less common than the other species in Britain and much less widely distributed. The two species often form pure stands on the shallow edges of ponds, slow-moving rivers or canals; they also grow together with other marshland plants like reeds, rushes and sedges, reinforcing the muddy bottoms of the water edges with their thick rhizomes. Both reedmaces are perennial plants and similar in appearance; they can be distinguished from each other by the flowering spadices, for in Lesser Reedmace the male and female flowers are some 1−3 cm distant from each other, while in Great Reedmace they are touching.

Family	**Typhaceae**	
Status	**Locally common**	
Distribution	**Mainly in central and southern England**	J F M A M J J A S O N D
Height	**100−300 cm**	

Branched Bur-reed
Sparganium erectum

The bur-reeds grow on the muddy edges of ponds and ditches, on the margins of slow-moving rivers and in marshes and wet meadows. Branched Bur-reed has erect sword-shaped, markedly keeled leaves growing from a creeping rhizome and thick flowering stems branched to form a large spreading inflorescence. Each branch bears several spherical heads, one or two lower ones being larger with female flowers and several male heads grow above them. The male flowers are each formed of three free stamens, the female ones of a single ovary and all possess membranous scales. After fertilization the female heads become large prickly spheres composed of angular pyramidal single-seeded fruits, each with a short pointed beak. The aggregate disintegrates when ripe, to be dispersed.

Family	**Sparganiaceae**	
Status	**Common**	
Distribution	**Throughout Britain**	J F M A M J J A S O N D
Height	**30−100 cm**	

Species featured
in this section

Species featured
in another section

Wood Anemone
Anemone nemorosa

This perennial plant grows in deciduous woodland as well as in shaded meadows or in hedgerows, on all but the poorest soils, sometimes colonising large areas. It is very common throughout Europe and eastern Asia from lowlands to mountain areas. The rapid spread of the species is due to the long slender underground stems from which grow pink white-tinged flowers on long stalks in spring. These are followed by long-stalked palmately lobed leaves, each with three deeply toothed lobes. The single-seeded fruits are borne in large round clusters. Wood Anemones were used at one time in herb medicine but have fallen into disrepute due to the acrid sap which they contain.

Family	Ranunculaceae		
Other names	Windflower		
Status	Common	J F M A M J J A S O N D	
Distribution	Throughout Britain		
Height	10—25 cm		

Goldilocks
Ranunculus auricomus

This spring-flowering plant forms a basal clump of variable leaves. They are either rounded or kidney-shaped, either palmately divided into broad lobes or undivided and entire. Several erect stems bear stalkless leaves, palmately divided into linear segments. A few golden-yellow, long-stalked flowers are borne in sparse inflorescences terminating the stems; they have five stunted petals, sometimes no petals at all, and numerous carpels which ripen into clusters of hairy single-seeded fruits. The plant grows in deciduous woodland, especially in damp mixed and oak woods on calcareous soils, in wet meadows and on rocky ground in foothill and mountain areas throughout Europe and northern Asia.

Family	Ranunculaceae		
Status	Common		
Distribution	Throughout much of Britain	J F M A M J J A S O N D	
Height	15—45 cm		

231

Yellow Wood Anemone

Anemone ranunculoides

Yellow Wood Anemone is found in damp shady woodland throughout much of Europe except the north, but it is not a common plant and is not native to Britain. It is sometimes grown in gardens and has escaped in a few areas of England to become naturalized in woodland. The flowers appear in spring before the basal leaves, growing from thin spreading underground stems; they are usually solitary and borne on short stalks together with a whorl of three deeply three-lobed toothed leaves. The stalks of these leaves are very short so that it may look as if nine simple leaves are present instead. The flowers resemble buttercups with five yellow petals and many stamens and carpels at the centre of the flower. They are followed by clusters of bristly single-seeded fruits which form at the same time as the basal leaves appear.

Family	**Ranunculaceae**	
Status	**Introduced**	
Distribution	**Occasionally natur-alized in England**	J F M A M J J A S O N D
Height	**10—20 cm**	

Traveller's Joy

Clematis vitalba

A native of the southern regions of Europe, this climbing plant is a most characteristic species of the chalk scrub thickets, limestone woodlands and hedgerows. It is a perennial twining plant which festoons shrubs, trees and fences, sometimes endangering its living supports with its rampant growth. The leaves are opposite, long-stalked and compound with toothed stalked heart-shaped leaflets and the stalks serve as tendrils; they thicken and become woody after twisting around a support. The fragrant white flowers are arranged in dense terminal clusters; they are hairy both inside and out with four white sepals, no petals and many white stamens and several carpels. These ripen into the characteristic 'bearded' single-seeded fruits which transform the 'Traveller's Joy' into 'Old Man's Beard' in late summer and autumn.

Family	**Ranunculaceae**	
Other names	**Old Man's Beard**	
Status	**Locally common**	J F M A M J J A S O N D
Distribution	**Mainly in southern England**	
Height	**80—150 cm**	

Columbine

Aquilegia vulgaris

An attractive clump-forming perennial plant with many long-stalked compound basal leaves and several erect flower-bearing stems. The drooping flowers grow in loose clusters forming a graceful inflorescence; they are very distinctive, usually blue in colour but sometimes white or reddish, with five petal-like sepals and five spurred petals, looking like miniature bonnets. The flowers are followed by clusters of many-seeded pods. The wild form of Columbine may be grown in gardens and there are also many cultivated varieties, usually with brighter colours and longer spurs. It grows in woods and damp grassland throughout much of Europe and Asia, especially on calcareous soils.

Family	**Ranunculaceae**	
Other names	**Granny Bonnets**	
Status	**Local**	J F M A M J J A S O N D
Distribution	**Throughout Britain except the north**	
Height	**40—80 cm**	

Wild Strawberry

Fragaria vesca

The wild form of this popular fruiting plant grows throughout all of the Northern Hemisphere, usually in sunny grassland and in woodland clearings from lowlands to mountain areas, adapting easily to many climatic and soil conditions. It often grows in large colonies, spreading rapidly with its network of slender rooting runners from which grow many new plants. Each plant has a woody rootstock which produces a ground rosette of compound leaves with three toothed stalkless leaflets and small clusters of white flowers growing on long stalks. The flowers are followed by the succulent fleshy red 'fruits' — actually the swollen receptacles — the true fruits are the pips scattered over the surface of the 'fruits'.

Family	**Rosaceae**	
Status	**Common**	
Distribution	**Throughout Britain**	J F M A M J J A S O N D
Height	**10—20 cm**	

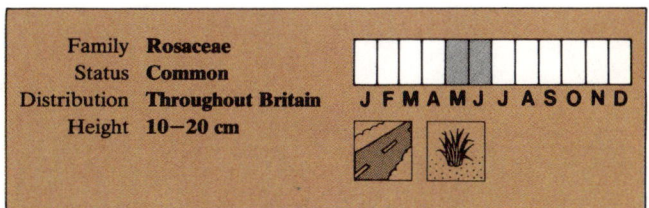

233

Narrow-leaved Everlasting Pea

Lathyrus sylvestris

This prostrate or climbing plant has long scrambling stems; these stems are flattened and winged, like those of many other *Lathyrus* species, with compound leaves. These have two narrow lance-shaped leaflets and large branched terminal tendrils which curl around other plants. From the leaf axils grow long-stalked racemes of large scentless flowers, like sweet peas, yellowish-green at first, turning reddish-pink when fully open. The flowers are followed by pods of pea-like seeds. This is a variable species with narrow-leaved and broad-leaved forms, growing in open deciduous woodland and in thickets and hedgerows, where its deep roots enrich the soil with nitrogen.

Family	**Leguminosae**
Status	**Local**
Distribution	**Scattered in England**
Height	**100—200 cm**

J F M A M J J A S O N D

Hautbois Strawberry

Fragaria moschata

This perennial strawberry is more robust than the common Wild Strawberry and was at one time grown in gardens for its fruit. It has now been replaced by *F. × ananassa* (the Cultivated Strawberry) and its present status and distribution in Britain are doubtful, for it can easily be mistaken for this latter plant. It grows in the wild in central Europe. It forms a rosette of compound leaves with three shortly stalked leaflets and it very rarely forms runners. The white flowers are borne in small clusters on long hairy stalks and are followed by a few typical strawberries. However, in this species the pips are not borne on the base of the fruit which often remains partly greenish in colour. The fruits have a musty flavour.

Family	**Rosaceae**
Synonym	*F. elatior*
Status	**Probably rare**
Distribution	**Mainly in England**
Height	**15—30 cm**

J F M A M J J A S O N D

Zigzag Clover

Trifolium medium

A straggling perennial softly hairy clover with slender weak zigzagging stems and long-stalked compound leaves. Each leaf has three long narrow leaflets, frequently with a faint white spot on each. The flowers are borne in solitary round flower-heads, growing on short stalks in the axils of a pair of leaves. The flowers are reddish-purple in colour, persistent and turning brown as they die. The pods which follow are membranous and split longitudinally to release the seeds. Zigzag Clover grows in dry woods and copses, also in pastures and on grassy slopes, from lowlands to the foothills throughout much of Europe except the far north and south.

Family	Leguminosae		J F M A M J J A S O N D
Status	Locally common		
Distribution	Throughout much of Britain		
Height	20—45 cm		

Black Pea

Lathyrus niger

Unlike the Everlasting Pea, this *Lathyrus* species has a wingless stem. It is an erect plant with a branched quadrangular stem which grows from a short thick rhizome. The leaves are compound, with 3—6 pairs of short-stalked lance-shaped leaflets, each leaflet with a short pointed tip. In the axils of the leaves grow long-stalked racemes of flowers, purple at first and later turning blue. They are followed by clusters of long black pods, each with up to 14 round seeds. This tall perennial plant grows in deciduous woodland in the warmer parts of Europe, mostly in lowlands and hills, but only in mountain areas in Britain where it is now largely extinct; it has been introduced into some southern parts of England.

Family	Leguminosae		J F M A M J J A S O N D
Synonym	*Orobus niger*		
Status	Very rare		
Distribution	Scotland and southern England		
Height	30—80 cm		

Broom

Cytisus scoparius

This shrubby plant is noticeable for its many long deep green twigs which are naked in winter and covered with small leaves in summer. The solitary pea-like yellow flowers grow in most of the leaf axils in early summer, transforming the green shrub into a blaze of yellow. They are followed by many black pods which open explosively to release the seeds, leaving the coiled twisted valves behind after opening. This is a western European species growing in the warmer regions of Europe only on sandy acid soils. It may form large colonies on heaths, on roadside verges and in woodland clearings and margins. Broom was used, as its name suggests, in broom-making for its tough slender twigs made it excellent for this purpose. It is also an important herbal plant used in the treatment of kidney and bladder complaints.

Family	Leguminosae	
Synonym	*Sarothamnus scoparius*	
Status	Locally common	
Distribution	Throughout Britain	
Height	50–200 cm	

J F M A M J J A S O N D

Rosebay Willowherb

Chamaenerion angustifolium

This is a most characteristic plant of woodland clearings from lowland areas up to the subalpine belt throughout all of the Northern Hemisphere, especially after a fire; hence its North American name of Fireweed. When in flower it transforms the clearings with the dark pink colour of its blooms which are followed by long fruiting capsules. On ripening these release numerous tiny seeds, each with long white hairs, to be carried by the wind in such numbers that the air may be full of flying seeds on a breezy day. It often forms large colonies with its spreading roots from which grow many tall erect stems with many alternate lance-shaped leaves.

Family	Onagraceae	
Other names	Fireweed	
Synonym	*Epilobium angustifolium*	
Status	Very common	
Distribution	Mainly in England, Scotland and Wales	
Height	60–120 cm	

J F M A M J J A S O N D

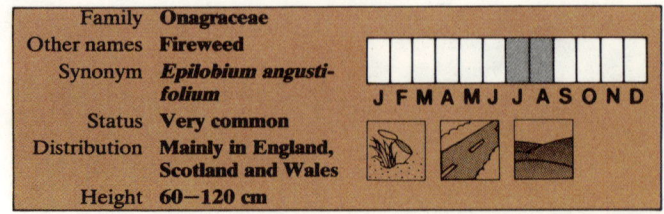

Broad-leaved Willowherb

Epilobium montanum

This common willowherb grows in woodland clearings, in gardens, hedgerows and walls, especially on calcareous soils, throughout Europe and western Asia. Like the Great Hairy Willowherb (*E. hirsutum*), it has a distinctive stigma divided into four spreading lobes. It forms a small basal rosette of bright green leaves from which grow side shoots in autumn, each one producing the rosette of a new plant. From these grow erect reddish leafy flowering stems in summer, with solitary pink flowers in the axils of the upper leaves, followed by long fruiting capsules. The capsules contain many reddish-brown hairy seeds which are dispersed by the wind.

Family	**Onagraceae**	
Status	**Common**	
Distribution	**Throughout Britain**	J F M A M J J A S O N D
Height	**10—80 cm**	

Sweet Violet

Viola odorata

From a short stout underground stem grows a low clump of long-stalked leaves, each with a rounded heart-shaped blade. Single violet-coloured fragrant flowers, on long stalks, appear among the leaves in spring and occasionally a few blooms may appear in autumn. The plant also produces inconspicuous closed green flowers, especially in summer, which are self-pollinated and followed by green many-seeded capsules. The seeds have white appendages for which they are carried away by ants. Sweet Violet also spreads by long rooting stolons. It is an important medicinal plant, used as a laxative and in the preparation of cough syrup. Its sweet-scented oils are used less in the production of perfumes than formerly since they have been largely replaced by artificial scents.

Family	**Violaceae**	
Status	**Quite common**	
Distribution	**Mainly in England and Ireland**	J F M A M J J A S O N D
Height	**5—10 cm**	

Hairy St John's Wort

Hypericum hirsutum

This perennial clump-forming plant has several erect rounded stems and many opposite stalkless ovate leaves, all covered with hairs. This hairiness distinguishes this St John's wort from the others. The yellow flowers are borne in loose clusters in the axils of the uppermost leaves. Each has five sepals edged with black dots, five petals and many yellow stamens. The flowers are followed by fruiting capsules. Hairy St John's Wort grows throughout Europe and Siberia in open deciduous woodland and damp grassland, especially on basic soils.

Family	Hypericaceae
Status	Locally common
Distribution	Scattered over England, Wales and Scotland
Height	40—100 cm

J F M A M J J A S O N D

Common Violet

Viola riviniana

This clump-forming violet has long-stalked broadly heart-shaped basal leaves and ascending stems with pointed leaves. The stipules of both leaf types are lance-shaped with long fringes. The solitary scentless flowers are borne on long stalks in the axils of the leaves; they are more than 2 cm across, pale bluish-violet in colour with 3 mm-long white spurs, and are followed by fruiting capsules with yellow-white seeds. This is a European woodland species which also grows in hedgerows, grassland and heathland from lowland to mountain areas, except where the soil is very wet.

Family	Violaceae
Status	Very common
Distribution	Throughout Britain
Height	10—40 cm

J F M A M J J A S O N D

Mountain St John's Wort

Hypericum montanum

Unlike the preceding species this plant has an erect simple stem bearing a few pairs of small opposite lance-shaped leaves, with black-dotted margins, which clasp the stems with their bases. The pale yellow flowers are borne in a dense compact inflorescence and are chiefly notable for the numerous yellow stamens in a ring around the centre of the flower. This perennial warmth-loving species grows throughout much of Europe in open woodland, also in clearings and on the margins of the woods, in hedgerows and chalk scrub, mostly on calcareous and other rapidly draining soils.

Family	Hypericaceae		
Status	Local		
Distribution	England and Wales		
Height	30—90 cm		

J F M A M J J A S O N D

Common St John's Wort

Hypericum perforatum

This species grows in woodland, grassland and hedgerows throughout Europe except the far north where it is replaced by the similar Imperforate St John's Wort (*H. maculatum*) which has quadrangular stems. Common St John's Wort forms a colony with many erect rounded stems growing from a spreading underground stem system. The erect stems bear many opposite stalkless leaves, in the axils of which grow the clusters of yellow flowers. The most characteristic feature of the flowers are the numerous yellow stamens in their centres. The flower-stalks, petals, sepals, fruiting capsules and leaf margins are all covered with black dots. Common St John's Wort is used in herb medicine as a mild sedative and anti-depressant.

Family	Hypericaceae		
Other names	Perforate St John's Wort		
Status	Common		
Distribution	Throughout most of Britain		
Height	30—90 cm		

J F M A M J J A S O N D

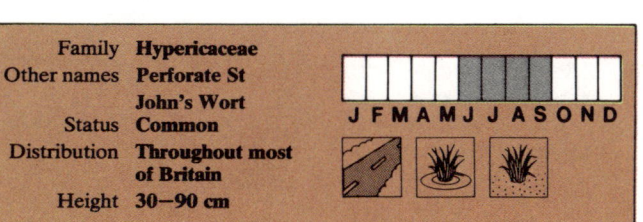

Bloody Cranesbill

Geranium sanguineum

This is a spreading clump-forming species with many invasive underground stems gradually increasing the size of the plant. From this underground network grow many slender reddish straggling stems with numerous deeply lobed palmate dark green leaves and bright pinkish-purple flowers growing in the leaf axils. Bloody Cranesbill grows on sunny grassy or rocky slopes and in open woodland, mainly in clearings and on the margins, in the lowlands and hills of Europe. There is also a prostrate subspecies which grows on stable sand dunes around the coasts, especially in the more northern areas. Both forms are grown in gardens, in flower borders and in rock gardens.

Family	Geraniaceae
Status	Local or rare
Distribution	Throughout much of Britain
Height	10—50 cm

J F M A M J J A S O N D

Masterwort

Astrantia major

This plant is rather different in appearance from all the other umbelliferous plants. It forms a clump of large rounded basal leaves, each with 3—7 coarsely toothed lobes, and several erect flowering stems. The flowers are borne in a wide-spreading compound umbel terminating each stem. Each umbel consists of several large, green-white finely-veined bracts which look like petals and many greenish-white or pink-tinged flowers; the whole umbel looks like a miniature posy. This is one of the few woodland species of this family. It grows scattered in the lowlands, but more often in the foothills of the European mountains, being most common in damp places in beech woods and in mountain meadows. It is often grown in flower borders.

Family	Umbelliferae
Other names	Astrantia
Status	Introduced
Distribution	Occasional
Height	30—75 cm

J F M A M J J A S O N D

Cowberry

Vaccinium vitis-idaea

This plant is found both in open birch and coniferous woodland and in heathlands on poor acid soils, where it is found growing with bilberries and heathers, throughout much of northern Europe especially in upland and mountain areas. It is a small creeping evergreen shrub with numerous erect and arching twigs and many small dark green oval leaves. The flowers are bell-shaped, white in colour tinged with pink and grow in small drooping terminal clusters. They are followed by round red acid-tasting berries which can be used to make jelly. The leaves are used in herb medicine as a treatment for rheumatism and arthritis.

Family	**Ericaceae**
Other names	**Red Whortleberry**
Status	**Locally common**
Distribution	**Mainly in Scotland, Wales and northern England**
Height	**5—30 cm**

J F M A M J J A S O N D

Bilberry

Vaccinium myrtillus

Bilberries grow throughout much of Europe in heathland and woodland on acid soils, usually in birch and coniferous woods, in upland and mountain areas and only on the mountains in southern Europe. It is a small creeping deciduous shrub with many erect branches and small bright green oval leaves. The solitary flowers grow in the axils of the leaves; they are bell-shaped, greenish-pink in colour and followed by round black sweet berries. These are good to eat and extensively used to make jams, jellies and fruit tarts. They are rich in Vitamins B and C when fresh and used in herb medicine in both fresh and dried conditions to treat intestinal disorders.

Family	**Ericaceae**
Other names	**Blaeberry, Whortleberry**
Status	**Common**
Distribution	**Throughout most of Britain**
Height	**15—50 cm**

J F M A M J J A S O N D

241

Common Centaury
Centaurium erythraea

This attractive annual plant has a basal rosette of oval, often spoon-shaped leaves and an erect leafy flowering stem with several opposite pairs of stalk-less, prominently veined leaves. The flowers are borne in a large terminal compound cluster; each one is tubular and funnel-shaped with five pinkish-red petals, and stamens inserted at the throat of the tube. Centaury grows throughout much of Europe and Asia, in woodland, wood margins and in dry grass-land; there is also a variety found on stable sand dunes in coastal areas. It is used in herb medicine as a tonic, to stimulate the appetite and to cleanse the liver and to purify the blood.

Family	Gentianaceae												
Synonyms	*Erythraea centaurium,* *C. umbellatum*												
Status	Common	J F M A M J J A S O N D											
Distribution	Mainly in England and Ireland												
Height	10—50 cm												

Oxlip
Primula elatior

A decorative spring-flowering plant which resembles the Cowslip. Both flower almost at the same time, often sharing habitats in Europe, but Oxlips grow at higher elevations in open woods whereas Cowslips are more often found in grassland. In Britain Oxlips are restricted to a few woods on chalky boulder clay in certain counties of East Anglia, where they replace Cowslips. Both species form rosettes of large toothed leaves but the flowers of Oxlips are larger than those of Cowslips, funnel-shaped and pale yellow with an orange mouth. The flowers grow in terminal droop-ing clusters on leafless flower-stalks. Both species are protected by law in certain European countries.

Family	Primulaceae												
Other names	Paigle												
Status	Very local	J F M A M J J A S O N D											
Distribution	East Anglia												
Height	10—30 cm												

Blue Gromwell

Lithospermum purpureocaeruleum

This perennial warmth-loving species grows mainly in central and southern Europe on calcareous soils, in limestone and chalk areas, in woodland margins and shrubby places from lowlands to the foothill areas. It has woody creeping stems with many sterile shoots and erect flowering shoots, all covered with narrowly lance-shaped leaves. The funnel-shaped flowers are borne in terminal clusters, opening bluish-purple and later turning to blue, as suggested by the Latin name. The flowers are followed by four glossy nutlets enclosed by the persistent sepals.

Family	Boraginaceae
Status	Very local
Distribution	Mainly around the Bristol Channel
Height	30—60 cm

J F M A M J J A S O N D

Lesser Periwinkle

Vinca minor

This perennial plant grows in the herb layer of open deciduous woodland where its slender trailing, root-ing stems often cover large areas. They are covered with many evergreen opposite, broadly lance-shaped leaves, in the axils of which grow the solitary flowers. These are bright blue in colour and funnel-shaped, opening in spring and followed, in the Mediterranean where the plant is native, by pods of several seeds. These are rarely produced in Britain or in the other areas of northern Europe where it has been intro-duced. The leaves of this plant and those of the Greater Periwinkle (*V. major*) are used in folk medicine as a laxative and to stop internal bleeding.

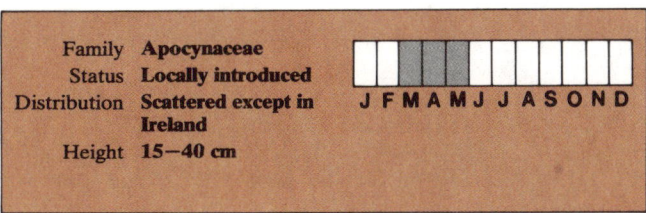

Family	Apocynaceae
Status	Locally introduced
Distribution	Scattered except in Ireland
Height	15—40 cm

J F M A M J J A S O N D

Betony

Stachys officinalis

In time this plant forms a spreading leafy mat of many rosettes growing from short woody rhizomes. The basal leaves are long-stalked, oblong and deeply toothed, dark green in colour and rather hairy. From this mat grow many erect stems with leaves similar to the basal ones, but smaller, and terminal spikes of large reddish-purple two-lipped flowers. Several cultivated varieties of Betony are grown in the flower border; in the wild it grows in grassland and heaths, open deciduous woods and hedgerows, more often on sandy soils than on clay soils, throughout much of Europe. It is used in herb medicine to alleviate intestinal discomfort.

Family	**Labiatae**
Synonyms	***Stachys betonica, Betonica officinalis***
Status	**Common**
Distribution	**Mainly in England and Wales**
Height	**30—80 cm**

J F M A M J J A S O N D

Bastard Balm

Mellitis melissophyllum

From thick underground stems grow erect angular stems bearing large opposite, coarsely toothed, strongly scented leaves. The whole plant is covered with soft hairs. The flowers grow in whorls in the axils of the upper leaves, they are large and two-lipped, white in colour and often tinged or spotted with pink, with large bell-shaped sepal-tubes. The sepals persist to enclose the fruits — four smooth nutlets. This rather rare plant grows in central and southern Europe in open deciduous woodland and hedgebanks, from lowlands to mountain elevations.

Family	**Labiatae**
Status	**Very local**
Distribution	**Southwest England, Sussex and South Wales**
Height	**20—50 cm**

J F M A M J J A S O N D

Deadly Nightshade

Atropa belladonna

A bushy perennial plant with large pointed-oval leaves and a few solitary drooping flowers, growing on short stalks in the axils of the upper leaves. The bell-shaped flowers are conspicuous in size but not in colour, for they are up to 30 mm long but greenish-violet in colour. They are followed by characteristic shiny black berries cupped in the persistent sepals. Like the other members of this family already described, Henbane and Woody Nightshade, this plant is deadly poisonous. The juice of the berries causes dilation of the pupil of the eye and it is now used carefully by opticians for eye examinations, unlike the days when beautiful women used it as a cosmetic to enlarge their eyes — a risky proceeding. The plant grows in wasteland, woodland and hedgerows throughout central and southern Europe, especially on calcareous soils.

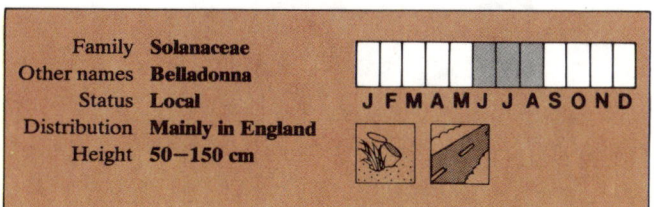

Family	Solanaceae														
Other names	Belladonna	J	F	M	A	M	J	J	A	S	O	N	D		
Status	Local														
Distribution	Mainly in England														
Height	50—150 cm														

Common Speedwell

Veronica officinalis

This small mat-forming plant grows in Europe from lowlands up to the subalpine belt, often in open woodland, but also in sunny meadows, on roadside verges and in hedgerows, usually on dry soils. It has many creeping hairy stems which form roots wherever they touch the ground and which bear many opposite pairs of oval leaves. The flowers are borne in erect racemes on long stalks growing from the axils of some of the leaves. They are lilac in colour, funnel-shaped with four petals of which the uppermost is the largest; they are followed by capsules with many tiny seeds. Speedwell is used in herb medicine to alleviate coughs and to treat skin complaints.

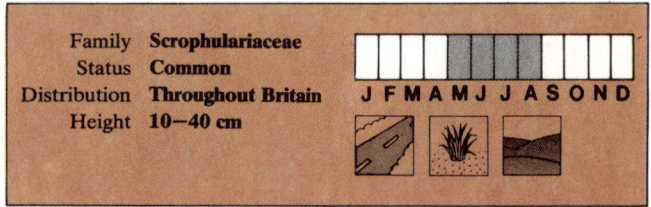

Family	Scrophulariaceae	J	F	M	A	M	J	J	A	S	O	N	D
Status	Common												
Distribution	Throughout Britain												
Height	10—40 cm												

Common Cow-wheat
Melampyrum pratense

An easily identifiable annual plant of deciduous woodland clearings and heathland, especially on rocky banks of streams and hillsides, throughout much of Europe. It has thin erect or ascending stems with many opposite lance-shaped leaves and horizontally borne flowers in the axils of the uppermost. The flowers are distinctive, each with a long thin, pale whitish-yellow tubular base and a more or less closed mouth, deeper yellow in colour. The flowers are followed by four-seeded capsules. This is one of the semi-parasitic members of this family partially dependent on the grasses, with which it grows, for its water and nutrients and its roots become attached to those of its hosts.

Family	**Scrophulariaceae**	
Status	**Locally common**	
Distribution	**Throughout Britain**	J F M A M J J A S O N D
Height	**10—50 cm**	

Foxglove
Digitalis purpurea

A biennial plant with a rosette of downy, broadly lance-shaped, dark green leaves in the first year and a tall flowering stem in the second, with many pinkish-purple tubular flowers, opening in long succession from the bottom upwards. The flowers are followed by rounded capsules, each with a long persistent style, and partially enclosed by the sepal-tube. This plant is very characteristic of open deciduous woodland, mountain rocks and heaths on acid soils in western Europe. It is a valuable medicinal plant for the vital heart medicine, digitalis, is extracted from its leaves. However, it is very poisonous in the fresh state causing drowsiness, convulsions and even death.

Family	**Scrophulariaceae**	
Status	**Common**	
Distribution	**Throughout Britain**	J F M A M J J A S O N D
Height	**50—150 cm**	

Crosswort

Galium cruciata

This branched trailing perennial plant has many slender, creeping and ascending stems, densely clothed with many whorls of four narrow leaves and many spreading hairs. Numerous honey-scented yellow funnel-shaped flowers grow in whorls in the axils of the leaves, followed by pairs of single-seeded fruits growing on curved stalks. Crosswort grows in open deciduous woodland, in hedgerows and scrubland, on roadsides and in grassland throughout central and southern Europe, especially on calcareous soils. It was used at one time in herb medicine, as an effective treatment both for internal and external wounds, although it is little used today.

Family	Rubiaceae			
Synonyms	*Valantia cruciata,* *Cruciata chersonensis*			
Other names	Mugwort	J F M A M J J A S O N D		
Status	Common			
Distribution	England, Wales and southern Scotland			
Height	20—50 cm			

Wood Cow-wheat

Melampyrum sylvaticum

This is a low-growing annual plant growing in open woodland, particularly in the coniferous forests of the mountain regions of northern Europe; it is rare in Britain and confined to mountain woodland, almost entirely in Scotland. It has branched stems with opposite lance-shaped leaves and solitary brownish-yellow flowers, half the size of the flowers of the Common Cow-wheat and borne more or less erect in the axils of the upper leaves. The flowers are open-mouthed, unlike those of the Common Cow-wheat in which the mouths of the flowers are closed. They are followed by two-seeded capsules. Like the other cow-wheats this plant is a partial parasite in its way of life.

Family	Scrophulariaceae			
Status	Rare	J F M A M J J A S O N D		
Distribution	Central Scotland			
Height	10—30 cm			

Peach-leaved Bellflower
Campanula persicifolia

This decorative bellflower grows in open deciduous woodland, on roadsides and in hedgerows throughout Europe and western Asia in lowlands and foothill areas, although it is introduced in Britain and only found growing as a garden escape. Many varieties and cultivars are grown in flower borders, including white and double-flowered forms. This bellflower forms slowly spreading mats of lance-shaped leaves from which grow tall erect flowering stems. These bear alternate lance-shaped leaves and a terminal raceme of large bell-shaped light blue flowers, which are followed by many-seeded capsules. Like all *Campanula* species, the stems of this plant are full of milky sap.

Family	**Campanulaceae**	
Status	**A well-established garden escape**	J F M A M J J A S O N D
Distribution	**Scattered in England and Scotland**	
Height	**30—80 cm**	

Bats-in-the-Belfry
Campanula trachelium

A non-flowering specimen of this plant resembles a Stinging Nettle with erect quadrangular stems bearing many alternate nettle-like leaves, all covered with bristly hairs. However, once the flowers appear in the upper leaf axils there is no mistaking it for anything other than a bellflower. The flowers often grow in small clusters; they are large, up to 4 cm long, bell-shaped and blue-violet or occasionally white in colour, with long whitish hairs inside and along the margins. The plant grows in open woods and in hedgebanks throughout Europe from lowlands to foothills, especially where the soil is heavy and moist.

Family	**Campanulaceae**	
Other names	**Nettle-leaved Bellflower**	J F M A M J J A S O N D
Status	**Local**	
Distribution	**Southern areas of Britain**	
Height	**60—100 cm**	

248

Spiked Rampion

Phyteuma spicatum

A strange-looking hairless perennial plant that grows in deciduous woodland and meadows, in lowland and upland areas, throughout much of Europe although it is very rare in Britain. It has a rosette of long-stalked heart-shaped basal leaves and a single erect flowering stalk with similar leaves and a cylindrical terminal spike of flowers. The flowers are greenish-yellow in colour, with linear petals which are joined at the tips in the bud, later separating and spreading out to expose the stamens and style. The fruiting spike which follows is larger with many capsules each crowned with stiff teeth.

Family	Campanulaceae		
Status	Very rare		
Distribution	East Sussex		
Height	30—80 cm		

J F M A M J J A S O N D

Leafy Hawkweed

Hieracium umbellatum

Unlike many hawkweeds, this species has no basal rosette of leaves; instead, its stems are densely covered with alternate, narrowly lance-shaped, irregularly toothed leaves, the lowermost of which wither during flowering. The yellow flower-heads are borne in an umbel terminating the stem, in late summer. Each has an involucre of blackish-green bracts and many yellow ray florets, and is followed by heads of hairy single-seeded fruits. This plant grows in open deciduous woodland, on roadside verges and heathland, in stony and rocky ground throughout the lowland areas of the Northern Hemisphere.

Family	Compositae		
Other names	Umbellate Hawkweed		
Status	Common		
Distribution	Throughout Britain		
Height	10—80 cm		

J F M A M J J A S O N D

Golden Rod
Solidago virgaurea

A frequent, very variable plant of dry woodland, grassland and hedgerows, often growing on rocky slopes and cliffs and on sand dunes near the coast throughout Europe, Asia and North America. It produces a clump of erect straight stems with many dark green lance-shaped leaves. The flower-heads are formed of bright yellow ray florets and are arranged in spray-like inflorescences, like racemes, in the axils of the uppermost leaves; the overall effect is of a characteristically-shaped terminal cluster of flowers, immediately recognisable as belonging to a Golden Rod. The single-seeded fruits which follow bear many short hairs, giving them a fluffy appearance in the mass. Golden Rod is used in herb medicine as an effective treatment for kidney stones and gravel and externally to promote the healing of wounds.

Family	**Compositae**
Status	**Mostly common**
Distribution	**Throughout much of Britain**
Height	**15—100 cm**

J F M A M J J A S O N D

Wood Cudweed
Gnaphalium sylvaticum

A perennial plant with short leafy shoots producing no flowers and simple erect flowering stems. The leaves are linear to lance-shaped, becoming smaller towards the tops of the stems. The flowers are borne in flower-heads in the axils of the leaves, the whole inflorescence forming a large spike. Each flower-head has an involucre of pale brown, green-striped membranous bracts and brown tubular disk florets. They are followed by heads of bristly fruits with reddish hairs. The whole plant is covered with whitish woolly hairs. Wood Cudweed grows in open woodland, in margins and clearings, in dry meadows and pastures and on heathlands, on dry acid soils, throughout Europe and the eastern parts of North America from lowlands to alpine areas.

Family	**Compositae**
Other names	**Heath Cudweed**
Status	**Locally common**
Distribution	**Throughout Britain**
Height	**10—60 cm**

J F M A M J J A S O N D

Martagon Lily

Lilium martagon

This decorative plant grows in deciduous mixed woodland in many scattered areas of Britain, probably as a well-established escape from flower gardens. In Europe it grows in the hills in deciduous woodland as well as in high-mountain meadows above the timberline. It is protected in some countries. It has a yellow scaly bulb, located deep in the ground, from which grows a single erect stem. The lance-shaped leaves are mostly arranged in a whorl about halfway up the stem, with only a few smaller single leaves growing separately. Several large pink purple-spotted flowers grow on drooping stalks at the top of the stem. They are supposed to resemble turbans, hence the name Turk's Cap Lily. The flowers are followed by large egg-shaped capsules containing many flattened seeds.

		J F M A M J J A S O N D
Family	**Liliaceae**	
Other names	**Turk's Cap Lily**	
Status	**Scattered, possibly introduced**	
Distribution	**England and Wales**	
Height	**40—100 cm**	

Saw-wort

Serratula tinctoria

From a stout rootstock grows a single tall stem with many variable toothed lance-shaped leaves on its lower part, branching to form a loose inflorescence higher up. The flower-heads are borne in many small clusters; male and female florets grow in separate heads, male heads being smaller than female. Both kinds are composed of tubular reddish-purple florets and the female heads are followed by heads of pale brown single-seeded fruits with yellowish hairs. Saw-wort grows in moist woodland and damp grassland on basic soils throughout much of Europe and Siberia. It was used at one time for the yellow dye which can be extracted from its leaves.

		J F M A M J J A S O N D
Family	**Compositae**	
Status	**Local**	
Distribution	**England and Wales**	
Height	**30—100 cm**	

Bluebell

Hyacinthoides non-scripta

Perhaps the one plant more commonly associated with the open deciduous woodlands of western maritime Europe, than any other. It forms wide-spreading colonies in oak and beech woods, especially on light acid soils, growing from numerous underground bulbs. From each bulb in early spring grows a clump of soft grass-like leaves, followed by a leafless flowering stalk with a terminal nodding raceme of blue, sometimes white or pink, bell-like flowers. Bluebell bulbs were used as a source of starch for stiffening collars in mediaeval times but the digging up of the bulbs is now illegal. The flowers are less common than formerly for, in picking them, flower collectors cannot help but trample the leaves thus starving the plants which depend on healthy leaves to manufacture next year's bulbs.

Family	Liliaceae
Synonyms	*Endymion non-scriptus, Scilla non-scripta*
Other names	Wild Hyacinth
Status	Common
Distribution	Throughout Britain
Height	15—40 cm

J F M A M J J A S O N D

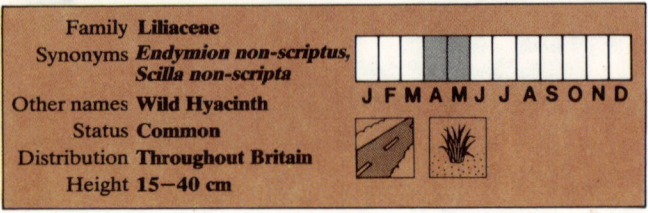

Lily-of-the-Valley

Convallaria majalis

From long creeping rhizomes grow erect shoots, each with two long-oval leaves sheathed at the bases of the leaf-stalks and a leafless flowering stalk emerging from the sheath. The flowers are borne in one-sided nodding racemes; they are white in colour, globular bell-shaped and sweetly scented, each growing from the axil of a tiny bract and followed by a red berry. Wide-spreading colonies of this plant may grow in suitable conditions in gardens and dry woods, usually on calcareous soils, throughout much of Europe. It is protected in many areas for it has been seriously threatened by pickers and it seems to be very particular in its habitat requirements. The plant is used in medicine, for the chemicals it contains form an effective heart stimulant. The flowers are used in perfumery.

Family	Liliaceae
Status	Local
Distribution	Mainly in England and Scotland
Height	10—20 cm

J F M A M J J A S O N D

Lady Orchid
Orchis purpurea

A most attractive but quickly disappearing wild flowering plant, growing in southern and central Europe particularly in woodland on chalk and limestone. In Britain it is now found only in Kent and is extinct in the other southern counties. It has a large ovoid tuber which produces a clump of several glossy leaves, 6—15 cm long, the largest at the base and the uppermost growing on the erect stem. The spurred flowers are borne in a rich cylindrical inflorescence which terminates the stem. Each has a hood, dark reddish-purple in colour and mottled with purple inside, and a paler lower lip with many tufts of reddish hairs and reddish spots. The Lady Orchid is now protected by law in many countries.

Family	Orchidaceae
Status	Rare
Distribution	Southeastern England
Height	30—70 cm

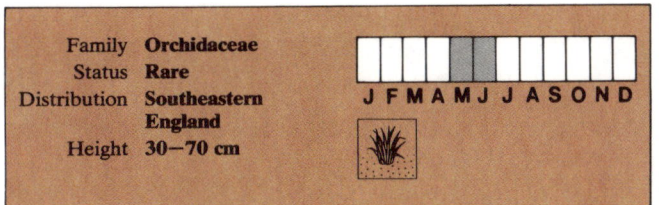

J F M A M J J A S O N D

Lesser Butterfly Orchid
Platanthera bifolia

The lowlands and foothills of Europe and western Asia are the home of this relatively common orchid. It grows mostly in deciduous oak and beech woodland or sometimes in mountain meadows, especially in chalk and limestone areas and on other basic soils. From an underground tuber grows a pair of elliptical leaves and an upright stem with more leaves sheathing its base. This is terminated by a sparse spike of white flowers, fragrant at night and pollinated by moths. It has typical orchid flowers, hooded with a long downcurved spur and a long drooping strap-shaped lower lip. The Lesser Butterfly Orchid is protected by law in many countries.

Family	Orchidaceae
Synonyms	Orchis bifolia, O. montana
Status	Relatively common
Distribution	Scattered throughout Britain
Height	20—55 cm

J F M A M J J A S O N D

Lady's Slipper
Cypripedium calceolus

This wild orchid is native to the temperate woodland of Europe and Asia, but its spectacular appearance has been the cause of its widespread disappearance. Many people have attempted to dig it up and transplant it to their gardens, without success for it does not move well and the gardens did not provide the woodland conditions it needed. What few plants remain are now strictly protected by law. In the wild it grows in open deciduous woods in limestone or dolomite areas. Lady's Slipper has a creeping rhizome from which grows an erect stem with three or four ovate leaves. Two or three flowers are borne at the top of the stem, each with a pale yellow lip resembling a slipper, and maroon upper and side petals.

Family	**Orchidaceae**
Status	**Very rare**
Distribution	**Northern England**
Height	**20—45 cm**

J F M A M J J A S O N D

Broad Helleborine
Epipactis helleborine

This orchid has a short rhizome from which grows a sparsely hairy, erect flowering stem, clothed with spirally arranged broadly ovate leaves which clasp the stem, becoming smaller towards the top. The stem is often violet-tinged at the base, becoming whiter near the top. The flowers grow in a loose terminal spike; they are greenish-brown in colour with a prominent purplish lower lip and a small hood. Unlike those of many orchids, the flowers of the helleborines are spurless. This helleborine grows in open deciduous woodland, in wood margins and hedgerows particularly in the beech woods of the chalk, throughout much of Europe and western Asia.

Family	**Orchidaceae**
Synonyms	*E. latifolia*
Other names	**Common Helleborine**
Status	**Local**
Distribution	**Mainly in England, Wales and Ireland**
Height	**20—70 cm**

J F M A M J J A S O N D

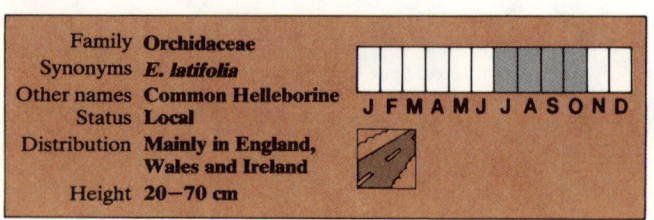

Species featured
in this section

Species featured
in another section

Baneberry
Actaea spicata

A species of shady deciduous woodland, growing only in ashwoods in limestone areas and on limestone pavement in northern England in Britain, but found in beech and mixed woods as well in Europe and western Siberia, where it grows in rocky wooded gorges, screes and under rocky overhangs in foothill and mountain regions. It has a black creeping rootstock from which grows a clump of long-stalked compound leaves, dark green and hairless like the rest of the plant. Several erect leafy flowering stalks bear terminal racemes of pure white flowers, followed by black berries. These berries are acrid and poisonous, as is the whole plant, blistering the skin and causing sickness and diarrhoea if eaten.

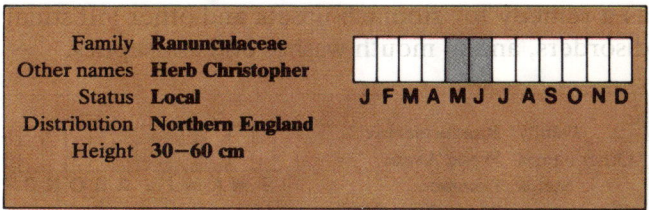

Family	Ranunculaceae		J F M A M J J A S O N D
Other names	Herb Christopher		
Status	Local		
Distribution	Northern England		
Height	30—60 cm		

Lesser Celandine
Ranunculus ficaria

Damp shady and sunny places, in deciduous woodland and hedgerows, in damp meadows and beside streams; all are good habitats to look for Lesser Celandines. This is a perennial plant with many rosettes of stalked heart-shaped, dark green leaves growing from underground clumps of club-shaped tubers and often forming wide-spreading carpets. The solitary shiny-yellow flowers grow on long stalks in spring, often transforming the carpet from a green one into a yellow one. In some forms of this plant few flowers are produced and instead white reproductive tubers are formed in the axils of the leaves. Lesser Celandine can be used, like watercress, in salads and sandwiches and its buds can be pickled as a substitute for capers. It is used in herb medicine as a remedy for piles and scurvy.

Family	Ranunculaceae		J F M A M J J A S O N D
Synonyms	*Ficaria verna, F. ranunculoides*		
Other names	Pilewort		
Status	Common		
Distribution	Throughout Britain		
Height	5—20 cm		

Herb Bennet

Geum urbanum

This is a perennial plant forming a ground rosette of compound leaves. The leaves resemble those of the related Water Avens (*G. rivale*), the rosette leaves being lyre-shaped with small leaflets alternating with large ones while the leaves of the flowering stems are basically three-lobed with large stipules. The small yellow flowers grow on long stalks in the axils of the upper leaves; they have five reflexed sepals and five petals and are followed by the characteristic *Geum* fruits. These are round clusters of hooked single-seeded fruits which catch in the fur of passing animals. Herb Bennet is a common plant of mixed deciduous woodland, hedgerows and other shady places, especially where the soil is damp, throughout much of Europe and Asia. It is used in herb medicine as a remedy for stomach upsets and other intestinal disorders, and in mouth washes and antiseptics.

Family	**Ranunculaceae**	
Other names	**Wood Avens**	
Status	**Common**	J F M A M J J A S O N D
Distribution	**Throughout Britain**	
Height	**30—60 cm**	

Common Enchanter's Nightshade

Circaea lutetiana

This plant often covers large areas in shady woodland, in areas where the light is too dim for other plants to grow; it does not do well in more open places. It grows throughout Europe on moist basic soils. It is a perennial herb with slender creeping rhizomes and large dull green, heart-shaped leaves covering the ground. The flowers are borne on straggling flowering stems; they are whitish in colour, each with two petals joined at the base, and they are followed by distinctive drooping fruits which are covered with hooked bristles. These catch on the fur of mammals or on birds' feathers and so the fruits are dispersed. The strange name 'Enchanter's Nightshade' is apparently derived from Greek times when the plant was named after Circe, the mythical enchantress.

Family	**Onagraceae**	
Status	**Common**	J F M A M J J A S O N D
Distribution	**Throughout Britain**	
Height	**20—60 cm**	

Coral-wort

Cardamine bulbifera

A perennial plant growing in deciduous and mixed mountain woodland or occasionally in lowland woods, mainly in central Europe; it is rare in Britain. It is most common in beechwoods on loose humus-rich soils. It resembles Lady's Smock and is often placed in the same genus as that plant (*Cardamine*) but may be classed separately in the genus *Dentaria*. Coral-wort has a creeping fleshy rhizome, like all species of *Dentaria,* with an erect stem, compound leaves with 5−7 lance-shaped leaflets and a terminal raceme of lilac flowers. Conspicuous dark brown bulbils, formed in the axils of the leaves, overwinter under fallen leaves and produce new plantlets in the spring.

Family	**Cruciferae**	
Synonym	***Dentaria bulbifera***	
Other names	**Coralroot**	
Status	**Very local**	J F M A M J J A S O N D
Distribution	**Southeast and southwest England**	
Height	**30−60 cm**	

Dame's Violet

Hesperis matronalis

An interesting biennial or perennial woodland herb with a pleasant fragrance which becomes most noticeable towards evening. It has oval toothed basal leaves and an erect stem with lance-shaped leaves, becoming smaller higher up the stem. There is a terminal raceme of stock-like flowers. The flowers have four petals, usually violet in colour but occasionally white, and they are followed by long slender pods each with a row of seeds. This plant is grown in flower gardens and sometimes seeds itself to grow wild in Britain. It is native to Europe and much of Asia, growing in damp shady woods and hedgerows.

Family	**Cruciferae**	
Other names	**Sweet Rocket**	
Status	**Garden escape**	J F M A M J J A S O N D
Distribution	**Occasionally naturalized**	
Height	**40−100 cm**	

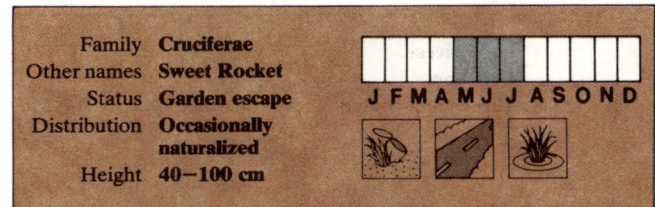

Small Balsam

Impatiens parviflora

Small Balsam is native to central Asia. It is an annual species which has spread to central Europe in the last 50 years or so, to become naturalized in shady deciduous woodlands, hedgerows and wastelands, where it grows on good soils from lowlands to upland areas. It has an erect hairless stem with alternate pointed leaves and racemes of flowers borne on long stalks in the leaf axils. The small flowers are pale yellow and red-dotted inside, with a straight spur; and they are followed by fruiting capsules which burst on touch, the valves coiling into a spiral and shooting the seeds to a great distance away from the parent plant.

Family	Balsaminaceae													
Status	Locally naturalized	J	F	M	A	M	J	J	A	S	O	N	D
Distribution	Mainly in England and Wales													
Height	30—60 cm													

Wood Sorrel

Oxalis acetosella

From a network of thin underground creeping stems grow the small leaves and flowers of the Wood Sorrel, in many small rosettes. The compound leaves are a distinctive bright green, with three heart-shaped leaflets; they exhibit sleep movements by folding down along the central leaf-stalk in the evening or in rain. The solitary flowers are white with violet veins, growing on long stalks in late spring or early summer. Wood Sorrel also produces small closed flowers, close to the ground and resembling buds that never open; these are self-fertilized and produce capsules with many seeds. The name *Oxalis* refers to the oxalic acid content of the leaves; they can be used in herb medicine to combat scurvy and to reduce fever. It is found in shady deciduous woods and hedgebanks throughout Europe and northern Asia.

Family	Oxalidaceae													
Status	Common	J	F	M	A	M	J	J	A	S	O	N	D
Distribution	Throughout Britain													
Height	5—15 cm													

Sanicle
Sanicula europaea

This woodland plant has a basal clump of long-stalked glossy, palmately-lobed leaves and several erect leafless unbranched flowering stalks, each with a compound umbel of white or pink flowers at the top. The male and female flowers are separate and the female ones are followed by tiny fruits covered with hooked bristles. Sanicle is particularly likely to be found in beech woods and oak woods, especially on loamy calcareous soils where it may form large colonies. It grows throughout Europe and parts of Asia Minor in lowlands and mountain areas, but only in mountain woods in southern Europe. It is used in herb medicine as a remedy for throat and mouth infections.

Family	Umbelliferae
Status	Locally common
Distribution	Throughout Britain
Height	30—60 cm

J F M A M J J A S O N D

Wild Angelica
Angelica sylvestris

This biennial or perennial plant has a stout rhizome from which grows a hollow longitudinally grooved purplish stem with many compound divided leaves. The leaves are dark green with ovate leaflets and swollen sheaths around the base of the grooved leaf-stalks, where they join the stems. The small white, pink-tinged flowers of Wild Angelica are borne in compound umbels at the top of the stem. They are followed by paired winged fruits, each with a single seed. This is not the Garden Angelica (*A. archangelica*) that is used as a candy and in herb medicine, but it can be used in some of the same ways to treat throat and chest infections. It grows in damp woodland, marshes, fens and damp meadows in Europe and much of Asia, commoner in the north than in the south.

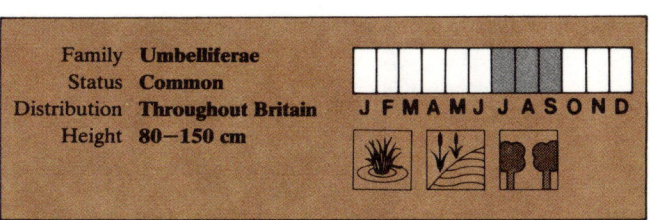

Family	Umbelliferae
Status	Common
Distribution	Throughout Britain
Height	80—150 cm

J F M A M J J A S O N D

Wood Spurge

Euphorbia amygdaloides

This plant forms a clump of shoots, sterile in the first year, lengthening, flowering and setting seed in the second year, while a new set of first-year shoots is formed at the same time. The leaves of the first year shoots are dark green and lance-shaped; they persist in the second year, when the shoots lengthen, to form a whorl beneath the inflorescence. The flowers are tiny, males and females separate in small clusters cupped by conspicuous green kidney-shaped bracts. Like all spurges the whole plant is filled with milky white sap. Wood Spurge grows in damp areas of mixed deciduous woodland, in central and southern Europe in lowland and mountain areas.

Family	Euphorbiaceae	J F M A M J J A S O N D
Status	Locally common	
Distribution	Mainly in southern England and Wales	
Height	30—80 cm	

Dog's Mercury

Mercurialis perennis

Dog's Mercury has many slender creeping rhizomes from which grow numerous erect angular stems with opposite dark green lance-shaped leaves — it often forms wide spreading carpets beneath the trees. From the axils of the upper leaves emerge flowering spikes of green flowers, male and female on separate plants. The female flowers are borne in ones or twos on long stalks and are followed by paired rounded hairy fruits, each with a single seed. The male flowers grow in slender multiflowered spikes. Dog's Mercury grows in shady woodland in the lowland and mountain areas of Europe, especially in beech woods on the chalk downs, in mountain woodland and amongst shady rocks. It may dominate the field layer to such an extent that little else grows. It is highly poisonous.

Family	Euphorbiaceae	J F M A M J J A S O N D
Status	Very common	
Distribution	Throughout Britain	
Height	15—40 cm	

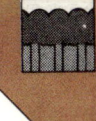

Red Campion

Silene dioica

A clump-forming plant, usually a short-lived perennial but sometimes surviving for only a year. It forms many small non-flowering shoots and several or many taller flowering shoots, all with opposite lance-shaped leaves and covered with spreading hairs. The bright reddish-pink flowers grow in pairs, grouped into larger clusters terminating the stems. Each has a large sticky brownish sepal-tube, five forked petals joined to form a tube within the sepal-tube and several white scales at the throat of the flower. Male and female flowers are borne separately and the female flowers are followed by toothed brown capsules with many seeds. Red Campion grows in many different places, in woodland, in clearings and margins, in hedgerows and on rocky cliffs and screes, especially on basic soils throughout Europe, western Asia and north Africa.

Family	Caryophyllaceae	
Synonyms	*Lychnis dioica, Melandrium rubrum, M. dioica*	J F M A M J J A S O N D
Status	Locally common	
Distribution	Throughout Britain	
Height	30—90 cm	

Greater Stitchwort

Stellaria holostea

This pale green perennial plant has many weak ascending stems forming a loose straggling clump, and many opposite pairs of linear, horizontally spreading leaves, fused together across the stem at the base. The large white satiny flowers are borne in pairs on long stalks, grouped together into large loose clusters. In each flower the five petals are deeply cut into two, so that it might appear to have ten petals. The flowers are followed by rounded capsules cupped in persistent sepals and containing many brown seeds. Greater Stitchwort grows in woodland and hedgerows throughout Europe and the Near East. The name 'Stitchwort' comes from the ancient use of the several species of stitchworts in herb medicine, for they were believed to ease a 'stitch' in the side.

Family	Caryophyllaceae	
Other names	Satin Flower	
Status	Common	J F M A M J J A S O N D
Distribution	Throughout Britain	
Height	15—30 cm	

Serrated Wintergreen

Orthilia secunda

A semi-shrubby herb with a woody base and a long creeping rhizome, which very much resembles members of the genus *Pyrola*. It has long-stalked ovate leaves which are leathery, frost-resistant and evergreen. The flowers are borne in dense one-sided racemes growing on long stalks from the axils of the leaves, in contrast to the inflorescences of *Pyrola* in which the flowers face in all directions. Serrated Wintergreen flowers are greenish white, rather bell-like in shape but with free petals and a long style. The plant grows from lowlands to mountain areas, on damp rock ledges and in coniferous and mixed deciduous woodland on acid humusy soils. It is scattered throughout all of the Northern Hemisphere, but is not very common and is protected in many countries.

Family	**Pyrolaceae**
Synonyms	***Pyrola secunda, Ramischia secunda***
Status	**Local**
Distribution	**Mainly in Scotland**
Height	**5—20 cm**

J F M A M J J A S O N D

Large Wintergreen

Pyrola rotundifolia

This plant grows in shady woodland as well as in bogs, wet marshes and meadows, and damp rocky ledges in mountain areas in Europe and Asia. A subspecies also grows in damp areas in sand dunes. The branched creeping underground stems produce rosettes of leathery rounded evergreen leaves and leafless stems, with white flowers in short dense flower sprays. A conspicuously long, curved style protrudes from the broadly bell-shaped flower. The name *Pyrola* comes from the shape of the leaves which are pear-shaped. The leaves are used in herb medicine in the treatment of skin disorders, in healing infected wounds and in treating urinary problems.

Family	**Pyrolaceae**
Status	**Rare**
Distribution	**Scattered throughout Britain**
Height	**15—30 cm**

J F M A M J J A S O N D

Chickweed Wintergreen

Trientalis europaea

From creeping slender underground stems grow erect unbranched stems, each with a single whorl of shining oval or lance-shaped leaves at the top and a few small alternate leaves lower down. A solitary white flower grows on a long stalk from the centre of the leaf whorl. It is broadly funnel-shaped with seven white petals spreading horizontally and is followed by a rounded capsule containing a few seeds. Chickweed Wintergreen forms spreading colonies in pine and birch woodland, in heathland and grassland, in humus-rich acid peaty soils throughout the Northern Hemisphere. It has been used in herb medicine in ointments to speed the healing of wounds.

Family	**Primulaceae**	
Status	**Local**	
Distribution	**Scotland and northern England**	
Height	**10—20 cm**	

J F M A M J J A S O N D

Yellow Bird's-nest

Monotropa hypopitys

One of a small group of plants lacking chlorophyll, not a parasite, however, but a saprophyte living on rotting leaves and other decaying organic material. This perennial plant has a simple whitish-yellow waxy stem, bearing many entire leaf-scales, at first with a drooping tip which becomes erect when the flowers, 10—15 to a plant, begin to open. These are arranged in a short terminal raceme, they are yellow in colour, bell-shaped with short stalks and are followed by multi-seeded capsules. Yellow Bird's-nest grows in scattered localities throughout much of Europe, in mixed deciduous woodland on acid soils. It is also found in a rather specialised kind of stable sand dune community, growing on dunes colonised by Creeping Willow (*Salix repens*) where the fallen leaves from the willow form a decaying layer beneath the shrubs.

Family	**Monotropaceae**	
Synonym	*Hypopitys multiflora*	
Status	**Local**	
Distribution	**Scattered, mainly in southern Britain**	
Height	**10—25 cm**	

J F M A M J J A S O N D

Common Cyclamen

Cyclamen purpurascens

Black flattened spherical tubers of this decorative plant produce many roots growing from all over their surface (in contrast to the other hardy cyclamen species, *C. hederifolium,* in which the roots grow only from the top of the tuber) and long-stalked rounded heart-shaped leaves. These are leathery in texture with a white pattern on the green surface. Many sweetly scented pale purple flowers grow on long stalks in summer with the leaves; they have the typical cyclamen shape with recurved petals, each with a crimson blotch at the base. The flowers of *C. hederifolium* appear before the leaves in autumn and are scentless. The flowers are followed by spherical capsules which are distinctive, for the long flowering stalks become coiled drawing the capsules down into the ground. It grows in deciduous woodland in Europe, especially in beech woods on chalk and limestone.

Family	**Primulaceae**	
Synonym	***C. europaeum***	
Status	**A garden species**	J F M A M J J A S O N D
Distribution	**Occasional**	
Height	**5—15 cm**	

Asarabacca

Asarum europaeum

Thick creeping rhizomes beneath the ground produce many short shoots, each with two kidney-shaped dark green leaves on long hairy stalks and a single terminal flower. The flowers appear in spring and are very inconspicuous, reddish-brown in colour and bell-shaped; they are followed by rounded capsules containing flat seeds. The plant is most likely to be seen in the non-flowering state for the leaves are almost evergreen and persist throughout much of the year. Asarabacca grows mainly in central Europe, in wet deciduous and coniferous woodland. At one time it was widely grown in Britain for its use as an active ingredient in snuff but it is now rare.

Family	**Aristolochiaceae**	
Status	**Rare**	
Distribution	**England and Wales**	J F M A M J J A S O N D
Height	**5—10 cm**	

Tuberous Comfrey

Symphytum tuberosum

This clump-forming perennial plant grows locally in wet deciduous and mixed woodland, along streams and hedgerows and in shaded clearings in the mountains and lowlands of Europe. The tuberously thickened underground rhizomes produce erect un-branched hairy stems with many simple, coarsely hairy leaves, ovate or lance-shaped depending on whether they are growing at the base or the top of the stem. The bell-shaped yellow-white flowers are borne in terminal one-sided clusters and each is followed by four nutlets, enclosed in a persistent sepal-tube. Tuberous Comfrey can be distinguished from its relative, the Common Comfrey (*S. officinale*), by its lack of winged leaf bases — the leaf bases of the Common Comfrey are winged and appear to run down the stem.

Family	Boraginaceae
Status	Local
Distribution	Most common in Scotland
Height	20—50 cm

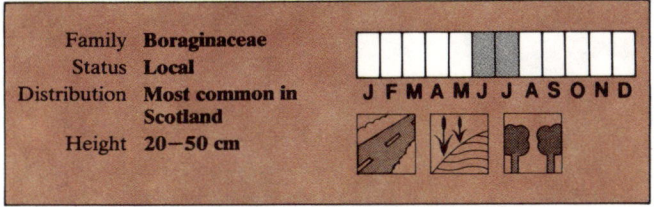

J F M A M J J A S O N D

Wood Forget-me-not

Myosotis sylvatica

An erect perennial plant, like the familiar garden forget-me-not but larger, with a rosette of spoon-shaped basal leaves and spreading stems bearing stalkless lance-shaped leaves, all covered with spreading hairs. The flowers are borne in loose one-sided clusters which become looser and more elongated as flowering progresses and fruits are formed. The flowers are funnel-shaped with flattened edges, bright blue in colour with an orange ring at the centre. The nutlets which follow are dark brown and shiny. Wood Forget-me-not grows in damp deciduous woods in Britain and in similar habitats in Europe, where it is also found in mountain woods and high altitude meadows.

Family	Boraginaceae
Status	Locally common
Distribution	Mainly in central and eastern England
Height	15—45 cm

J F M A M J J A S O N D

Hedge Woundwort
Stachys sylvatica

From long creeping rhizomes grow many erect, finely hairy, quadrangular stems with many pairs of opposite long-stalked leaves. The leaves are heart-shaped, coarsely toothed and densely hairy all over, with an unpleasant scent when bruised. The reddish-violet flowers grow in many whorls, of about six flowers in each, in the axils of the uppermost leaves. The flowers are two-lipped with a helmet-shaped upper lip and a three-lobed lower lip, patterned with white markings. Hedge Woundwort grows in damp deciduous woodland, hedgerows and shady waste places throughout lowland Europe and western Asia and in spruce woods in mountain areas.

Family	**Labiatae**
Status	**Common**
Distribution	**Throughout Britain**
Height	**30—100 cm**

J F M A M J J A S O N D

Yellow Archangel
Lamiastrum galeobdolon

An invasive trailing plant with far-flung prostrate stems which soon cover large areas of ground. These stems bear many opposite toothed pointed-ovate leaves, as do the erect flowering stems which are produced in late spring. The flowers are two-lipped, yellow with reddish-brown markings, borne in several whorls in the axils of the leaves. Yellow Archangel is very similar in appearance to the deadnettles (*Lamium* species), but is now separated from them because of differences in the colour and shape of its flowers. It grows in woodland and hedgerows, especially in damp soils, throughout much of Europe. It was used in herb medicine, like the deadnettles, to treat sores and ulcers and to stop bleeding.

Family	**Labiatae**
Synonyms	***Galeobdolon luteum, Lamium galeobdolon***
Other names	**Yellow Deadnettle**
Status	**Common**
Distribution	**Mainly in England and Wales**
Height	**15—50 cm**

J F M A M J J A S O N D

Toothwort

Lathraea squamaria

A true chlorophyll-lacking parasite growing in damp woodland throughout Europe and western Asia on the roots of deciduous trees like alder, hazel and beech, from which it draws nutrients and water through specialized root-suckers called haustoria. Toothwort has branched creeping rhizomes from which grow the special roots. Early in the spring, fleshy pale pink or dead white stems appear with a few oval whitish scales and dense one-sided racemes of whitish purple-tinged flowers. The top of the stem is drooping, becoming erect only when the flowers start to open. The flowers are tubular, two-lipped with a tubular purplish sepal-tube and are followed by rounded capsules with many seeds.

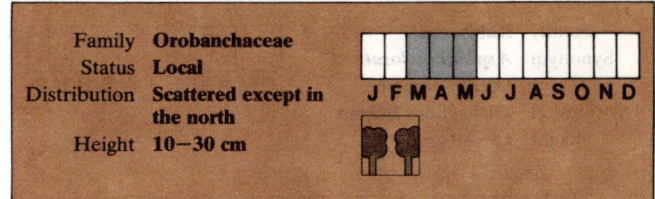

Family	**Orobanchaceae**
Status	**Local**
Distribution	**Scattered except in the north**
Height	**10—30 cm**

J F M A M J J A S O N D

Figwort

Scrophularia nodosa

An ancient medicinal plant, reputed to be an effective treatment for 'scrofula' — skin eruptions, abscesses, sores and ulcers — hence the name *Scrophularia*. It is a distinctive perennial plant with an erect branched stem and opposite pairs of large toothed ovate leaves. The curious flowers are borne in clusters on long stalks in the axils of the upper leaves. They are tubular, rather rounded in outline with two small lips, reddish-brown in colour and unpleasantly scented, a source of great attraction to wasps. They are followed by rounded conical capsules with many pitted seeds. The plant grows in damp deciduous woods, wet hedgerows and waste places throughout much of Europe and the temperate regions of Asia.

Family	**Scrophulariaceae**
Status	**Common**
Distribution	**Throughout Britain**
Height	**50—100 cm**

J F M A M J J A S O N D

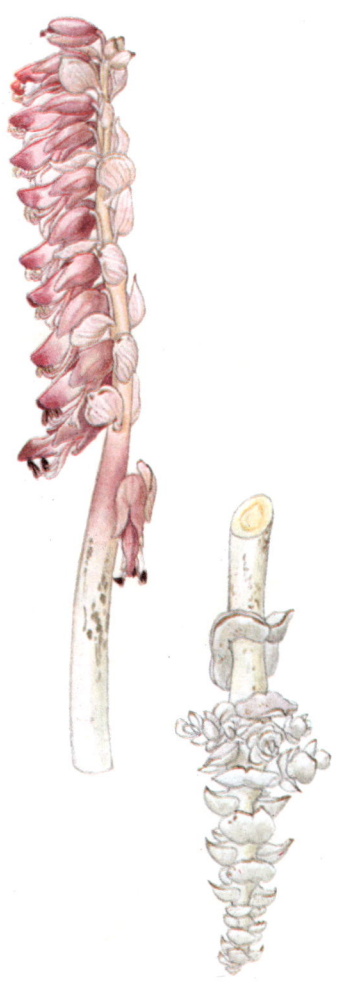

Sweet Woodruff
Galium odoratum

In the shade of deciduous woodland, this perennial plant may form dense continuous carpets growing from far-creeping rhizomes, especially in beech woods and on calcareous soils, but it cannot survive in more open areas where the light intensity is higher. It forms many small erect shoots, clothed with whorls of lance-shaped leaves and bearing several terminal clusters of white flowers on long stalks. The flowers are funnel-shaped with four white petals. The whole plant smells of coumarin (new-mown hay) especially when dried, and it is used in herb medicine as a remedy in circulatory disorders and to prevent blood clots. It is also used to flavour 'may cups' and other drinks and in perfumery.

Family	**Rubiaceae**
Synonym	***Asperula odorata***
Status	**Locally common**
Distribution	**Throughout Britain**
Height	**15–40 cm**

J F M A M J J A S O N D

Moschatel
Adoxa moschatellina

A unique plant, only species of a single genus with a family of its own, which seems to be unrelated to any other plants. It has creeping rhizomes with many clumps of attractive light green leaves; each leaf has a long stalk and three lobed leaflets. The flowers are borne in heads on long stalks and cannot be mistaken — five flowers form a head, four facing in four opposite directions and the fifth directly upwards, hence the common names 'Townhall Clock' and 'Five-faced Bishop'. The flowers are musk-scented, most strongly in damp weather and when the dew falls. Moschatel grows in woodland and hedgerows with humus-rich fertile soils and beneath shady mountain rocks.

Family	**Adoxaceae**
Other names	**Townhall Clock, Five-faced Bishop**
Status	**Local**
Distribution	**Throughout Britain, except Ireland**
Height	**5–15 cm**

J F M A M J J A S O N D

Spreading Bellflower

Campanula patula

A biennial or short-lived perennial plant that grows in shady woodland, hedgebanks and meadows in central and northern Europe. It forms a basal clump of lance-shaped, somewhat spoon-shaped leaves from which grow many slender branching stems. These bear many lance-shaped leaves and many bell-shaped purple-blue flowers which quite transform the plant. The capsules which follow are like upside-down rounded cones, cupped in the persistent sepals which project upwards like spikes around the capsule. The numerous minute seeds are released through pores at the top.

		J F M A M J J A S O N D
Family	**Campanulaceae**	
Status	**Local**	
Distribution	**Scattered in England and Wales**	
Height	**30—60 cm**	

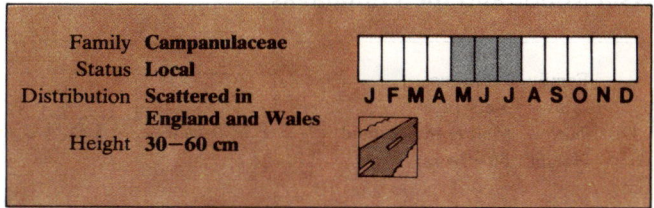

Yellow Star of Bethlehem

Gagea lutea

This bulb-forming plant is most often found in deciduous woodland and damp meadows but is not always easy to identify, for it often goes for years without flowering. Its leaves are like those of a bluebell, but it only forms one to three leaves per bulb, and these are strongly ribbed on the undersides. The infrequent flowers are borne on erect fleshy flowering stalks in small clusters, with one or two leaf-like bracts beneath. The flowers are star-like, glossy yellow in colour with a green stripe on the outside. They are followed by capsules with many rounded seeds.

		J F M A M J J A S O N D
Family	**Liliaceae**	
Synonym	***G. sylvatica***	
Status	**Very local**	
Distribution	**Scattered in England and Scotland**	
Height	**10—30 cm**	

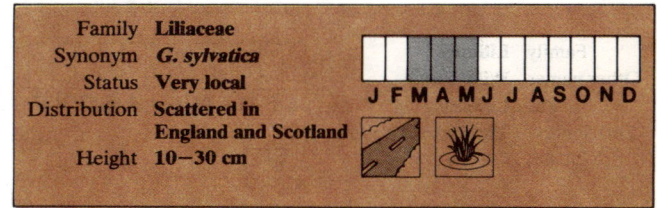

271

Ramsons

Allium ursinum

This perennial bulbous plant can be recognised from a distance by its pungent garlic-like smell. It often colonises large areas of the ground in ash, beech and mixed woodland on damp soils throughout much of Europe, forming dense growths in spring and early summer. The leaves die back by late summer and the bulbs remain dormant beneath the ground until the following spring. Each bulb forms two deep green, broadly ovate leaves, each with a twisted stalk, and a leafless flower-stalk terminated by an umbel of white star-like flowers. When the flowers are in bud the whole umbel is sheathed in a membranous spathe. Fresh leaves can be used to promote digestion and to lower blood pressure. It can be chopped up in salads and sandwiches or cooked in soups and stews but it is then less effective. It has the same effect as the cultivated garlic but is stronger in flavour.

Family	**Liliaceae**	
Other names	**Wild Garlic**	
Status	**Common**	
Distribution	**Throughout Britain**	J F M A M J J A S O N D
Height	**20—50 cm**	

Whorled Solomon's Seal

Polygonatum verticillatum

This is an easily recognized woodland perennial with erect angular stems and narrowly lance-shaped leaves arranged in several whorls of 3—6. The upright stems grow from long creeping underground stems. The flowers grow on long stalks in whorls in the leaf axils; they are greenish-white and bell-shaped with a constriction around the middle. They are followed by spherical blue-violet berries, poisonous like the rest of the plant. This is a mountain species which grows in mixed deciduous woodland and in spruce woods, also in high mountain meadows above the tree line, throughout the mountain areas of Europe, Asia Minor and the Himalayas.

Family	**Liliaceae**	
Status	**Very rare**	
Distribution	**Mainly in Scotland**	J F M A M J J A S O N D
Height	**30—70 cm**	

May Lily

Maianthemum bifolium

This small woodland perennial has slender creeping and branched underground rhizomes, from which grow long-stalked heart-shaped basal leaves which wither before flowering, and small erect stems bearing two similar leaves arranged one above the other. A dense terminal inflorescence of tiny, pleasantly fragrant white flowers is borne above the upper leaf; the flowers grow either singly or in groups of 2−3 and are followed by red spherical berries. May Lily grows in shady deciduous and coniferous woods in northern Europe and Asia, on damp acid soils in lowlands and foothill areas, but is not common anywhere in Europe.

Family	Liliaceae		J F M A M J J A S O N D
Synonym	*M. convallaria*		
Status	Very rare		
Distribution	Eastern England		
Height	5−20 cm		

Solomon's Seal

Polygonatum multiflorum

A much more common species than the previous one, growing usually in deciduous woodland in lowlands and foothill areas throughout much of Europe. It is sometimes grown in gardens. Like Whorled Solomon's Seal it has long creeping rhizomes, but it differs in that it has rounded arching stems and leaves arranged not in whorls but alternately. They are large and broad, ovate with pointed tips and usually stalkless. In their axils grow dangling clusters of greenish-white cylindrically bell-shaped flowers with small green lobes and a constriction in the middle of each. The flowers are followed by poisonous blue-black berries. The related Angular Solomon's Seal (*P. odoratum*) has an angular arched stem and solitary flowers and grows in more open drier woodland.

Family	Liliaceae		J F M A M J J A S O N D
Status	Local		
Distribution	Scattered over Wales, England and Scotland		
Height	30−80 cm		

Herb Paris

Paris quadrifolia

Damp shady woodlands provide a home for this distinctive, dangerously poisonous plant. It has creeping underground stems from which grow erect hairless stalks, each topped by four large pointed-ovate leaves in a whorl with a single flower in the centre. It has green lance-shaped sepals and wider green petals spreading downwards, and a ring of erect stamens surrounding the ovary in the centre. The fruit that follows is a fleshy berry-like capsule, round and black in colour and deadly poisonous like the rest of the plant. It is a narcotic, inducing vomiting, sweating and convulsions and may lead to death if consumed in large enough quantities, but it has a nauseously bitter taste. The leaves are unpleasantly scented when bruised.

Family	Trilliaceae												
Status	Local												
Distribution	Mainly in England and eastern Scotland	J	F	M	A	M	J	J	A	S	O	N	D
Height	10—40 cm												

Snowdrop

Galanthus nivalis

In February, in mild winters as early as January, this little plant produces its single flower and two green linear leaves from a perennial bulb. The modest nodding flower has become a symbol of the passing of winter and the arrival of spring. It has three outer long, pure white petals and three inner short broad ones, white with pale green-blotched tips. The flowers are followed by fleshy green capsules with many seeds which often drop close to the parent so that a small colony is formed. Snowdrops grow in damp deciduous woodland and beside streams throughout many parts of Europe. The wild form and its cultivated varieties are often grown in gardens together with several other species of *Galanthus*.

Family	Amaryllidaceae												
Other names	Fair Maids of February, Bulbous Violet	J	F	M	A	M	J	J	A	S	O	N	D
Status	Local												
Distribution	Mainly in England and Wales												
Height	10—20 cm												

Spring Snowflake

Leucojum vernum

A bulb-forming plant which produces three to four linear dark green leaves in early spring and a leafless flowering stalk bearing one or occasionally two drooping, broadly bell-shaped flowers growing from a sheath-like bract at the top of the stem. The six white petals bear greenish-yellow spots close to the tips. The flowers are followed by pear-shaped capsules and pale seeds, each with an appendage which attracts ants; these insects are responsible for the dispersal of the seeds, carrying them away from the parent plant. After flowering and fruiting is over, the whole plant dies back and the bulb remains dormant beneath the ground until it starts back into growth again in the following winter. Spring Snowflake grows in damp mixed woodland and hedgerows, beside streams and in meadows mainly in central Europe. It is grown in British flower gardens.

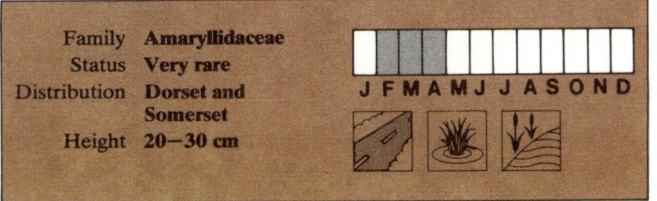

Family	Amaryllidaceae
Status	Very rare
Distribution	Dorset and Somerset
Height	20—30 cm

J F M A M J J A S O N D

Cuckoo Pint

Arum maculatum

A distinctive hedgerow and shady woodland plant, often growing in deep shade where other green plants do not thrive, mostly on basic soils throughout Europe except in the north, and in north Africa. It forms a clump of large long-stalked leaves shaped like arrow-heads and often marked with black spots. The strange flowers appear in late spring, they are borne at the base of a dull purple spadix and enclosed in a constriction at the base of a large erect spathe, yellowish-green in colour and sometimes marked with purple spots. The flowers are pollinated by small flies which are trapped by hairs in the constricted base of the spathe and only released when the hairs wither after pollination. The flowers are followed by a spike of berries, green at first and turning bright red when ripe, very poisonous and irritating to the skin.

Family	Araceae
Other names	Lords and Ladies
Status	Common
Distribution	Throughout much of Britain
Height	15—50 cm

J F M A M J J A S O N D

Coral-root

Corallorhiza trifida

Another saprophytic species, like the previous one depending on decaying vegetation for its food, but growing in wet alder woods or pine and birch woodland on acid peaty soils, or in wet hollows in sand dunes (dune slacks) where the ground is moss-covered and damp throughout the year. It is a rare plant protected by law in the northern European countries where it grows. It is also found in North America and Siberia. Coral-root has no roots but only a coral-shaped rhizome, from which grows a pale yellow or brownish slender erect stem with 2−4 scale-like leaves at its base. The sparse inflorescence contains 2−10 small flowers with inconspicuous bracts, each flower yellowish-green in colour and hooded, with long lateral petals and a small whitish red-spotted lower lip.

Family	Orchidaceae
Synonyms	*Ophrys corallorhiza, C. innata*
Status	Rare
Distribution	Scotland and northern England
Height	5−25 cm

J F M A M J J A S O N D

Bird's-nest Orchid

Neottia nidus-avis

Bird's-nest Orchid is a saprophytic plant which lacks chlorophyll and which lives with a fungus on rotting leaves; the fungus digests the decaying remains which can then be absorbed by the orchid. It is found in shady woodland, especially in beech woods and on humus-rich calcareous soils, often growing in such deep shade that green plants cannot grow there. It has a short creeping rhizome covered with thickened fleshy roots and forming a nest-like clump. The thick erect waxy stem is brownish-yellow in colour, not green, and bears stunted scale-like clasping leaves. It is terminated by a dense inflorescence of fragrant brownish-yellow flowers, each one hooded with a broad lower lip cleft into two spreading lobes.

Family	Orchidaceae
Synonym	*Ophrys nidus-avis*
Status	Local
Distribution	Throughout much of Britain
Height	25−50 cm

J F M A M J J A S O N D

Species featured
in this section

Species featured
in another section

Tormentil

Potentilla erecta

One of the most characteristic small flowering plants of acid soils, growing in grassy moorland and in grassy patches between heathers and gorse on heathlands, also in fens and sand dunes from lowland to mountain areas throughout Europe. It is a small plant with straggling flowering stems and small yellow four-petalled flowers, opening throughout the summer. The leaves are compound with three toothed leaflets, long-stalked ones growing in a basal rosette and stalkless ones on the straggling stems. Tormentil has a long folk history — its name comes from the Latin *tormentum,* which means torture and comes from the use of the plant to relieve the torture of colic and intestinal inflammation, also of toothache and mouth ulcers. The roots of the plant yield a red dye and were used instead of oak bark as a tanning agent for leather.

Family	Rosaceae	
Synonym	*P. tormentilla*	
Status	Common	J F M A M J J A S O N D
Distribution	Throughout Britain	
Height	10–30 cm	

Grass of Parnassus

Parnassia palustris

An attractive little plant with a basal rosette of numerous long-stalked rounded, rather heart-shaped leaves, glossy and hairless in texture. The solitary flowers are borne on long stalks, each with one clasping leaf about half-way up the stem and one attractive flower. The flower has five white petals, with conspicuous veins and five gland-tipped fringed sterile stamens, alternating with five normal stamens. Grass of Parnassus grows throughout much of Europe in damp peaty moorland and marshes, on mossy rocks and screes, more often in upland moors but sometimes in lowland areas, also in dune slacks on the coast. It is used in herb medicine as a remedy for diarrhoea and nervous irritation.

Family	Parnassiaceae	
Status	Local	
Distribution	Northern England,	J F M A M J J A S O N D
	Ireland and Scotland	
Height	10–25 cm	

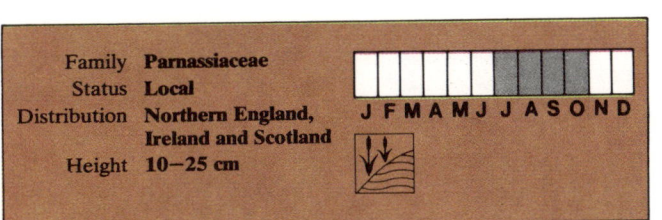

Marsh Cinquefoil

Potentilla palustris

A rather different plant to many other cinquefoils, it has been classed in a separate genus, *Comarum,* by some botanists. It has a creeping woody rhizome, with many ascending stems forming a clump. The stems bear alternate compound leaves, the lowermost with 5—7 toothed leaflets while the upper ones have only three leaflets. The flowers grow in loose terminal clusters; they are purplish in colour with purple sepals and petals and are followed by rounded clusters of single-seeded fruits, borne on spongy receptacles and partially enclosed by the persistent flowers. Marsh Cinquefoil grows in marshes and wet heathland, peat bogs and moors throughout much of Europe and Asia.

Family	Rosaceae
Synonyms	*Comarum palustris, P. comarum*
Status	Locally common
Distribution	Throughout most of Britain
Height	15—50 cm

J F M A M J J A S O N D

Common Sundew

Drosera rotundifolia

A plant with an unusual lifestyle for this is an insectivorous plant. It forms a small rosette of long-stalked leaves with round blades, on the margins of which are many reddish sticky hairs. When an insect lands on a leaf, attracted by the glistening sticky drops on the hairs, it becomes trapped and the leaf curls inward, enclosing the insect which is then digested and absorbed. The small white flowers are borne in long clusters terminating the erect leafless flower stems in summer. Sundews grow in *Sphagnum* bogs and in wet acid heaths, sometimes forming a floating edge around moorland pools, throughout Europe, northern Asia and North America. It is thought that its carnivorous lifestyle may be an adaptation to its nutrient-poor habitats.

Family	Droseraceae
Status	Locally common
Distribution	Throughout Britain except the southeast
Height	5—25 cm

J F M A M J J A S O N D

Marsh Violet
Viola palustris

This little violet has long creeping rhizomes from which grow several rosettes of long-stalked glossy, rounded kidney-shaped leaves, often somewhat furled at the base and funnel-shaped. The solitary flowers are borne on long stalks with tiny bracts half-way up the stem; each flower has five pale violet petals, the lowermost with dark purple veins and elongated into a spur at the back. The flowers are followed by triangular capsules, erect at first but the stalks on which they are borne droop at maturity. This perennial plant can be found in marshlands, fens and bogs, in heaths and wet meadows on acid soils, particularly in the mountain areas of Europe and North America.

Family	Violaceae				
Status	Common				
Distribution	Throughout much of Britain				
Height	5—15 cm				

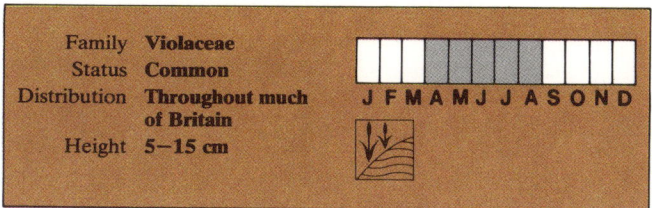

J F M A M J J A S O N D

Trailing St John's Wort
Hypericum humifusum

A small sprawling plant with leafy thread-like stems, rooting where they touch the ground to form a low spreading mat. The whole plant is hairless, with many opposite oblong stalkless leaves and a few small solitary pale yellow flowers growing in the leaf axils. These have many tiny black spots on the petals and 15—20 stamens in the centre. The flowers are followed by multiseeded capsules. This tiny, usually perennial plant grows scattered in dry grassy moors, on heaths and in open woods and clearings, on lime-deficient soils throughout western and central Europe.

Family	Hypericaceae				
Status	Locally common				
Distribution	Throughout much of Britain				
Height	5—20 cm				

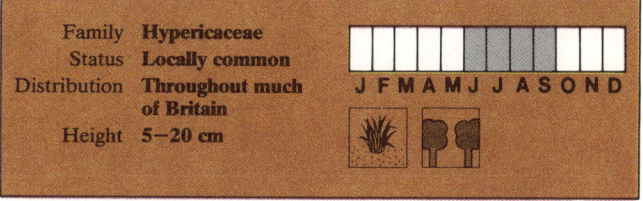

J F M A M J J A S O N D

Spanish Catchfly
Silene otites

This biennial or perennial species grows in poor soils in warm localities like stony slopes and dry grassy hillsides in central and southern Europe and in western Asia; it is confined to the Breckland Heaths of East Anglia in Britain. It forms a clump of non-flowering shoots with paddle-shaped leaves, and a few taller flowering shoots. The flowers are borne in long narrow inflorescences, they have pale yellowish-green petals and the male and female flowers are borne on separate plants. The flowers are scented in the evenings and pollinated by moths; they are followed by long ovoid capsules with kidney-shaped seeds.

Family	Caryophyllaceae
Synonym	*Cucubalus otites*
Status	Very local
Distribution	East Anglia
Height	20—80 cm

J F M A M J J A S O N D

Sheep's Sorrel
Rumex acetosella

A small lime-hating species which grows on poor acid soils in dry localities like stony grassland, sandy fields, heaths and grassy moorland throughout many of the temperate regions of the world, in both Northern and Southern Hemispheres. The plant has a perennial rhizome with a mat of lance-shaped leaves in spring, from which soon grow several erect stems. These have long-stalked leaves, usually with arrow-shaped bases and white ochreae clasping the bases of the leaf-stalks. They are terminated by branched inflorescences, composed of many whorls of tiny reddish petal-less male and female flowers on separate plants. The female flowers are followed by small three-sided reddish fruits. Like the other sorrels, this plant has acid leaves which can be used, to combat scurvy, in salads and soups, also in herb medicine to treat kidney disorders.

Family	Polygonaceae
Status	Common
Distribution	Throughout Britain
Height	10—30 cm

J F M A M J J A S O N D

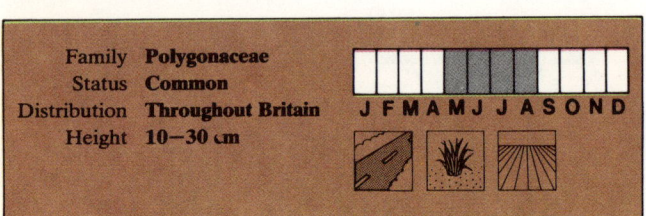

Bell-heather

Erica cinerea

A similar plant to the previous one and growing with it on the drier parts of the moorlands and heaths in western maritime areas of Europe. It is a low-growing shrub, with many ascending branches and whorls of dark green linear evergreen leaves growing in threes, on short side-shoots. The bell-shaped flowers are relatively large, reddish-purple in colour and borne in terminal inflorescences, in whorls in the axils of the leaves. There are numerous varieties of bell-heathers cultivated in heather gardens, with flowers of many different shades of pink, red and white.

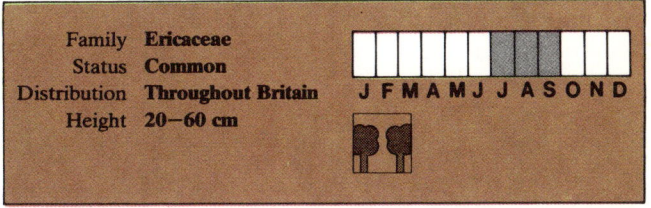

Family	**Ericaceae**													
Status	**Common**													
Distribution	**Throughout Britain**	J	F	M	A	M	J	J	A	S	O	N	D	
Height	**20–60 cm**													

Heather

Calluna vulgaris

A woody low-growing shrub that forms miles of monotonous dark-green growth on heaths and moors throughout many parts of Europe; it forms larger plants and is most common in the western maritime areas, where it grows with several *Erica* species and with Gorse (*Ulex europaeus*). It is a branched twiggy plant, with evergreen linear stalkless leaves growing in four rows on many short side-shoots on the main branches. The many reddish-purple flowers grow in loose spike-like inflorescences in the axils of the topmost shoots and terminating the branches. Heather played an important role in rural economy for hundreds of years. It was used to make baskets and brooms, to stuff mattresses and for thatching; mixed with peat it was used as a building material and for making fires. Its flowers are a good source of nectar and pollen for honey bees.

Family	**Ericaceae**													
Other names	**Ling**													
Status	**Common**	J	F	M	A	M	J	J	A	S	O	N	D	
Distribution	**Throughout Britain**													
Height	**30–80 cm**													

Cranberry

Vaccinium oxycoccus

A smaller shrub than the heathers, with slender prostrate woody stems creeping in the moss of peat bogs or in wet heathland, where it grows with sundews (*Drosera* species) or with Bog Whortleberries (*V. uliginosum*) throughout much of Europe and North America. The stems bear many small alternate leaves, dark green on the upper surface and with greyish undersides. They are tough, leathery and evergreen. Up to four deep pink flowers, with reflexed petals, are borne in a terminal raceme at the end of each creeping stem. They are followed by the cranberries — the ripe red berries are edible when raw but they are best cooked and are traditionally used in fruit sauces which accompany turkey, especially in North America.

Family	**Ericaceae**
Synonyms	*Oxycoccus palustris, O. quadripetalus*
Status	**Local**
Distribution	**Throughout much of Britain**
Height	15—20 cm

J F M A M J J A S O N D

Bog Whortleberry

Vaccinium uliginosum

Bog Whortleberries grow in the northern temperate regions of the Northern Hemisphere, mostly at mountain elevations but also in the foothills and in the lowlands, on moors and heaths, in open pine and birch woods, often with Bilberries (*V. myrtillus*). It is a deciduous shrub with creeping underground stems and many erect twiggy branches clothed with numerous oval bluish-green leaves. These have many prominent veins. The small whitish-pink flowers are like small round bells and are followed by sweet blue-black berries. These should not be picked since the plant is not common and protected by law in many countries.

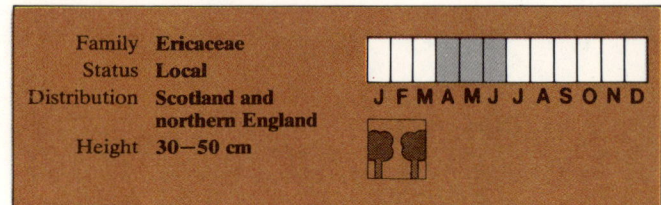

Family	**Ericaceae**
Status	**Local**
Distribution	**Scotland and northern England**
Height	**30—50 cm**

J F M A M J J A S O N D

Marsh Gentian

Gentiana pneumonanthe

This beautiful gentian is rapidly disappearing from its native areas in Europe and western Asia and is now protected in many countries. It is threatened mostly by the gradual disappearance of its natural habitats — wet meadows and wet heathlands in lowlands and hill areas which are drained for agricultural reasons. Marsh Gentian is a small perennial plant, with a few simple stems bearing linear alternate leaves and terminal inflorescences. Up to seven flowers grow in the axils of the upper leaves; they are bright blue with green stripes on the outside, bell-shaped and erect. They are followed by many-seeded capsules.

Family	**Gentianaceae**	
Status	**Very local**	
Distribution	**Northern and south-eastern England**	
Height	**10—40 cm**	

J F M A M J J A S O N D

Common Dodder

Cuscuta epithymum

All dodders are parasites. As soon as a seedling emerges from the seed its threadlike stem performs circular movements, until it finds a support around which it grows in an anti-clockwise direction. Its hosts are usually Gorse and heathers which may become covered with dodder stems in a bad infestation. The slender reddish stems have special sucking roots (haustoria) which penetrate the vascular bundles of the host, drawing the water and nutrients necessary for its growth. The stems also have traces of leaves and balls of pink bell-shaped flowers followed by fruiting capsules. This annual plant produces a large number of seeds.

Family	**Convolvulaceae**	
Synonym	***C. trifolii***	
Status	**Local**	
Distribution	**Mainly in England and Wales**	
Height	**20—60 cm**	

J F M A M J J A S O N D

Lousewort
Pedicularis sylvatica

A small perennial plant which forms loose mats or rosettes of divided leaves in spring, each leaf with many small toothed lobes. From these mats grow short erect flowering stems with similar leaves and dense terminal racemes of pink flowers. These are hooded with a three-lobed lower lip and they are followed by capsules enclosed in the distinctive bladder-like sepal-tubes. Lousewort grows in damp heathland and peat bogs, in wet meadows and marshes throughout much of Europe. The name 'Lousewort' comes from the old belief that sheep which ate this plant became infested with parasites, but their poor health was probably due to the poor pasture on which the plant grows, which was not good for the sheep.

Family	Scrophulariaceae
Other names	Dwarf Red Rattle
Status	Quite common
Distribution	Throughout Britain
Height	5—25 cm

J F M A M J J A S O N D

Wall Speedwell
Veronica arvensis

An annual plant, a weed of arable fields and dry grassland also growing on heathland and more particularly on grassy moorland, on dry soils in open places and on rocks and walls throughout Europe and Asia. It is a small leafy plant with hairy branched ascending stems, liberally clothed with rounded toothed leaves, the lowermost with stalks while those higher up are stalkless. The flowers grow on long stalks in the axils of most of the leaves, they are bright blue with four petals and they are followed by heart-shaped fruiting capsules with many flat seeds.

Family	Scrophulariaceae
Status	Common
Distribution	Throughout Britain
Height	5—30 cm

J F M A M J J A S O N D

Field Southernwood

Artemisia campestris

A small perennial shrubby plant with creeping woody branches and tufted non-flowering shoots of finely divided leaves. The flowers are borne on taller shoots with similar leaves, although the leaves do become less divided towards the top of the plant. The tiny flowers grow in small flower-heads, in a complex inflorescence terminating the tall shoots; the flower-heads are reddish-brown in colour and followed by smooth single-seeded fruits. This *Artemisia* species grows in sandy fields and dry grassland in Europe and Asia, in lowlands and upland areas, but it is rare in Britain and confined to the Breckland Heaths of East Anglia.

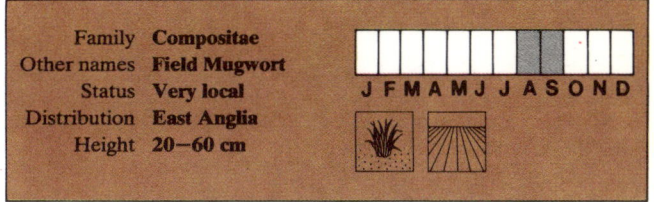

Family	**Compositae**	J F M A M J J A S O N D
Other names	**Field Mugwort**	
Status	**Very local**	
Distribution	**East Anglia**	
Height	**20—60 cm**	

Common Butterwort

Pinguicula vulgaris

A small perennial plant forming a ground rosette of semi-succulent, pale yellow leaves. The leaf margins are usually rolled inwards and the upper surface is covered by a sticky fluid exuded by numerous glands. The leaves serve as insect traps; when an insect lands on one the leaf closes around the victim which is then digested and absorbed. The remains are then blown off by the wind. One or several leafless flowering stalks bear solitary pale violet two-lipped spurred flowers. The plant grows in wet heathland and in peaty *Sphagnum* bogs throughout much of the Northern Hemisphere, but it is not common except in some parts of Britain and is protected in many countries.

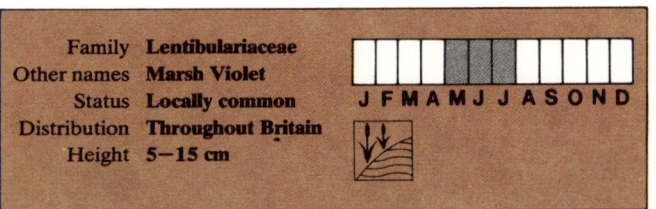

Family	**Lentibulariaceae**	J F M A M J J A S O N D
Other names	**Marsh Violet**	
Status	**Locally common**	
Distribution	**Throughout Britain**	
Height	**5—15 cm**	

Cat's-foot

Antennaria dioica

A rosette-forming plant with numerous rooting runners from which grow new rosettes, so that a spreading mat of rather paddle-shaped, grey woolly leaves is formed. From this mat grow erect flower-bearing stems with terminal globular flower-heads, male and female heads separate. The male heads are whitish in colour; the female ones are pinkish-red and followed by hairy single-seeded fruits which are dispersed by the wind. Cat's-foot grows in northern and central Europe, Asia and North America in heathland and dry grassland usually on basic soils in upland and lowland areas. It is used in herb medicine as a treatment for diarrhoea and for gall bladder problems.

Family	**Compositae**
Synonym	*Gnaphalium dioicum*
Status	**Relatively common**
Distribution	**Throughout Britain except in the south**
Height	**5—20 cm**

J F M A M J J A S O N D

Slender Cudweed

Filago minima

A slender annual plant with an erect branched stem clothed with spirally arranged linear or lance-shaped leaves, all covered with grey silky hairs. The small flower-heads are borne in small clusters in the axils of the leaves and terminating the stems; each head is formed of a few tubular florets enclosed in membranous bracts which open out to resemble a star when the heads are in fruit. The single-seeded fruits bear rows of hairs which soon fall off. Slender Cudweed grows in sandy fields, on dry sunny hillsides and in heathland throughout much of Europe and Siberia on acid and sandy soils.

Family	**Compositae**
Status	**Locally common**
Distribution	**Scattered, except in Ireland**
Height	**10—20 cm**

J F M A M J J A S O N D

Bibliography

Aichele, D., 1975, *A Field Guide in Colour to Wild Flowers,* Octopus.

Balfour, E. B., 1975, *The Living Soil,* Faber and Faber.

Clapham, A. R., Tutin, T. G. and Warburg, E. F., 1962, *Flora of the British Isles,* Cambridge Univ. Press.

Fitter, R., Fitter, A. and Blamey, M., 1974, *The Wild Flowers of Britain and Northern Europe,* Collins.

Fitter, R. S. R., 1971, *Finding Wild Flowers,* Collins.

Forsyth, A. A., 1968, *British Poisonous Plants,* H.M.S.O. Bulletin 161.

Gilmour, J. and Walters, M., 1954, *Wild Flowers,* Collins New Naturalist Series.

Grieve, M., 1980, *A Modern Herbal,* Ed. C. F. Leyel, Penguin.

Grigson, G., 1958, *The Englishman's Flora,* Paladin.

Halliday, G. and Malloch, A., 1981, *Wild Flowers, their habitats in Britain and northern Europe,* Peter Lowe.

Hepburn, I., 1952, *Flowers of the Coast,* Collins New Naturalist Series.

Keble-Martin, W., 1969, *The Concise British Flora in Colour,* Ebury Press and Michael Joseph.

Lancaster, R., 1983, *In Search of the Wild Asparagus,* Michael Joseph/Rainbird.

Launert, E., 1981, *The Hamlyn Guide to Edible and Medicinal Plants of Britain and Northern Europe,* Hamlyn.

Phillips, R., 1977, *Wild Flowers of Britain,* Pan.

Polunin, O., 1969, *Flowers of Europe, a Field Guide,* Oxford Univ. Press.

Raven, J. and Walters, M., 1956, *Mountain Flowers,* Collins New Naturalist Series.

Reader's Digest, *Field Guide to the Wild Flowers of Britain,* 1981, Reader's Digest.

Sikula, J. and Stolfa, V., 1978, *A Concise Guide in Colour to Grasses,* Hamlyn.

Useful Addresses

Botanical Society of the British Isles, 68 Outwoods Road, Loughborough, Leicestershire.

British Trust for Conservation Volunteers, 10–14 Duke Street, Reading, Berkshire, RG1 4RU

Countryside Commission, John Dower House, Crescent Place, Cheltenham, Gloucestershire, GL50 3RA

Countryside Commission for Scotland, Battleby, Redgorton, Perth, PH1 3EW

Conservation Trust, 246 London Road, Earley, Reading, RG6 1AJ

Fauna and Flora Preservation Society, c/o Zoological Society of London, Regents Park, London, NW1 4RY

Field Studies Council, 62 Wilson Street, London, EC2A 2BU

Forestry Commission, 231 Corstorphine Road, Edinburgh, EH12 7AT

Henry Doubleday Research Association, 20 Convent Lane, Bocking, Braintree, Essex

National Trust, 42 Queen Anne's Gate, London SW1H 9AS

National Trust for Scotland, 5 Charlotte Square, Edinburgh, EH2 4DU

Nature Conservancy Council, 19–20 Belgrave Square, London SW1X 8PY

Royal Society for Nature Conservation, The Green, Nettleham, Lincoln, LN2 2NR

The addresses of the County Trusts for Nature Conservation can be obtained by writing to the Royal Society for Nature Conservation.

Index of Scientific Names

Numbers in **bold** type refer to main entries

Index of common names

Numbers in **bold** type refer to main entries